TALES FROM RABBI'S DESK

VOLUME 4

BY

RABBI DR. WALTER ROTHSCHILD

ISBN: 9798755526982

Front Cover -
Portrait of Rabbi Walter Rothschild
Painted by Michail Schnittmann, Berlin

CONTENTS

FOREWORD

This is the fourth selection of 'Tales from the Rabbi's Desk' presented to the non-reading public. It would be good to say this is due to public demand but in fact it is due more to an inner demand; When one has to write, one has to write - and there is no way around this, if one is to find any inner peace. Maybe God felt the same way – there is after all no biblical verse that explains WHY God felt that God had to start the ball rolling through space. Perhaps it was just an idea in the Divine Mind that had to find a way out, to be turned into something seven-dimensional?

In gathering together a fourth collection of these 'Tales' the obvious question is what they have to offer that the other volumes did not. The answer is merely: More of the same. Several of these 'Tales' have actually been on my computer for many years, originally dated back to 2007 or even 2001. Others were begun but 'stalled' unfinished for some years as I became unsure how best to continue, especially those that are a little closer to reality. Some are more 'true' and some are less so, but all are 'authentic'. They COULD have happened this way. As a Rabbi working in congregations in Northern England and in Europe from the 1980's to the 2020's one met all sorts of fascinating problems, one was approached by survivors and children of survivors and then even their grandchildren. But I have decided that, while nobody would be interested in an accurate Autobiography of a congregational rabbi, one can make many of the same points in meditative, semi-autobiographical but fictional short stories.

There are things that happened and incidents in my career that nobody would ever believe. I really did have a congregational member who dropped dead in Saudi Arabia where he was selling military equipment to Israel's enemies but where, as a Jew, he should never even have been let into the country, let alone be doing what he was doing, so we were faced with the interesting conundrum of how to get the body out. Or at least the undertaker and the local consulate would have to find some means of accepting whatever fake identity papers he had had with him. Which would not, presumably, help him much when he came to Judgement - Recording Angels, I am sure, know all the tricks..... In an overheated and creaky couchette coach on the way to Auschwitz one year my companion turned out to be a Catholic priest so excited at meeting a real live Jew that he wanted me to read him Psalms in Hebrew all night....

Please do be aware though that this is Fiction. I have drawn upon authentic experiences, mostly modified so as to make any characters into unidentifiable composites. Some of the more recent items are perhaps a little closer to the actual events, a little angrier, a little sadder, represent a little more self-indulgence, but even so they are fictionalised. In some cases it is just possible that someone may vaguely recognise a character or an incident, but I certainly hope not. Should anyone still feel personally insulted by being recognizably described as a liar or a criminal, dishonest or immoral, they are welcome to come to court and prove that they are NOT so. But first they would have to explain why they thought they recognised themselves in my description of a fictional character in the first place.

The Dalai Lama said once that "People are born to be loved and Things are made to be used, but the problems of the world come from the fact that we love things but use people." Neat, and true. We love Things. Sometimes some People are hard to love, and sometimes People consider other people Things.

****

Rabbi Dr. Walter Rothschild. Berlin. 2021

Dedicated to Esther Rothschild
who stood by me through everything

****

LOSS

She was a rather angry lady. I hadn't been expecting the anger - at least, not like this. Grieving, certainly, depressed, lost, disoriented, all sorts of negative words for weakness and loneliness. But not such anger. And it was my fault, with my thoughtless remark.

"I'm very sorry you have lost your husband," I had said.

"Oh, but I haven't lost him, young man," she said, peering at me with blazing blue eyes, an almost supercilious twist to her mouth. "He has died and he has left me. That is true. But that is all. I didn't LOSE him." She emphasised the word with a distaste, as though it were something one brings into the house on one's shoe from outside and rubs into the clean living-room carpet.

Maybe she saw my discomfiture, for she softened a little and sat back. "I'm sorry..." she began.

I jumped in, feet first, once again. "Oh no, it's really..."

She interrupted me with a stare and I dribbled into silence, the rest of the sentence sagging onto the floor by my ankles.

"Maybe I should explain to you," she began again. "When I came to this country, I came alone. I was just nineteen. And you might say, I had lost everyone, and everything. That in fact is exactly what people said to me and said about me. But that made me angry. And so I learned that I had one thing left that was important to me, and that was my anger. I have held on to that anger ever since and when the time comes to face the Lord - and I will NOT say 'the Good Lord' - I shall express it to Him as well." (You could tell how she spoke with a capital H.) "Maybe that is why He has been waiting so long to take me. Maybe He is afraid of the encounter. Maybe He is putting it off. Well, I can wait, and the anger is still here."

She sat back, and I sat up, really rather alarmed.

"I said to people, No, I have not lost everything. Everything has been taken from me. That is different. That means of course that I am still a victim, of robbery and theft and worse, but it does not make me into the passive victim. My home was taken away from me. My future was taken away from me. My school and my friends were taken away from me. My family...." She paused and now there was a lump in her throat too - "My family was taken away from me. Brutally. Cruelly. Needlessly. But I HATE it when people say things like 'She lost her family'. And you read that, don't you? In the obituaries and the biographies in the Newsletter. 'He lost his parents, she lost her sisters and her mother,' that sort of thing, It makes it sound so unimportant, so careless. But no, I did not lose my family. I know exactly where my family is. I know exactly where their remains are lying, though I have never, ever been back there. I did not 'lose' them. They were killed. No, not killed, they were murdered. No, not even murdered, because to me Murder means that the murderer at least knows his victim and murders for a reason, however evil it might be. No, my family was butchered. My father and my mother and my young sister were just butchered by people who did not know who they were and did not even care. They were butchered like animals that have no name and no identity. Who cares, when they slaughter a cow, if the calf misses her mother? Who cares, when they slit a chicken's throat, if she has a mate or siblings or chicks? It was an anonymous murder, it was a mass murder, and the murderers did not care that the people they were shooting in my village were fathers and mothers and husbands and wives and grandparents and brothers and sisters and aunts and uncles and cousins. They did not care that these people had lived here in this village all their lives, or that their families had lived here for generations. They did not care that we had a wonderful community and a rabbi whom we respected and adored and a cantor who really, really tried his best and that we had a school with teachers who tried to bring us to see the beauty of the world and of knowledge and tradition, and that we had festivals together and celebrated weddings and Bar-Mitzvahs and new babies. They did not care that few of us were really interested in politics or were informed about what was happening in the world, though we knew that it was bad and that it was getting worse. No, they didn't care at all. For them we probably weren't even more than a spot on the map. You know, they didn't even bother to count us as they lined us up to shoot us into a pit. I say 'us' - but I had managed to run away and I am still running, even now, all these years later, yes, Rabbi, I am still running away because that is the place where, I believe, God wanted me to die too, together with my mother and my father and my little sister, and all my friends and neighbours, and because I ran away God doesn't know what to do with me now. God lost me. I didn't lose God. I threw him out of my life. Quite deliberately. That was the anger, you see. When I stopped running that day, in the forest, hungry and cold and very, very scared, I said to the sky 'If You are there, do something. And if you don't do anything, then you are dead for me too. And if you can do something, then why didn't you do something today?'

There was no answer, Rabbi, no answer, so I curled up and went to sleep and next day I continued running and - well, I don't want to tell you the rest of the story right now. I am going through a lot of memories right now. And I can feel the anger inside me."

Sometimes it is good to be able to pick up a cup of tea. I tried, but I had already emptied it and now did not seem the right moment to ask for a second cup.

"I did not lose my husband, Rabbi. Hermann died. His body grew old as I watched him, until he could hardly move and hardly breathe, and then he died. Maybe God took him. That is possible. I have a God who takes, not gives, Rabbi.

And I live on, in spite of him, not because of him."

I had been sitting in the deep armchair in the cosy living room with its little lace-edged tablecloths on the occasional tables and the towel draped over the mirror, the large landscape of purple hills over the fireplace, the television set standing in the corner on a table laden with television programme magazines. On top of the pile lay the synagogue Newsletter, visible and recognisable by its particular logo and the colour of the ink.

She pulled herself together and continued in a quieter voice. "To lose something implies that you are careless, that you don't look after something properly, you don't remember where you put it. People do that all the time. But you don't lose things that are so important to you. Or people. They go. Maybe they go of their own accord, maybe they go because time passes and they fade, maybe they go because someone takes them and breaks them. I feel that they are no longer there. In that respect, and maybe in that respect only, I feel I could say I have 'lost' them. But I refuse, I totally refuse to take any responsibility for their loss!" The anger burned still. "When someone steals something of mine, then it still exists but they have it now, not me. When they kill someone of mine, then that person no longer exists and neither of us, not me and not he, has this person. They are gone, gone for ever, and it is almost as though they had never been. But I remember them. I have to. And I will."

She stopped speaking and the silence grew longer and I felt pretty helpless to do anything polite that would end it - which meant that any ending would be of necessity impolite, even rude. But I couldn't sit there for another half-hour or so. There were other calls to make and some things to write, letters, an article - I had planned a fairly full afternoon. I had, so to speak, no time to lose - or to throw away.

So I thanked her for the tea - she acknowledged that with a wave of her left hand - and I stood up and reached for my hat. I had not exactly brought the recently-widowed lady any comfort at all, so in that respect the visit had been, from a pastoral viewpoint, a failure. But I had learned a lot. About the power of anger, and the power of self-respect, about the importance of asserting one's innocence, and the strength that comes from such certainty.

The time had certainly not been lost.

****

ROUND THE BLOCK

Kalbah loves her walks. She loves it when I take her out. I get back from the office quite late sometimes, and quite often in a foul mood, but it is wonderful to have a creature in the house who, however late it is, however tired one is, whatever else one may have said earlier that day or even that week, is still always happy to see you. She barks, she jumps, she wags her tail, she pulls back her lips to make her teeth show in a happy grin. She is happy, because I am here, and because now we will take our walk around the block.

Ah. The Block. That's what we call it. Actually three streets and a linking footpath. It's our regular route, almost always clockwise, a routine, measured pace, pauses at the normal spots where there is almost always something interesting to sniff, occasionally a barking frenzy when the cat at No. 12 is out in the front garden. I use the time to think, to unwind, to compose ideas together in my head into essays or sermons or letters - and to observe.

And there is such a lot to observe. It is now over a year since Kevin died, the boy at No. 30, Terence and Sheila's son. A bright lad, a cheeky urchin, but at fifteen he came down with leukaemia and by sixteen he was badly ill and he never had his seventeenth birthday. That was sad, very sad. He was their only child. In the evenings Sheila still puts the light on in his room and from the pavement outside you can see the Airfix models still dangling from their strings from the ceiling, the Battle of Britain and the Blitz continuing endlessly and interminably as the Heinkel 111 and the Spitfire and the Messerschmidt 109 twirl one way and then another in the draughts by the window. The posters of footballers on the walls are also visible, and the bookshelves by the window - I bet Terence built those himself, just as he would have taught Kevin to use the glue and the paintbrush and how to put transfers carefully, so carefully in the right place and the right way up on a fuselage or a tailplane.

How long will they leave the room like that? No-one knows and no-one likes to ask. But every evening when they are at home the light goes on, soon after dusk, and it is never switched off until about 11pm - I know, because it is sometimes that late when I am walking past at the end of a long day.

Next door to Terence and Sheila at No. 28 live the Bonhams. Cynthia has threatened to leave Bernard several times, I know. Bernard is the sort of guy who will tell you, earnestly, looking you straight in the eye, that he is "one of those men not meant to be married just to one woman." The problem is, he is, and many of the other women he encounters are - at least technically - married to one man, each, and as a rabbi there is no way I can condone what he does or they do and yet they are all, theoretically at least, adults, capable of thinking for themselves and taking responsibility for their actions. Yet he talks as though this sentence, if repeated often enough, will excuse anything and everything.

The rumour is that Cynthia one day last year put him to the test. The obvious test. The test that says: "Let's see how YOU like it." He didn't, and there were loud words and sounds of crashing and Cynthia spent a few days not going out until the marks on her face had healed but maybe Bernard did get the message, at that, because my sources tell he me is home a lot more nowadays and certainly I see his car in the driveway on a lot of evenings as Kalbah and I take our walk.

They have no children. Maybe it is better so.

At 19, just across the road and a bit along on the left, lived George and Jenny Flinders and their brood of three, the twin boys and young Caroline. Until Jenny lost first one breast and then the other and finally, after three terrible weeks in the hospice, where they had such difficulty getting the pain control right, the ability to breathe any more at all. It was one of those cases where they had done everything right, where she had gone to fitness studios twice a week and had gone to her gynaecologist regularly and had her regular check-ups and all that, but still, when the growth was suddenly noticed, it was almost too late to do anything at all and certainly too late to save her and many of us in the congregation got a severe shock about that, because you like to think that an annual check-up is a sort of guarantee, just as you think that a certificate from the garage means your car won't ever break down for another twelve months. She was only thirty-six and it has taken George, understandably, a long time to get over it and the kids each went through bad times, the twins took it quite differently in many ways, but now it seems that things might perhaps be settling down and George has begun seeing Lottie Solomons, who has been bringing up her daughter on her own since the rather messy divorce when Henry went off with the receptionist whom he had made pregnant beforehand.

Well, let's hope George and Lottie can make each other happy, and let's hope the kids might get on with each other. Heaven knows they have, all of them, been through a dreadful three years.

Alan at No. 11 left the congregation last year and, since he had been an active member once and I had not been aware of any fight, I went round and rang the bell and asked him outright if there was a problem and could I get him to re-join? He took me into the kitchen and I counted four beer bottles on the ledge above the sink and he sat there and told me, almost in a whisper, that he had lost his job and was having to cut down on a lot of things, at least for the time being. Jeremy was already 11 going on 12 at that time and about to start preparing for a Bar-Mitzvah so I suggested I could have a word with Malcolm P., the Hon. Treasurer (not to be confused with Malcom L., the Hon. Secretary) to hint that the family be let off their subscriptions for the year but that we still go ahead with the plans. But Alan for some reason wouldn't accept that, he didn't want anyone to know his predicament, and though I went round once more and also sent a letter, he never responded and as far as I know Jeremy is already just thirteen but there is no Bar-Mitzvah planned. A pity. Pride can be such a destructive thing, the down-side of self-respect.

Then round the corner at No. 41 live the Pennyfeathers. Where can I start describing this family? Carol the elder daughter got pregnant at fifteen and either couldn't or wouldn't tell anyone who the father was. So all the boys at the youth club and in her class fell under some sort of vague general suspicion - until it turned out, after the baby was born and DNA tests were made, that it had been her Geography teacher. Who is now doing time. Though it could have been any one of a dozen men, it seems. So maybe he was just unlucky to have been the one caught, or caught out. A pretty girl, was Carol, with curly black hair and a happy smile, but that was then and now she lives in a home somewhere with her child and is still trying to finish her exams.

The younger daughter, Alice, turned punk or gothic or whatever about the same time - I get a bit confused about the latest slang words for the phase in a teenager's life where they feel incomplete without a face smudged in various colours, hair sticking into various shapes and bits of metal stuck into their lips, ears, nose and/or tongue. And maybe, for all I know, other places as well, though the general impression is so unattractive that I have never been even tempted to explore further.

The youngest is another Kevin, and the problem for the Pennyfeathers is that he is quite an attractive, feminine-looking boy and there was some business that I heard rumours of but never got to the bottom of - and no-one wanted to tell me more, which means it wasn't really my business anyway - about some accusations against Kevin's uncle. Yes, those sorts of rumours.

Well, Adam and Eve may have been the first parents to have problems with their children, but they certainly weren't the last.

Go along a little further and at 22 opposite the letter box and just before the bus stop is the house where the Cheadles lived, until their divorce. Now he is in London somewhere and she moved into a small flat in town. Next door is No. 20 where Harold lives alone now and does his best to stick to his Seven Steps programme, but it can't be easy for him that some of the local louts like to stand by the bus shelter of an evening and drink and leave their bottles either smashed on the pavement or thrown over the hedge onto his lawn. It is now eight years since Shiona, who was going through one of her heavy depressions, slit her wrists one evening while he was at the pub and he hit the bottle in a very big way after that for a while before somehow pulling up and trying to pull himself together, about four years ago now it must be but one loses count of the time. It was not her first attempt either, apparently, and if anything he had got so used to her threats and moans that it was, he told me once, rather guiltily, almost a relief when it actually worked at last. He missed her and he felt bad about it but now a sort of load had dropped from him, a tension, a waiting. None of us, not at the congregation nor any of the agencies nor the GP had really been aware of just how badly Shiona had been feeling; it was already some time ago - it happened before I came here - that they had had a cot death. Her funeral was one of the first I had to do when I came here and that's how I got to know Harold at the time.

I think I'll skip telling anything about the houses along the Lane. Especially the tall one with the high hedge and the dark windows and the door boarded up. At least that one wasn't one of our community. Another right turn and our house is in sight and I usually find myself walking quicker, and Kalbah, too, lifts her tail and seems to head straight for the gate, not dodging all the time to every tree, lamppost or clump of dandelions.

Kalbah loves her walks. She loves it when I bring her back indoors and go to the kitchen and give her a dog biscuit. And me - yes, for me too, there is often a feeling of relief when I can close the door behind me, and lock it, shut out the quiet, trim suburban streets, put the keys on the shelf, and concentrate at last on my own problems.....

****

SHIT HAPPENS

Mr. Katzenberg's daughter-in-law Rachel had asked me to pop round some time to see the old man and so late one Tuesday afternoon I did so. Their son Ben had got back from school just before I arrived and he was shouting at the toilet door on the landing upstairs as I took my coat off in the hall, "Grandad! Grandad! Can I come in? It's urgent, Grandad!" and even downstairs I could hear the old man call through the closed door "Yes, yes, I won't be long," So I followed Rachel into the kitchen and sat down at one of those wooden round-backed chairs and fiddled with my brief case while she put a kettle on to boil and made some tea.

"I'm sorry about this," she said, "But it's really become a problem. And I wanted to ask your advice. I mentioned it to Dad's social worker and she wasn't sure where to start. He keeps saying she wouldn't understand anyway. Mark's away again for a couple of days but he also doesn't really know what to do. It was he who told me to give you a call."

"Well, that's all right," I said, "but what actually is the problem?"

She looked a bit flustered. "Well, it sounds silly, embarrassing even, but the fact is - he seems to spend most of his time the last few months on the toilet. I mean, sitting on the toilet. I don't mean he's ill or anything - of course, at his age, that's what we thought first. Mark was very worried, took his dad to the doctor, was there some cancer of the, the, you know, bowels, was he always needing to go for any reason, but it seems, well, thank goodness, that's not the issue. And then, a couple of days ago, he said to Mark that he wanted to see you. So Mark asked me to call the Shul."

There followed a few minutes of activity and confusion. The old man came downstairs, the kettle began to steam, mugs clattered, and so on. I stood up as calm as I could and let it all happen around me.

So, in due course Mr. Katzenberg and I were alone in the living room. We sat and talked over a mug of tea. I was not at all sure how to start the difficult subject, but thank goodness he did it for me. "Well, Rabbi, I think I know why they called you in," he said, with almost a twinkle in his eye. "They say I'm spending too much time in the bathroom, eh?"

I nodded and stirred my tea further. "Yes, I understand people are getting worried. Though why they thought I could help is, to be honest, unclear to me. I mean, I'm not a doctor or anything."

"No, of course you're not. But I thought you might understand better than most, and that is why I want to explain it to you. Maybe you can find a way, a tactful way to tell Rachel to stop worrying, eh?"

"Well, I'll try. But first, you'd better tell me what I ought to be saying," I replied.

He sat back with his eyes on the ceiling and I let the silence grow gently. It was clear he was going to talk, he was just gathering his thoughts together, I didn't need to push. And so it was.

"It's perhaps a bit strange," he began, "or then again, perhaps it's not, but as I get older I get different memories. I mean, I forget some things I used to know and I remember some things I thought I'd forgotten. You understand?"

"Yes," I said. "I think it's normal and to be honest, I think that's starting with me too!"

"Well then, it all depends what it is that you remember. And how. And for me, these last two years or so, well...... Well, it's like this, Rabbi. A long time ago now, I was put on a train. One of <u>those</u> trains, you know. Everyone from my town, those who were still alive at least, fitted onto two trains and I was on the second one. No-one told us where we were going or how long the journey would be, but when the wagons were shunted into the local goods yard, they stank. We were marched along the cobbles along the train and it was a warm day and the smell was everywhere. Wagon doors had been opened and we were forced to get in. It was clear that the people who had been there before us had fouled the wagons, but I don't think anyone blamed them, even though a few of us cursed about the stink. Oh God, it stank. But we were forced in - lots of us, each wagon was filled and more than filled, we were standing pressed up together, and the door was pushed closed, and we were there in the dark, just some light coming in through the cracks between the planks, and there was no way out.

There are some things I remember about that journey, Rabbi, and some things I have spent years trying to forget. The man standing pressed up next to me was one of my teachers from the Primary School. He died, standing there, next to me, just like that, he faded away quite suddenly, but he stayed standing. He had to, there was no room to fall down. Next to him on the other side was also his wife - I had been to their home a few times for lemonade and cakes. She cried, but only a little. But then, what became very obvious was that time was passing, the train was either standing still or moving only slowly, and one by one each of us felt the urgent need to, well, to do what we had to do. Know what I mean? Even if you are thirsty, you need to pee. Even if you are hungry, your body wants to expel whatever is in it, after a while. When we got in, there wasn't actually anything that awful lying on the floor - I suppose they had hosed the wagons down after the first journey - but there was still enough excrement and stuff between the floor planks or wherever, and that is why it smelled. Well, we stood and strained and held back as long as we could, all of us, a few times people said things like "Can I get through to the corner please?" and there was some shuffling, and after the first day and night a few people had died and someone arranged it somehow so as to move the bodies to one side and lay them down and that made a little more space for the rest of us, but the fact was that there was no pause, the doors were never opened, and there was nowhere to go. So someone took command in a way, I don't know now who it was, but he said aloud, "All those who have to go - move to the back of the wagon and use the corner there", and there was a sort of standing musical chairs as people went past and bent down and those nearest turned their backs to allow just a little bit of modesty, it is awful, Rabbi, it is awful to have to undo your belt and lower your trousers and pants and crouch down and just, well, do it, in the same wagon as the girl you have been in love with since you were fourteen. And it must have been even worse for the women. There was of course no paper, no water, no nothing, just the initial feeling of relief combined with this shame, this pointless shame, that you had fouled up the place where we were all suffering together. None of us had any dignity, any privacy, well, we still felt that we <u>wanted</u> some dignity, but it simply wasn't there, the Rabbi in his wagon must have had the same problem as the teachers or shopkeepers in mine. The little children, those of them still alive, had even less control of course. Now I know that, technically, none of this was really our own fault - we all knew it - we hadn't asked to be transported like this - but still, Rabbi, that sense of shame reaches out through the years and reminds one that, well, like a baby filling a nappy, we were all of us, just, well, filthy. Fouled. Our clothes too, our hands. If there is no toilet paper or any way of washing, you begin to itch as well. Things dribble. It is all very, well, embarrassing and unpleasant. And the train just went on, slowly, with a lot of stops, and each time we hoped we could get out and wash, but they never opened the doors, never. Until we arrived, of course. And then we were hit by the noise of the shouting and the barking and by the bright sunlight in our eyes and also by the fresh air - yes, Rabbi, I say, Fresh Air - it was actually full of smoke and later on we knew why but, compared to that goods wagon, it smelled so sweet..... We breathed in large gulps of it while we shuffled in rows along the platform to be chosen.

The Chosen People, they call us. Well, some of us were chosen to live a little longer and to work, and the rest, we never saw again and never will. Not in this world. I was one of those and we were stripped and showered and our hair was cut and, Rabbi, it felt Good, so good after that time - I know that might shock you, of course. It meant they took away our identity, our clothes, our names and gave us just numbers, but we were washed free of that dreck. And then we were set to work, awful work, I won't describe it, and twice a day we were allowed to go to one of the barracks and sit on a plank for maybe ten minutes maximum until the whistle, along with everyone else, and do what we had to do, and sometimes at other times it was possible to find a quiet corner to pee in, but a lot of the time you spent holding your bladder in or your bowels and waiting for the official opportunity, as you didn't want to get beaten, or worse, if you were caught. The bastards loved calling us 'filthy', but they were the ones who made us that way."

He paused now, and my tea had gone cold, but I felt once again that all I had to do was to sit there, that was my role, that was my duty, that was my function. Just sit and be patient. And then he visibly pulled himself together, shot me a quick look and returned to his theme.

"Well, the time came when I was free again, free and alone, but free. And many things I put behind me and I began my life from scratch like many others. But you know, in these last months and years I keep going back in my mind to those days in the wagon and those days when I could only go to the latrine when the Blockälteste let me. It's the smell of the bodies and what came out of those bodies that I can still smell in my nostrils, still, all those years later. And so I love the bathroom,

Rabbi. It's my favourite place in the world now. I think of Heaven as a big bathroom. You can sit there and take all the time in whichever world you are in, and let your body relax and your mind relax and maybe your soul relax too, Rabbi, and everything smells of flowers, and the paper is soft and there is so much of it, I can sit alone, all alone, no-one is pushing me, no one stands against me, no-one hears me or sees me or smells me when I let my body muscles relax. It is more than luxury, Rabbi, it is heaven. Truly. It's the place where I can purify myself and think and even sometimes - only sometimes, mind you - I try to pray. When I was younger, Rabbi, I learned some Talmud, just a bit before everything was stopped, and I know that the Rabbis always called the toilet an unclean place - '*tamey*' - but that was Then. Now, it is the cleanest place of all.

I know Mark was getting worried and I know Rachel doesn't understand, she's a nice girl, she's good for Mark, but she really doesn't understand me at all, you know, her family was very different...... And I know sometimes I am in the way when other people want to come in and so I am normally able to leave when I have to. Really. I need a minute or two sometimes to pull myself together. But, well - what can I tell you? I love to feel the paper, I love to stroke and to smell the bars of soap, I love that flower spray Rachel buys, I love the rugs and the clean whiteness of it all. For me, this room is my place, my place where I can go and relax. Can you understand that? Can you explain that, maybe, eh, hm?"

They don't teach you this kind of thing in rabbinic seminaries but either you learn quick on the job or you fail. I was still learning, of course, one is always learning, but I didn't want to fail, or to let anyone down. I promised to do my best.

Mr. Katzenberg stood up, slowly, and reached out his hand. I took it and shook it. He smiled at me and left the toom.

I sat down again and could hear him going up the staircase. I sniffed my hand and it smelled of flowered soap. Within a minute Rachel came in. "Another tea, Rabbi?"

"Oh, sorry, I never finished this one," I said, looking at the mug still three-quarters full of cold brown fluid. Fluid. That set up an association in my mind. "Look," I said. "I think I understand your father-in-law. There really is no need to worry. He has some memories from the past, bad memories, you understand, and he likes to, well, to sit there and relax. Why exactly there - well, he told me, but it isn't really important right now. If I were you, I'd just let him stay on like this while he is with you here. You may eventually want to add a downstairs loo or something, if it gets, well, inconvenient. Maybe you can tell Mark that. When he's back, ask him to call me, and I can go over a few things with him. OK?"

She agreed, which was a relief to me, because it was now becoming clear to me that I needed another form of relief as well, and I knew that the bathroom upstairs was already occupied. The best thing to do would be to get in my car and get back to the synagogue as quickly as possible. Just hold on, and hold in, until then.

I managed it and all was all right, of course, even though the 'Gentlemen's Cloakroom' by the entrance always smells of damp and needs refurbishment and the heating is inadequate, but it struck me forcefully yet again how everyone has their own especial memories, their own strengths and their own weaknesses, and just how much we take for granted, we who are free to pee, we who - with those occasional inconveniences when the conveniences are closed - are never short of an opportunity to reduce the stress. The stress under which everyone of necessity lives who still inhabits their body, and the stress which also inhabits the soul.

****

ON A WING AND A PRAYER

"Rabbi, why don't you repeat the *Amidah*?" It was the sort of question I had been half-expecting because it is these questions that exercise the minds of those who occupy themselves with Ritual Committees or Service Committees or whatever they are called in the different communities. Theoretically these should be the most learned and committed of the congregants, those who wish to occupy their valuable time not with Fundraising or Security or Catering or Maintenance or Social Activities or even the Library and Education - all important in themselves - but with one of the main functions of a synagogue community, which is to organise religious services where people may come and pray. Who could argue with the importance of that? True, a synagogue community must be more than that, much more, for a synagogue performs several roles and functions, as a place of prayer but also as a place of study and learning, and a place of social contact and support. There are synagogues where many pray but no-one visits the sick, and there are synagogues where many come for dances and lectures but hardly anyone attends the services...... A synagogue in a provincial town, where there are not so many other Jewish buildings and facilities around, should be a focal point for a wide variety of needs and there are youngsters and young people and young families and not-so-young people and then frankly elderly people, there are Youth Groups and Sunday Schools and a kitchen and classrooms and toilets that need cleaning and an Office for the Administrator and a room for the Caretaker and hopefully a study for the Rabbi (is it called his 'Study' or his 'Office'? Even that will tell you a lot about the community).

"There is no need to, if we say it aloud together," I explained, patiently.

"But Rabbi, you are deviating from the Tradition! I

insist we return to the proper way of doing it."

Oh no, not again, not this old argument again. There is always someone who claims to know the one and only true and proper way to pray to God. Someone who is going to complain about what is left out of the prayer book and what has been left in, about the translations or even the lack of translations, about the need for a transcription into our own normal alphabet (which is impossible really as there are sounds in Hebrew which cannot really be represented with the limited alphabet at our disposal). There is always a dogmatist who knows that the prayer book and the ritual with which he grew up is the only one that Moses on Mount Sinai ever announced and ever authorised. Why, we even have some prayer books with the word 'Authorised' in gold letters on their spines! But authorised by some long-deceased 'Chief Rabbi' and a committee and not even from my own strand of Judaism.

But what is Prayer anyway, and what are our prayer books, and what our services? Here I can only explain the arguments I have had to use so many times - in conflicts which I have by no means always won. I have offered *shiurim*, sermons, articles - and the point just does not get through to some people, who see Prayer as a mechanical contraption that must not be modified or otherwise tinkered with, lest it stop working. These are of course the people opposed to any update on their computers!

There is a big difference between Prayer and Liturgy, which is in a way 'frozen Prayer', words someone has written down. But let us look at liturgy first.

One day someone sometime somewhere sat down and wrote, composed a prayer - a liturgical poem or whatever. With a few tiny exceptions, when something is quoted in a certain rabbi's name in the *Mishnah*, or maybe when they weave a part of their name into an acrostic, we have no idea who they were. But they were geniuses, that much is clear, for the prayers which have survived to be incorporated into our standard liturgies are tiny works of art, with structure, the repetitions only there when they are needed to add weight or emphasis, the personal appeal calling out from the black-printed letters. Of course, much other stuff may have been composed and since become lost, and some prayer books become overloaded with dross, packed by their editors with medieval poems that may have spoken to the medieval heart but fail to speak to the modern one. Sometimes one needs to learn what can be removed.

The point is, our prayers are never ever laid down in the Bible. Here and there we read about people like Jacob or Hannah going somewhere to pray, or Moses calls out to God to heal his sister Miriam, but these are tiny exceptions, whereas books are filled with detailed instructions for rituals, describing the building of altars and laying down what should be laid down upon them. There was in those days a very simple and practical way of approaching God. If God, despite being Everywhere, was also basically 'Up There', in Heaven, or in the Heavens, then one would want for specific purposes or on specific occasions to bring this God a present. This is in itself a slight contradiction, for everything on Earth was God's own creation in any case but, never mind, when a child brings their parent a present purchased with the same pocket money the parent has given them, the child is adding a new dimension, that of love and gratitude, to the simple act of purchasing and giving. In the same way a human might want to say "Thank you" or "I am sorry", and could approach God with a contribution - an animal, a basket of fruit, a handful of grain, a flask of the best olive oil - and give these things to God. NOT their first-born child, not any more, and not any prisoners-of-war either! These were defined as vile and barbarous practices, misunderstandings perpetrated by the followers of Moloch or Baal, of Marduk and Astarte, or ancient Pharaohs and Tuts and Phuts, and we were forbidden repeatedly to perform them - but the fact is that other peoples considered these also to be appropriate gifts of gratitude to their gods and there would have been no need to repeat the prohibition for us unless this repetition was also necessary....

So, we were told first how different patriarchs built some stone altar erected in the wilderness and later, following the Exodus from Egypt, which family could officiate as Priests and which family could act as their assistants, bringing the jugs and the firewood, and within a holy tented precinct or later in a massive complex of stone courtyards and staircases and towers and palaces a gift would be offered to God. But how? Gravity ensures that anything you throw up will fall down again, rather defeating the point of the exercise. But there is a simple method of transforming the physical properties of something solid into something gaseous - or at least into smoke, warm gases filled with tiny burnt particles - which can rise up into the sky and dissipate there into invisibility and infinity and which in so doing will bring God 'Up There' into a better mood and appreciative of our desires to appreciate the divine in our lives too.

So, the animal (properly slaughtered and drained of its liquid) and the grain and the fruit can be either burned or a part of it is burned and the rest shared with God in a holy meal just as with any other meal where each guest brings some of the meal with them, contributing one of the courses

It sounds messy - some people think it cruel as well, though these people have usually never seen how modern steaks and chops and roast chickens are prepared for this stage of their existence - and it was not cheap, to the extent that the price list for each type of sacrifice had to be modified in Leviticus with a cheaper discounted version for those whose finances were not up to the full version. It still counted though because, proportionate to their income, it was still a significant gift, but it meant they need not be publicly humiliated just because they could afford only a pigeon rather than a bullock. The idea was the same, the intention was the same, the effect was the same.

But then all that ended, violently - twice, in fact, the second time almost 2,000 years ago - and apart from a few nostalgic incorrigibles no-one really wants it all back. The *Cohanim*, presumed descendants of the ancient Priesthood, are reduced now to standing in front of the congregation at some morning services, in their stockinged feet and with their *tallitot* covering their faces, repeating an ancient sequence of blessings as the Chazan calls them out, word by word. That, and a few restrictions on whom they may marry and whether they may attend funerals, forms all that is left of their earlier role. The Levites don't even have that and are fully redundant, unless you count that they may be given an earlier call to the Torah reading and are allowed to add the title '*HaLevi*' to their Hebrew names.

Not only that, but the various Hebrew Prophets spent a lot of their time and effort in criticising the sacrificial rites - look at Isaiah, or Hosea 6:6 - whether they were performed in the 'divinely authorised place' in Jerusalem or whether - which was classed as even worse - they were carried out secretly on hilltops and under trees and inside private houses. They demanded instead that the Jews should focus on social action, on obedience to God's will but as manifested in the political and the social sphere, not the ritual one.

But at some time, and we don't know when or where or who it was, someone must have had the idea of gathering a few friends round and saying, "Well, as we cannot get to Jerusalem easily, because of the distance and so forth, shall we do something here to praise God?" And so the 'Beit Knesset', the House of Meeting came into existence, probably originally in a private room, then a rented room, then eventually special buildings were erected. There were no standard blueprints for such buildings because there were no altars and no holy courtyards, they were places where any Jew (and maybe Jewesses too) could come and join in. They would need a table and some seats and maybe a bookshelf or a niche in which the books (in those days, rolled parchments) could be kept. Presumably someone suggested they sing a few Psalms and someone else suggested they read from a copy of the Torah when they could save up enough to afford to buy one, and somebody else composed a couple of poems and showed them round, maybe shyly, and others said, "Hey, these are great, let's say them every week!" or "every time we meet!" and then maybe some visitor came and liked them and asked for a copy (all done by hand, of course) and took them back to HIS circle of friends, and so they got passed on further round, together with songs and various formulae.

And what would grab people's attention like this, when they were searching for some form of informal spirituality? Why, prayers that expressed what almost everyone was feeling, or maybe what some people were feeling some of the time, or things that were felt appropriate to specific festival occasions, or prayers to be said before reading from the Torah or later from one of the books of the Prophets, and when lighting the oil lamps so that there would be light to read by during the Sabbath Evening gathering, and a benediction over the wine and the bread that symbolised God's bounty in making food and drink available to us, and more prayers of thanks after the meal was concluded, and so on - once the basic idea had become established then creative people would have found many things to write and if they were good, they lasted and spread. Songs too and presumably melodies for them as well, though we don't have these anymore. Someone would have suggested that they study the Bible passage aloud, read it to each other and discuss it. Maybe it was decided to start at the beginning and work through on a regular if routine schedule, with additional readings outside this sequence for especial days - the New Moon, or a Festival Day. But five lengthy books is a lot to read and we know that in Babylon later they decided to take three years to plough through the entire work, whereas in Palestine they would do it in one year and then start again. Lists were prepared - different lists, echoes of these differences can still be found in the calendars of readings between Ashkenazim and Sephardim. From this someone would have offered to deliver a discourse on this or some other subject. But the important thing is to stress again and again that this was a gradual development and led by no-one. By the time Jesus was wandering around Galilee we know he found such 'Synagogues' (the Greek term for a Meeting House or Club House) in Nazareth and Kfar Nachum and that it was totally normal to go into one of these at a specific day and time and join in; We learn incidentally that it was also quite normal to ask a guest to join in and read something. These were not competition to the Temple, they were not alternative places of sacrificial ritual, they were places where Jews could meet to be Jews rather than farmers or traders, craftsmen or officials. Wherever Paul went in Rome, Greece and Asia Minor he found congregations of Jews who met like this; Jews who presumably spoke Hebrew and Latin, or Hebrew and Greek, or Hebrew and Aramaic, or Hebrew and Syriac, or whatever. Philo described a synagogue in Alexandria that was so large (and had such bad acoustics) that most of the worshippers couldn't even hear the prayers and had to be warned by flag when to respond 'Amen' - 'I agree' - to what was being said at the front. Sometimes we could do with that system in more modern synagogues with bad acoustics....

And then one awful day the Temple was not there anymore, Rome's Legions under Titus had burned it, had carried off the holy vessels and sacrificial equipment, had massacred the priests and burned their books. The Jews of Jerusalem witnessed it, others will have heard as the news spread like a ripple around the Mediterranean. Their God, their One and Only God, had allowed His House to be burned down, His People to be exiled. There was no royal dynasty, there was no priesthood, there was no way even to approach this distant God now - except through these crumbs that were left, these small, scattered groups of individuals who could form communities, who could read the texts and sing the songs and in some way strain to fill the enormous gap that was left. To make matters worse many of these Jews could hardly read Hebrew, the ancient Holy Language or '*Lashon Kodesh*', and their daily commerce and communication was usually in one of the regional forms of Aramaic. So we have prayers in Aramaic and Bible translations ('*Targumim*') into Aramaic too. But it was important that they should have something to use that they could understand.

What did they say, what did they sing? With the few exceptions of texts cited in the Mishnah - and even these refer only to those texts known to the rabbis who put the contents of the Mishnah together - we don't know. At some point seven hundred years or so after the temple had gone, had been taken away, a community in what is now Spain apparently wrote a letter to a wise old Rabbi, Amram Gaon, who lived and taught in what is now Iraq. How? Why? The Why? is probably easier to answer - there must have been endless discussions and conflicts and committee meetings until eventually someone with a loud voice had said, "Enough! Let's write a letter to an expert and ask him what it is we should be saying at our services!" And so they did so. How did they get the letter to Rav Amram? Did they give it to a merchant, or a special courier? To a sailor with the request that he pass it on to another sailor and eventually so it could get to the other end of the Sea and across the Fertile Crescent on some camel or donkey until it reached the person to whom it was addressed? How much did all this cost? We don't know. How long did it all take? We don't know. But the tradition tells us that Rav Amram responded to this request from so far away courteously and humbly on the lines of, "Well, I cannot really tell you what you should pray, but here is a copy of what we use here." And this ancient manuscript, the so-called 'Siddur Rav Amram', is the earliest evidence we have for what has come to be accepted as the standard on which all prayer books are based.

For there is no end to the making of new prayer books. There are additional pieces, there are additions and omissions for Zionist or anti-Zionist purposes, for purposes of adding '*kavvanah*' or spiritual intensity during meditations before and during the prayers; there are Hasidic and feminist and egalitarian versions. There are versions where everything possible is added to make a service last several hours even if read at great speed, and versions which have been stripped down to a bare minimum in the hope that the worshippers will at least take their time and think on the content of what they are praying and that the service need not take more than an hour.

Almost all prayer books - '*Siddurim*', meaning just 'Orders of Service', have the Hebrew text of the liturgy; many for use in the Diaspora have the Hebrew text - usually on the right-hand page when one has opened the book from the right - and a translation on the left - into English, German, Russian, Spanish, French, Danish, whatever; some even have transliteration, the Hebrew text printed in the local alphabet (whereby the Hebrew letter '*Shin*' could be 'sh' in English, 'sch' in German, 'sj' in Dutch 'ch' in French....)

But then, what are we doing in Prayer? In Judaism, we talk directly to God - we do not need to go through any intermediary, not through a Son or a Mother or a second-Cousin of God, not through a priest or a Saint. No, we say quite clearly and with great familiarity, "Blessed are You", and the You is the intimate form of the second person singular. (The fact that it is also masculine is one of those 'givens' -

Hebrew grammar has only the masculine and feminine forms, no neuter.) Much of this is based of course on the Psalms as a model for how an individual pleads with or praises his personal God.

We talk - to an invisible God whom we cannot even name correctly, so we address this god as 'Him' (which infuriates some) or 'The Eternal One' or 'The Holy One, blessed is His Name' or 'Lord' or a variety of other euphemisms. But - Must a prayer be said aloud? If so, then in which language? Surely God, who initiated the confusion of languages at Babel, understands them all? Must one, may one address God only in the Holy Tongue, especially if one does not understand it? Many think so, though the question varies from religion to religion - should God be addressed in Latin or Greek, and not Hebrew? This is the purpose of the Transliterations which theoretically allow the worshipper to pretend that they understand - but oh dear, oh dear, when someone is reading or stumbling through the transliteration aloud it is so clear to everyone that they have not understood the rhythm, the music of the text, they put all the stresses and pauses and emphases in the wrong places, it is like playing a piano piece using just the one key and pretending you have got the melody right.... It is like reading something in Czech or Croatian aloud when you have no real idea what all those funny squiggles over the 'c' and 's' letters really mean....

And what if one prays silently? Is the language then important at all? If God can hear silent prayer, then why should it be necessary to speak the words aloud? And if God hears the individual, what is the difference with a communal prayer? Does God hear the many individuals or just the single joint voice? These are not trivial questions, because we seek to encourage people to come to services rather than to stay at home - many of course claim they could "pray just as well at home" though they rarely admit the frequency with which they actually do that. There IS a difference between being alone, or in a small group of three or four, or in an actual community. There is the difference between singing alone, in a barbershop quartet and in a choir. There is a difference between kicking a ball around by yourself, kicking a ball with a couple of friends, and playing in a proper team.

None of these arguments are new but.... how can one convince a dogmatist in the Ritual Committee? The *Amidah* is the shorthand term for the 'Standing Prayer' - that's all the word means, really - but the *Amidah* is the kernel of the liturgy, it forms the centre of all services, and it comprises several passages – it comes in longer and medium and shorter versions for weekdays and the Sabbath, extra passages are added for certain festival or intermediate days, and there is a tradition in some places that one stands and reads it silently – and then the prayer leader, the '*Shaliach Tzibbur*', repeats the whole thing again, aloud. Why? Because, explain the apologists for this repetitive time-wasting, there are some worshippers who cannot read the Hebrew for themselves and therefore it is important to give them the opportunity to hear the words and say "*Amen*". No-one says what should happen if these worshippers cannot understand the Hebrew when it is read aloud, either. Should one then repeat it again, but in English? Does God need to hear it all twice over? (God can, presumably, hear both the silent and the loud versions equally well.)

Another name for this sequence of prayers is the '*Shemoneh Esreh*' which is simply Hebrew for 'Eighteen' and is used because the daily version has, er.... Nineteen paragraphs. Yes, that is really so. One may add, it seems, but one may not take away, and once a name has been settled it may not be changed even to match a new reality. This is another symptom of the same neurotic, obsessive syndrome.

Mr. Fishman, Abe to his (few) friends, Mr. Fishman to everyone else, was one of those who believed in repeating things. The service should have quantity, he felt; the quality was less important. Anything under an hour didn't count as a real service to him and he personally preferred a service that lasted at least two and a half.

One of the earliest reforms of what became known as 'Reform Judaism' (not 'reformed' and certainly not always 'reforming') was to eliminate unnecessary prayers from the encrusted liturgy of the time. Some of these were classed as unnecessary because they prayed for things that the people didn't really want any more - the restoration of the Temple, the Priesthood, the Sacrifices, the Davidic Kingdom; Some were even politically suppressed because, being good and satisfied and loyal citizens of modern European states, it was felt impolite to keep praying for an own land. Others were suppressed or removed because they were simply repetitions, adding nothing to the content of the service but making it drag on and on. And this is the simple answer: I do not repeat it because I believe that once is enough - at least, once per service.

Quite often it is people who have converted to Judaism who want to wallow in what they consider to be the entire 'traditional' liturgy. Those who grew up in traditional synagogues and escaped from them to a more modern, open, liberal community with shorter services have little desire to go back to the repetitions and the interpolated psalms and medieval pietistic poetry and the additional sections of rabbinic texts and the '*Mussaf*', the Additional Service which comprises little more than a repetition (AGAIN!) of the *Amidah* and an account of all the animal sacrifices that were once slaughtered upon a given day. But those who have never experienced this form of ritual have a hankering for it, a yearning for it, they want to double and re-double, they want to feel that Nothing is Being Left Out. Why? Will God somehow remain unsatisfied, perhaps even wrathful?

Incidentally - I have yet to meet any member of any Ritual Committee in any congregation who says that he wishes the Rabbi's sermon to be longer, or to be repeated......

If you feel that I have been going on at some length here and repeating the same basic point again and again, you will have some indication of what a traditional synagogue service can be like - albeit this was at least in a language you could read and (hopefully) understand. Now imagine starting at the beginning again and reading it aloud!

People like Mr. Fishman - and one finds them in every congregation - will never be convinced by lengthy explanations concerning the historical development of liturgy. This is something I learned a while ago. Though it did take me a long time, too long, to do so. Such people are authoritarian and will only accept an authoritarian answer.

So I looked at him and said, "We will do it this way, because I am the Rabbi and I have decided that it should be so."

Ah! Wonderful! Synagogue democracy at its finest - the principle of "One Man - One Vote: I am that man, and I have that Vote!"

Of course, the fight will be repeated - again and again, in years to come. I know that, deep in my bones. People who believe in authoritarian structures always assume that they will be the ones in authority! And they complain bitterly about the need for reform when they are not. But for now, at least, we will not repeat the *Amidah*. We will not repeat the *Amidah*. We will not repeat the *Amidah*. We will.....

****

THE MENTOR

All young rabbis are on a learning curve, as is the way in any profession I suppose. There is no substitute for experience and experience is often bought dearly, usually by making mistakes. During one's training one can be taught the basic mechanics of any job, sometimes by experienced practitioners themselves, sometimes by those who have chosen an academic rather than a professional career and have never had to face the reality themselves. You can study to become a doctor, a lawyer, a teacher, a policeman, a clergyman. But once 'out on the road' or 'in the field' or whatever other metaphor is used – 'at the chalk face' for a teacher – one is often alone and in dire need of advice or mentoring. The lucky ones get the right advice, the unlucky ones sink rather than swim. Several years spent studying ancient texts or possibly taking part in abstract seminars on liturgy and homiletics are certainly not wasted years - but they do not prepare you for officiating at your first funeral for a baby, your first counselling of a couple who have just suffered a miscarriage, the first time a fist-fight breaks out at a synagogue board meeting, the first battered or betrayed wife who comes to you for advice and support.... the first time your contract is blatantly broken..... Sooner or later you will encounter brutal and hidden realities of human existence from which you were sheltered in the seminary or the college.

There is a nice old statement from a Chasidic rabbi that we say the words "Our God and the God of our Fathers" (well, nowadays it is more politically correct to say "our Ancestors") because these represent two different experiences of God – the direct encounter, which inspires you, and the indirect encounter through the experience of previous generations, which can educate you. This applies to other areas too of course. Some mistakes you simply have to make yourself, or you will never understand how to avoid repeating them; other mistakes you can however avoid, because you can learn from others, and so they do not need to be repeated. Wise old colleagues are not always easy to find (old ones are less hard to find) but it is important to seek them out, for every rabbi also needs a rabbi and since we have no hierarchy of bishops and others whose task it is to provide pastoral care for the pastors, we are otherwise left very much alone. So - when one can find such a rabbi, for oneself, it pays to listen. It is even better if he or she listens to you too....

So here are a few – just a few - of the basic lessons one can learn. Many of them apply universally and of course to other religions, to other organisations and institutions too.

"It took me years to learn you couldn't trust even the people you could trust" was one sentence burned early into my brain. Of course, there are such wonderful, friendly people in the congregation, so considerate, so supportive! Until.... Until there comes some problem in which they have a different viewpoint to you, or different interests; they want something told to them that you wish to keep confidential, or they wish (or demand) you to keep secret something which should be a public scandal. There are the situations where whatever you do is going to be wrong, to speak or not to speak, to preach or not to preach.... There are times when you know the truth, but everyone wants to hear the more comfortable lie. And it is true, amazingly true, that it is so often the people with whom one has become closest on a congregational and even a personal level who then, to your horror, vote against you at some meeting.... or start to spread rumours.... and the hurt is doubly deep. The people whose children have played with your children, the people you have invited to dinner or been invited to them, the people you have worked closely with on some committee..... The people whom you thought you could trust. "*Et tu, Brute*?" - the cry of amazed disappointment and pain resounds down the centuries.

There are only two kinds of congregation - and it is irrelevant to which denomination they nominally belong. There are those that think they will solve all their problems if only they get a Rabbi, and those that think they will solve their problems if only they get a different rabbi. Rather than looking inwards to see where the problems lie, they place their expectations on the newcomer, the outsider, to see the issues and deal with them. The problem is that often the newcomer can indeed see the issues, but they do not really want the new Rabbi to deal with them.... only to leave things as they are! Which means that after a few years there is a gentle, barely perceptible switch from being Type 1 to Type 2 and the intrigues begin and the way is slowly prepared again for a change of rabbi, because the next one will surely see the issues and deal with them better than the current incumbent....

Then there is the temptation, on arriving in a pulpit, to listen eagerly to all sorts of people who tell you what is wrong with the current leadership, how the congregation would be improved out of all recognition if only one would support their party and not the Establishment. Beware such people - one learns. They love complaining about the people currently doing the congregational work, but they will rarely if ever step forward to take the work on themselves when they could, or should, or when they are needed. Their role in life is to stand outside the lay leadership and complain, and they do this with amazing subtlety and convincing expertise, and if you make an alliance with them you will merely isolate yourself from the people who are already doing the work, addressing envelopes, keeping accounts, arranging repairs and the myriad other tasks involved in keeping the congregation running. Yes, these people have wonderful suggestions, but if you ask THEM to follow through, to come to services and to bring ten of their like-minded friends with them, you will wait in vain before an empty synagogue.

Of course, there is the parallel danger that you let yourself be swallowed up by the existing establishment who have all been in office on the Board for twenty years or more and who steadfastly resist any suggestion for even slight change to the ritual, the customs, the liturgy.... The type who will complain that no new faces are coming forward and then, when you do find volunteers prepared to get involved, discourage or reject these, "No, I can see I will have to do the job myself..." they say - and then a year later complain once again that there are no new faces.....

Some communities are still fairly new and some are a hundred years old. It is usually rare that the communities that are a hundred years old are still being run by their founders..... which is an interesting lesson for those who believe that they are irreplaceable and must remain in office for ever, to prevent everything falling apart. No-one is irreplaceable. Including You.

Be aware of those who spend too much time in the synagogue or on synagogue business. They can be like those people who retire from a job and then constantly drop into the office again to chat to the current staff and reminisce about how things used to be and how they used to do them. When someone spends too many hours in the office or counting the prayer books - what is going wrong with the rest of their life, at home?

Never let yourself get blackmailed. When someone threatens to resign unless something or someone else is changed, you look grave and say "I am very sorry to hear that, but if you really feel that way, then I have no option but to accept your resignation." They will not do this a second time and word will quickly spread. If someone is behaving destructively and threatens to split the congregation on ideological grounds - encourage him or her to go. Do not fight them, do not expel them, do not forbid them from entering the building - no, this would merely reinforce their anger. Instead, you say "You are clearly looking for a different kind of service or community, I think this is wonderful and wish you success in finding it." And tell everyone that you have said this, before any rumours begin. They will leave, perhaps to their own surprise, and they will take with them a few malcontents, and then there will be more chance of peace for everyone else than if they stayed and spent the next years harassing everyone else for being too frum, not frum enough, too ignorant, too knowledgeable, too kosher, not kosher and more. Let the new community be formed through this organic division and do what it will, this is no longer your problem. The malcontents will from now on have a choice. And if they wish to come back, a little chastened perhaps, because it is always much more difficult than they thought it would be, then of course the door is always open.

You must learn to work with the people who come, whoever they are, rather than with those who say they will come "if only" something can be changed to suit them. If only the synagogue were bigger, or smarter, or in a different street, or if only the prayer books were different, if only there were more Hebrew or less Hebrew, if only there was an organ or if only the choir would be disbanded, if only the services would begin half an hour later or be half an hour shorter - THEN they would come. They say. But in the meantime they cannot be bothered to change their attitudes or their schedules or their expectations. There are those who would come "if only So-and-so stopped coming" - but the fact is that So-and-so IS coming and so he is the one you can work with, not the one who stays away. The absentees seem to see no problem in leaving you alone with So-and-so, who may indeed be slightly disturbed, slightly smelly, slightly too talkative, slightly too taciturn, but who is also (as one must remind oneself) a creature of God and a member of the community.

The people who never came will be the ones most upset when you leave. They may even urge you not to leave and promise to do their best to ensure you do not leave. They may even try. But their best will never be enough and should never be relied upon.

You learn that when a congregation or an organisation, a movement, really wants to commit suicide, to shoot itself in the foot or whatever metaphor you wish, when the psychopaths have taken over and no-one else is prepared to resist - then there is nothing you can do except prepare your exit strategy. You will not win if you fight alone, and alone is the only way left for you to fight.

You learn that it is often an advantage not to be a tenant of the congregation where you serve, however cheap it might seem to be, and it is also better to have your own, personal and transferable pension fund..... that independence may cost a little more than accepting favours from congregants who are lawyers, dentists, garage mechanics, gardeners, but then you are free to say 'No' and to keep distance.

You learn that you have to love the people or else you cannot fulfil your tasks - though Love does not need to be unconditional and indiscriminate. The congregations are organic, they grow and shrink, people come, people go, people grow older, though some do not and have to be brought to the cemetery and their places filled..... The congregation is not 'yours', it was there before you came and it will (hopefully) continue after you have left, whether you leave through retirement, death, dismissal or just a better offer elsewhere.

Three sentences:
Never believe what you hear at the kosher café.
Always believe what you hear at the kosher café.
Learn the difference between the above sentences.

You can expect a life that is never boring but you need your own ways to deal with the stress, your own hobbies, interests, relationships, family. You need time to withdraw and time to study and time to pray... if you can. But your place is on the bimah, not in the cemetery - do what you can to keep it that way.

At the end of the day you are not a friend, you are an employee, someone who is paid to get closely involved with their family life, with their personal problems, with their religious doubts, to console them in their mourning, to share in the joy of their new children or new partners, you are paid to criticise them tactfully when they are heading down the wrong path in life.... and as long as it is someone else you are criticising you can usually get away with it, or maybe you give up criticising totally and just smile at everyone and shake hands and keep your mouth shut - you are not doing your job then, but you are also avoiding a lot of the risks. But sometimes the criticism may apply to a sinner who has influence, who is a major donor (but no-one knows where the money comes from) or who is a regular worshipper (but with a secret record of domestic violence) or a particularly pious scholar (but a promiscuous one)...... and then you sometimes have a choice of Doing your job or Keeping your job.

And what would a wise old rabbi recommend in such circumstances?

Well, you had better go and find one and ask................................

****

THE DEALER

He dealt in 'Kunst', a general word that means more than Culture and implies a certain sense of élitism, for whatever object is declared to be 'Kunst', however ordinary and everyday or even ugly it may seem, is by definition now somehow worth more, is better than normal, is extra-ordinary rather than ordinary, and people do not buy or sell, they 'deal' in Kunst. So he was a dealer. He dealt - still, even now in his old age - in things which were in themselves useless or at least were not meant to be used, merely admired, or locked away, but that did not matter, for what is anything worth, if there is no-one to value it?

He had come out of the Camps, he said, barefoot and without anything at all. No family, no qualifications, no home, no security. No friends, no belief. No nationality. Just his bare life. So he had started with nothing and built himself up, made profits, made gains, it didn't matter how, he needed a sense of material security because it was the only security left to him and even that was only provisional. For he knew how someone could come and take the family home, steal the family bank account, throw the family itself into trucks and steal their very lives. He knew this, he had witnessed it. But now, here, he was still alive, at least, and this was the aim he unconsciously set himself. He knew that people could take away your name, your identity, your nationality, and give you just a number and even tattoo it into your flesh. They can take your hair, and your health. They can take a person's pride and his self-respect and his will to live - though with this last, they had not succeeded, not with him. With many others from his barrack, with many others on the Death March, but not with him.

So he lived now where had lived for decades, alone now, widowed and childless, in a large flat filled with what could only be called Objects of Art - I won't use the fancy French term, there was little tasteful or cultural or beautiful about them, at least not to me, they were just 'Objects' but for him they had the value of possession and of familiarity, they were his and they had stood on this shelf or in this cabinet or hanging on that wall for years and he wanted it to stay that way. He did not want to leave, not to any Home. He would stay here, he had decided. Till the end.

I wondered if he ever asked where the items came from with which he dealt? I even asked him, indirectly, obliquely, once, but he was sharp enough to know what I was getting at. "They are objects," he told me. "Commodities. Do you ever stop to ask who used a banknote before you got it in your change? No, of course not. Whoever once had it, no longer has it. Maybe they spent it, maybe it was stolen from them by a burglar or a pickpocket, maybe they got it in a quiet deal when they were paid in cash to avoid paying the taxman. Who knows, who cares? It is in your wallet now, your pocket, and when the time comes you will pass it on to someone else in exchange for something else you want more. That is the only way to think about these things, you see. The painter, for example - did he paint out of love, out of inspiration, out of a burning desire to paint? Or did he paint because some rich man commissioned him to do so, to make a portrait of himself or his wife or his daughter or his horse or a copperplate engraving or a watercolour of his house or palace? The sculptor, did he one day stand in his studio and think "I shall carve an abstract figure that will represent the person I love?" or did he hack at the stone with his chisel, using all his skills, to create some statue for someone who would pay him for it, and with this money he would pay his rent and pay his mistress and maybe even feed his children? These embroideries - they were done to commission too, no-one would sit down and embroider twelve cushions identically in this pattern and with this expensive brocade in the hope that someone would come along and say "How pretty! I'll buy them all!" This furniture too. Sets of chairs, a sideboard, an escritoire. They were commodities when they were made. Maybe one owner sold them to another owner, maybe one owner went bankrupt through gambling and was forced to sell up, to put everything to auction; maybe one owner killed a previous owner and took possession, maybe they were looted one day by soldiers from an invading army, maybe they were hidden in an attic by people who never came back and were found by someone else who moved in. There is no end when you start thinking like this, so it is best not to begin. Whoever made these things, whoever bought them first, they are all dead now anyway. The fancy chair is for looking at, not sitting on. The instrument is for looking at, not playing. Or it is just an investment."

He was very emphatic about this and I took the hint. It is strange, because arguments still rage about who stole what from whom, who forced someone to sell an item cheaply as they were forced to dispose of their assets or prepare for a forced emigration, which museum acquired large collections at knock-down prices when the former owners, or better the last previous owners, were no longer there to bargain a better one. Sometimes there are bitter disputes and heirs emerge from somewhere abroad and old documents from the past can be found in archives. But here was a man who, himself Jewish, a survivor, a sole survivor, found nothing wrong in buying and selling a set of crockery, with golden edges and paintings of flowers and a certain mark on the back, and all that mattered was that the price he got for selling was higher than the price he paid when buying. Commodities. Objects. Neutral. No memories. They go to someone now and they will go to someone else later and it doesn't matter anymore. Morality has no part to play in dealings in art. How many of the painters, sculptors, writers, printers, silversmiths, composers who made these masterpieces died in poverty, rejected by all, wallowing in squalor, in hunger and cold and coughing up their own blood - all so that, a century later, philistine millionaires could compete at auction for a manuscript or a painting or a piece of porcelain? So that big businesses could acquire 'assets' to hang in boardrooms and conference rooms. So that state museums could fight over the spoils and then deposit most of the items in their Depôts, lacking space to display them anyway. What would an author think if he were to know that now, two hundred years later, the binding of the book is worth more than what he wrote to put inside it? Or what would an instrument maker or a composer think to know that the keyboard on which they worked so creatively is now worth much less than the marquetry of the casing?

The body, not the soul. This man had kept his body but, he said, he lost his soul back then, in the camp. Fighting with a dying man for a piece of bread because you knew he was going to die in any case and so it would be a waste to let him have it, consume it, swallow it, it would not help him but it might just help you. They treated people like Objects, he said, but they treat Objects like valued people. So he dealt in Objects.

"Would you like another biscuit? I rather like these, they come from...." and he named a rather exquisite and expensive Patisserie near the Zoo. The porcelain teapot was nearly empty, and when we had finished the tea this would be a sign that I could go. In the meantime, the biscuits were indeed delicious, thick and creamy and chocolaty - is that the right adjective? Never mind. You will know what I mean and I took yet another as well. It would be a shame to leave them on this silver dish with the fretted edgings and a mermaid or something growing out of one side. Tacky.

In the meantime, there was still a heaviness in the air between us and I knew that, actually, he wanted to talk but that at the same time he did not know how to start. And I, too, felt blocked somehow, aware that I needed an opening that was not too tactless and yet got to the point. I am not a dealer, I don't bargain, I don't look for the cheapest price, I don't make offers I do not really mean in the hope that one can start a haggling. I like to ask a question I really mean and to get a response that is honest and true. If I wanted to deal in polite lies I could have become a diplomat, I suppose, but instead I want to get, if not all the truth, at least some of the truth. What was going on right now inside this man's head?

The walls were lined with paintings, young girls smiling uncomfortably and stiffly in tight eighteenth-century corsets and a red sash across the shoulder and chest - it is amazing what effect a sash or a band can have, how it makes someone look important and aristocratic just by being there. A young man on a brown horse. A hillside with a castle and trees in blossom. On the glass-topped table was an ugly porcelain fake straw basket and a heavy bronze lamp stand. Under the glass were wooden carvings, three-dimensional, of eagles and - for all I cared - vultures, staring up at you with beady eyes through the glass, quite unnerving.

But also on the glass was still the old photograph. A couple, not old, not young, staring confidently at the camera, she with bobbed hair, pretty, a frock that came down to her knees, a modest necklace, he with a small moustache, a little heavier, in a suit with a high collar, clearly prosperous and proud, and between them, in front of them, a teenage boy with short hair and an earnest expression and ears that stuck out the way they do at a certain age, and a girl, a little younger, pretty, blooming, just developing the shape and the poise that would get all the boys and half of the men in the small town following her with their eyes as she walked down to the marketplace or to the school. The boy with the sticking-out ears, I had learned, was now the old man in front of me on the settee across from the glass-topped table, still smart and erect but now with grey thinning hair, wrinkles, a flap of skin under his chin, liver spots on his wrinkled hand. The others - went up in smoke, decades ago. This slightly faded photograph was probably the only evidence that they had ever existed.

I found the question I needed. I asked it. "Do you still talk to them?" I asked him.

His eyes, already red-rimmed, turned redder and became moist. I had found a way in. One that gave him the excuse to say what he wanted to say. "Yes," he said. "The older I get, the more I think about them. For years I didn't, I tried not to. But now, now, yes. Yes, I feel closer to them now than I ever did before." He paused. "I'm ninety-two, you know."

He did not believe. Not in a soul, not in God, not in afterlife, even. Or so he said. This I understood, I have met many people in my career as a rabbi who didn't believe in God and few of them ever bother to apologise for this, instead they state it openly and challenge me to prove them wrong. Which of course I cannot and even if I could, would that be a good way to start a pastoral visit? So confrontational? Things have happened, long before I was born, and things still happen, when people get ill or have strokes or lose their beloveds. I am not going to apologise to them, either, for my quaint habit of continuing to try to believe in spite of all the evidence. I don't need to get theological or philosophical, I don't need to use jargon and above all I must never, ever whine. No, God can sort His own mess out, and approach the people any way he wants, in a dream, in a vision, in an encounter with some natural beauty, or whatever else there is in the tool box. That is not my job. My job is to minister, to visit, to listen, to prompt when necessary, to loosen the spiritual blockages. Like a plumber confronted with a blocked lavatory. Full of excrement that I myself didn't put there - but I must ensure the system is flushed through and works again. Not perhaps a very nice metaphor for the work of a clergyman, but can you think of a better one? Shit happens,

God can hide behind a cloud, invisible, ineffable, and we down here, maybe on our knees, get to deal with the effects. And we do our best, because we believe in the system even if the taps run dry or the drains don't work and the effluent builds up.

So, this man who dealt in objects had distanced himself from subjects and he did not believe. And yet - he did, or at least, even if he did not, he still spoke to his family, as though they were there, as though they could hear, as though - perhaps - they could answer. As though, perhaps, they would all meet again. Soon. Not straight away but, at ninety-two, "soon" is already something one does not care to dwell upon too much.

There was not a lot for me to say. I had no follow-up questions. I did not intend to ask him what he said or whether they answered. It was enough. That "Yes" had been enough. He had been able, for a moment, to open up a part of himself that had been closed, closed to everyone, and for a long time closed to himself. There had been a part of him that had been a son and a brother and a part of him still was. And now he had admitted this, to himself and to me, and that was enough. We sat in silence for a while but now it was a different silence.

The tea was gone and I was determined not to succumb to the temptation of another of those biscuits. Well, some battles with yourself you might win, but not all of them. It really was delicious and the taste remained with me as I walked down the steps and down the path to the gate and turned to walk past the villas and the modern blocks of expensive flats towards the bus stop. I assumed that in each one there lived a solitary person, a survivor, a widow or a widower - more of the former, of course - in a silent flat filled with thick carpets and genteel furniture and expensive paintings and little silver trays and wardrobes filled with things that would never be needed again. Maybe some of them had been his customers - no, his 'clients'. In the world he had lived in one had 'clients' and 'connoisseurs' and 'collectors'. After all that had happened he had chosen to come here, to build a life here, to deal here, to make money, to acquire what some would call Kunst and some would call bric-à-brac and some would merely find as bits of rubble in an archaeological dig in another thousand years. Objects. He lived alone now, childless and widowed, a visiting housekeeper kept order and dusted all these items. He had come a long way since the Americans encountered the survivors of the Death March all those years ago and he had been freed to find himself again in a world that had not cared and still did not care. Alone and penniless and even with the wrong language for the place where he was freed and where he decided to stay. But inside him, in his heart, there were indeed still Subjects, subjects of affection and of love. In his empty flat filled with Things he still spoke to the ones who meant most to him. And when the time came to leave it all behind, he would make that deal, that transition, effortlessly and without fear. Whatever he lost, he knew, the gain would be greater.

It was a cold day and my hands got cold as I stood waiting for the bus. But inside I felt a little warmer, and not just because of the tea from that fine antique bone-china teapot.

****

PARENTS

Poor Samuel. Samuel grew up without parents. Oh, he had a father, and a mother, but he didn't have Parents. Parents - that is when Mummy and Daddy live together and you see them almost every day, and sometimes they smile and sometimes they are sad and sometimes they are happy and sometimes they quarrel, but they are There. For Samuel, like so many kids, it was different. Sometimes he had a Mother Here and a Father There, and sometimes he had a Father Here and a Mother There. At different sides of town. Samuel grew up even as a small impressionable child knowing that a Father can hate a Mother and that a Mother can be very, very angry and bitter at a Father, and he grew up learning words that other children don't necessarily learn, words like 'Custody' and 'Access' and 'Arranged' and 'Supervised'. He met not just dentists and speech therapists like so many children, he met also counsellors and therapists and child psychiatrists.

Many kids bring their school report home and their parents read it and are either happy or, well, not quite as happy as they would like to be. But Samuel grew up knowing that if he brought back a school report that was not of the best, it would be quoted at the next meeting at the Family Court as proof that his mother was neglecting him. And this would make his mother cry. And so he tried harder, so that she would not need to cry.

There are naturally many kids who grow up with only one parent - usually though not always the mother - and with the knowledge that there had indeed once been a loving father but that he had been killed in a terrible war or had died out on the distant seas or had become ill, his heart had stopped, whatever, he was somewhere, out of sight, but he was still a part of the family, and the child should love his memory, however vague and childish it might be. These are family tragedies but the important thing is that they are Family tragedies, the tragedies took place within the Family and they may have removed one member but they did not destroy the Family.

It's different when the missing member of the family simply lives in another suburb of the same town, or maybe in another town but still not so far away that you cannot be expected not to visit every second weekend. It is one thing to have a Father in Heaven, another a Father who seems to drive all to Hell.

There are children whose parents go to the Parents' Evening at the school - and those whose Father or Mother go separately, just as they come separately to different performances of the same play or who attend the same concert but sit at different sides of the room. There are children who are collected from Kindergarten or school on, say, a Thursday or a Friday by a different parent than the one who brought them and are then taken to a different home - each is Home, they have two homes with two rooms and two sets of toys or books or clothes and neighbours and neighbours' kids. Many children have two sets of grandparents but there are occasions when all get together for a family celebration such as a birthday, their own or their mother's or their father's - and then there are children who, even if all the grandparents are all still alive and healthy, know that one set never ever meets the other set - or maybe never even wants to meet them..... Such feelings cannot be kept secret for long from an inquisitive and sensitive child, however much the adults try not to speak about them aloud, in the child's presence. You can tell which photos are where, and which are missing. Schools and class teachers and the other kids in the class - many of them in similar positions - adapt but the fact is that there are effectively two families, or partial families, not one Family with one set of parents.

There are children who have two birthdays and two birthday parties every year. No wonder they grow older quicker.

There are children who learn early on not to believe in Romance, because they have seen the bitter after-effects. They know that when the handsome Prince and the Miller's Daughter fall in love they do not necessarily remain 'Happy Ever After'. They know that behind every picture of a happy wedding there are other shady characters, lawyers and others, awaiting their turn, their share of the spoils.

To make matters more complicated, Samuel's Father - let's call him Alan, though that was not his name - was Jewish and a member of my congregation, and his mother Alice - which is also not her name, but we can look at her through a mirror, just like the other Alice - was not. So, on two weekends a month Samuel was brought to the synagogue on a Saturday morning, from the time he was old enough for the Junior Service anyway, and on two weekends a month it seems he was taken to church. One God, two Parents - an unholy Trinity.

Alan wanted Samuel to be Jewish. Jewish law says Samuel was not, for we have understood for centuries that the influence of the Mother is usually the important one. In Biblical times of course things were different and the father decided everything. But we live, thank goodness, no longer in Biblical times and rabbinic Judaism perceived the world differently. Though there are debates nowadays about how to be consistent.

Fortunately, at the time Samuel had been born his Mother and his Father had been still together and so he had been circumcised as a baby. So this at least was not an issue. The split had come later. All before my time, but by all accounts it had been as much an earthquake as a split. And since then Alice had given up even pretending to be interested in her husband's rituals and had gone back to her own religion and so Samuel celebrated both Easter and *Pesach*, Christmas and *Chanukah*.

Alan, by the way, had re-married, to Samantha, who was not Jewish and not much else either and who had brought two small children with her into her second marriage - the first from her first husband, the second, according to some wagging tongues, from Alan himself.

Now Samuel was twelve and was approaching the age for a *Bar-Mitzvah* and Alan had gone to the Family Court again - he was truly an expert there, it seemed he almost always won the sympathy of the court, he must have had a good lawyer - and he had argued that at age 13 a Jewish child becomes a Man and therefore Samuel should be prepared for this important stage in life, like Confirmation, and that Alice must agree to this, and that Samuel should come even more often to the synagogue or to classes, and so forth. The result was a piece of paper, well, actually three pieces of A4 with the usual letterheads and case numbers and file references and seals and titles, which stated that the Minor, Samuel, should be entitled to be prepared for and celebrate a '*Bar-Nitzvah*'. The clerk had made a slight spelling mistake but that didn't matter, it was obviously a valid piece of evidence in this long-running battle between Father and Mother.

There was only one slight problem, and that was that, according to the *halachah*, the Jewish legal system, the "way we walk" - for this is what the word means - Samuel was not actually Jewish. There are some rabbis and some communities where the existence of a Jewish father is considered sufficient, and some movements - especially in America - which tried for reasons of 'fairness' and 'non-discrimination' and 'consistency' to argue that it was enough if only one parent were Jewish, and it doesn't actually matter which one. This is a debate which is threatening to split the Jewish people (yet again - we are already split in so many ways) and I have my own opinions and this whole incident I am describing happened a couple of decades ago now and the argument has moved further on since then but, at the time I describe, the principle was clear. Someone who wished to be accepted into the Jewish People as represented in our congregation had to appear before a *Beit Din,* a House of Judgement, a Court, formed of three qualified rabbis, and explain themselves, their motivations, their interests, and demonstrate that they knew enough - even if only a minimum - so as to be able to function within the community; that they could say some specific prayers and blessings, that they knew how the synagogue services worked and the Jewish calendar and what festival came when and what one does on each festival, how one celebrates, what one eats; and very importantly, that they were not at the same time a member of another religion or another religious group.

This way, goes the theory, anyone who really sincerely wants to come in can come in and their acceptance is assured. They must prove, if they are men, that a certain piece of skin has been removed, the sign of the covenant; they must demonstrate they have learned to the best of their ability - and not everyone is a good linguist or an academic, some people are childlike in their faith, some have real problems with learning a new language with a new alphabet, but at least they can show that they are doing their best - and then they are interviewed, in a friendly, calm manner, and hopefully all goes well and they are invited to enter the *Mikveh,* the cleansing waters into which one steps down, into this special bath of flowing and purifying waters, and their past is washed away and they come out again spiritually cleansed and transformed and able to be accepted fully into our community. It may not sound a big deal, but it is. And if they are ambivalent, if they want to cling to their former religion as well, then they are politely turned away. We do not want potential missionaries for another faith active within our community! And these guidelines are really universal. No valid church would baptise someone who wanted to remain an active atheist or Moslem, who was not taking the new faith seriously. (In the days of forced baptism, the Catholic Church did force people to be baptised against their will, and then discovered - logically enough - that there was no guarantee of the loyalty or religious purity of these forced converts, and so the Inquisition was set up to root out a problem of their own making. When Islam was spread on the basis of "Accept the Prophet or I will chop your head off" many people must have said "OK, I accept the prophet" - with a small 'p' perhaps, in the heat and fear of that moment - who had actually very little idea of what the *Koran* said or what this new religion would demand of them but who felt that their heads were worth keeping on their necks and their hearts should be kept beating as before. It is sad that there are still religions and religious movements that have not yet learned the perils of an enforced monopoly.)

So, if someone wishes to be accepted, they come and ask and we can say 'Welcome'; but we do not force them to come. If they can prove they have or had a Jewish mother, the process is basically automatic (albeit we still wish to know that they have not retained other religious affiliations and beliefs, that they do not accept a certain person as the Messiah); but if they had a Jewish father, then we do not make it automatic. It could be that of the children of a Jewish man, one is interested and another two or three are not, so why should one assume that all of them are Jewish? Let the one for whom it is important make a conscious decision, make a formal application, make the move and that way the others are also respected and allowed to stay as they are.

When it comes to the Jewish Mother, the matrilineal

line, one works on the assumption that we usually know who a child's mother is - the tragic exceptions may be orphans found after a war or a catastrophe - but that, until the days of DNA testing, one could never be wholly sure who the father was..... The Mother usually lived in the village and was present within the village society - even if she had been the victim of a seduction or a rape - whereas what the putative father got up to outside the village, on a military campaign or a business trip, could be anyone's business or none. The same questions still turn up when someone comes along and claims a passport because their biological father, whom they never knew, had clearly been a foreign soldier in their country. Or a travelling musician. What counts as important? Genes, DNA, blood, upbringing? Culture and language? The wishes of the parent, of the siblings? Who sets the rules and what proofs are required by the local bureaucracy? Can one speak of 'Jewish' sperm, or 'Jewish' eggs? Some people do. Is it not somehow racist to assume that a person is so affected by factors that worked before he or she was even conceived, let alone born or raised?

I have known women who have had three or four children by three or four different fathers. But the children grow up together as one family within the community. And I am sure I have known men who have fathered children in several parts of the world, even if they do not boast of it. What right do they have, should they have, for access, for deciding upon the child's education or faith? What responsibilities should they have, for paying towards the child's upkeep and education? Difficult questions. One chap told me, with a smile, when he heard where I was going for my next post, "You may find a few people there, Rabbi, around in their thirties by now, who look a bit like me. I was stationed there shortly after the war, you see." As a Rabbi I am usually only involved when a father wants access to his child and wants a Rabbi to write a letter for him. But this must be a tiny minority of cases.

Something deep and wonderful happens inside a human body when pieces of two humans come together and spark and make a third - but what part does religion or culture play in this? We know much more, now, about some genetic issues, about different and sometimes incompatible rhesus factors in the blood, about hereditary conditions and diseases. We know much more, now, about the effects of smoking or alcohol or drugs during pregnancy, or even of the HIV virus, on an embryo, a foetus, an unborn child. But what makes the new person into the new person he or she will be?

Jewish tradition in the Talmud speaks of there being three partners necessary in the creation of the child - the Father, the Mother and God. The man - and this is logical, for men often produce a white fluid - gives the child all that is white, the bones, the teeth, the whites of the eyes; the mother - and this is logical, for women often produce a red fluid - gives the child all that is red or dark, the flesh, the hair. And God? God gives the invisible spirit, the *Nefesh* and *Neshama*, the soul, the life. The rabbis of the talmudic age were not stupid; they may not have had all the scientific apparatus but they had their eyes and they knew how to use them. It is all written down, how they examined still-births of different stages, how they describe the development of an embryo from the size of a pea, no more than a blood clot, mostly fluid, to a full-formed and yet soul-less child born and not born at the same time. They knew that tall fathers often had tall children and small fathers small children; they knew how the colour of eyes and hair could indicate - sometimes embarrassingly so - who the father may have been. In Niddah 30 Rav Simlai explains how a foetus is positioned. They were aware of possible malformations and causes of premature birth.

What they did not know was that a time might come when a person could be thrown out of their career and home and loaded onto a goods wagon and sent to be murdered, just because one of their grandfathers had been Jewish..... This is of course the most extreme example of the effects of such definitions, but it acts as a warning not to carry the concepts too far.

In the case of Minors, however we choose to define that - a child till the age of 13? or 16? or 18? or 21? - we have laws now that define when a child may drive a moped or a car, may vote or purchase a weapon, may sign a contract or may be called to the army - in the case of such Minors an Adult has to take the responsibility and, where there are two adults, even if they live separately from each other and their behaviour is not always what we would like to define as 'adult', they both have to agree. At least in writing. Alice, I suspect reluctantly, had signed a letter - it was in my file, and that was vital - which stated that she had no objection to her son Samuel being prepared for a *Bar-Mitzvah*. At least <u>she</u> had spelled it correctly.

And so we came to the *Beit Din*. These court sittings are held when necessary, usually when we have enough cases presented by enough colleagues to make it worth setting up the day and for colleagues to travel to meet together. Since I was the local rabbi and the 'Sponsor' for this case and had to stay neutral, for the longer-term interests of all concerned, three of my colleagues formed the Court and I just sat there at the side and took the Minutes. It was a session I shall never forget. A Revered Senior Colleague, whom I shall not name, but he had been my teacher and my own Rabbi, took the chair.

Maybe I should add here - a *Beit Din* is a place where people with needs come on their own initiative to be helped, it is not a criminal court where suspects are tried. I had the good fortune to be taught by a colleague, now passed on to a Higher Court, who stressed this, that our task was to be - like

God - tempering Justice with Mercy. So often in the liturgy we appeal to God to be not just, but merciful, for if God were to be just we would get the punishment we feel we deserved, whereas in fact we want a second chance.....

Alas, some of my colleagues, I have observed, seem to enjoy the sense of power they have, for a *Beit Din* is really the only place, the only time that a Rabbi can truly change a person's life, with a signature and a rubber stamp. On the Ordination certificate is the traditional formula that the bearer is now qualified to teach and to judge, and the hope is that they know what they are doing in both respects. Our task is to help people who need papers to get papers, who need advice to get advice, and to get them what they really need - which may not always be what they think they need. We are actually there for them, my teacher said, and not the other way around. Of course, if a Court cannot ever say 'No' then its 'Yes' has little meaning, and so each case needs to be heard carefully and judged on its merits and demerits, each case has to be prepared in advance, a file prepared, statements collected, forms filled in, relevant documents copied. Jewish texts are full of warnings about judges who let themselves be influenced, either by excessive sympathy for an underdog, or through excessive obeisance to the mighty. There are warnings against taking bribes of any sort (and a bribe need not be money, it can be an offer to help one's career or publish a book) and the fact that these warnings were needed even then shows that human nature has not changed all that much. One word for Judge in Hebrew is *Dayan*, one who applies the *Din*, the Law, and another word is *Elohim*, which also means God - for the judges represent the Creator of the Law and the one who supervises its application.... and the worst form of a dysfunctional society is one in which there is neither *Din* nor *Dayan*, no rule of law, no sense of justice available to all, but just anarchic chaos, the rule of the strongest, the trampling of the weakest. Christians often complain that Judaism is a 'Religion of Law' - but what alternative can they recommend?

Alan was nervous, obviously, and perhaps this made him a little brash, but there was nothing new there and experienced rabbis, judges, know to look beneath the surface. So they did. And my colleagues, my revered colleagues, looked deep.

"Do you bring Samuel to the synagogue services?" he was asked.

"Yes, yes I do, every other week. I had to fight through the Court to get the right to do that, but I won, and so every second week we are here."

"Very good. And what do you do the other weeks?"

"Well...." and here there was some embarrassment, some confusion, "You understand, my business - I often have to be away, I am often travelling."

"How often?"

"Oh, three or four times a year. Trade fairs and such."

"I see. You keep a Jewish home?"

"Of course."

"But I understand your new wife, Samantha, Samuel's stepmother, is not Jewish?"

"Well, that is so, but she supports me in everything I do."

"So, what do you do? Do you light the Sabbath candles?"

"When Samuel is with us, yes, of course."

"And on other occasions?"

"Well, you see.... I don't want to push her."

"I see." Clearly pushing Samuel, or Alice, was something different.

"What about *Chanukah*? Do you all light *Chanukah* candles?'

"Yes. At least, on the nights Samuel is with us."

"And the others?"

"Well, sometimes we are away, or, well...."

The questioning went on, polite, almost friendly, it is important to put people at their ease. The task of a *Beit Din* is not to be an inquisition, not to intimidate, it is to find out what is really going on and this is not always what people at first say is going on. It is a formal informal court, or an informal formal one, there are no ushers calling, we sit at a table, witnesses are not summoned in chains or under police escort, lawyers do not huddle, no public and no member of the press sits and watches. We might be able to change lives, but we do not issue death sentences!

The trouble was, we were not quite going round in circles and yet at the same time we were not actually getting anywhere. The answers were all largely correct and yet there was an overall impression that was not. One could sense an unease amongst the colleagues, an atmosphere building up. The chairman of the Court tried to sum the problem up.

"It seems to me," said my Revered Senior Colleague, "that you want Samuel to live a Jewish life - or one as Jewish as possible in these circumstances - and yet you, yourself, do not live a Jewish life. You attend services only when Samuel is with you, you try to observe the Sabbath only when Samuel is with you, you celebrate festivals only when Samuel is with you. You have made a very good impression..." - here everyone seemed to relax for a moment, but too soon, too soon.... "You have given us a very good impression, of a father who wants his son to be Jewish. But I am afraid to say, you have not given the impression of someone who lives very Jewishly himself."

"Indeed," he went on after a grave pause, "One could almost get the impression, <u>Almost</u>, that it is as important or more important to use Judaism as a means of annoying Samuel's mother. As a tool against her, even a weapon against her. Would that be a fair impression?"

There was a shocked silence.

"I believe it would be in everyone's interests if Samuel himself were to be asked. But alone, without either of his parents in the room, yes? Of course, he is a Minor still, but I don't think you need to be afraid we shall eat him up!"

The slight attempt at jocularity fell flat, but Alan nodded, got up and left the room, and I went out to the waiting area (actually just the corridor outside) and asked Samuel to come in with me.

It is tough being a boy of twelve and I am glad I do not have to go through it again. You have just got used to your body, you can run and jump and play sports with it, and then it starts to change. There are new dreams and new worries and new fears of being found out. There are spots and itches and greasy places and hairs that tickle as they come pushing through the skin. Some develop a little moustache already. The hair is oily and won't flow or lie like it used to. Your voice squeaks and changes. It is hell. People start to expect different things of you, get critical of you. It doesn't really help that some of the boys at school are going through the same process - whereas others are not, not yet. It certainly does not help that some of the girls at school are also changing, wearing different clothes that emphasise different parts of themselves, tights not socks or leggings, funny straps that appear around their necks, layers of something that can be seen mysteriously under blouses or sweaters. You are attracted and appalled at the same time. They smell different, they start to act different. Oh, there are lessons and books and posters and things and these days also videos on computers but none of this tells you really What is happening or Why it is happening to You, it is just abstract stuff, fantasy stuff, school stuff.

And it must be hard, when you don't really know who you are yet, to have to explain to some elderly gentlemen (for so we all appear to a boy of twelve), even if they are smiling and trying to be friendly, Who you think you are or Who you want to be? But Samuel was a bright lad and he had been well prepared and he was not afraid, and that was the important thing. One could talk to him. One could ask him to read a short passage from a prayer book. One could ask him what his favourite festival was. One could even ask him - and this was the sensitive bit - about his father and his mother. How did he feel, going to synagogue one week and church the next? Was he interested also in the New Testament? Did he have many friends in the youth club attached to the church?

It was a pity, but Alice was not there - she had been sent an invitation but I suppose she felt that, having written a letter to keep Samuel's father happy, that was enough. It was a pity, because I think she would have found the next stage interesting and it would have meant that both parents were present.

We invited Alan in again. He looked nervous, he had clearly been uneasy sitting outside while his son was in here with us. But we welcomed him and asked him to take a place and pull up a chair and so forth. Little comments, little gestures, but they can be important in setting the atmosphere.

My Revered Senior Colleague, having drawn breath, looked around at us and nodded, then spoke to Samuel, not to Alan.

"Samuel, we have had a very interesting talk with you and I should like to say, here, that we enjoyed it." The rabbis all nodded, solemnly. "You are clearly a young man who has thought a lot about things and it is also clear to us that you want to do what is right. For both your father and your mother."

We nodded again. Alan looked at each rabbi in turn, then at the floor.

"We have decided that, in these special circumstances, it would be better not to rush. When you are sixteen I should like you to come to us again, yes? Just to talk to us, just to tell us how you feel then. That might seem a long way ahead, at your age, four whole years, but take it from me, it isn't really that long at all. And then, you can make up your own mind."

The result was that Samuel did have a Bar-*Mitzvah,* but when he was sixteen. It went quite well, in the circumstances. By now Alice had also got a new friend - at last - a partner to support her. A teenager of sixteen is quite different from a not-quite-teenager of thirteen. Initial puberty has passed and there are different issues, different perspectives, different problems to deal with. Alan was there, and proud, and I called him up to the scroll to say the blessings. The journey had taken a little longer than he had planned, and had involved an unexpected detour, but all had got there safely in the end. And - at my suggestion - Alan and Alice sat together at the top table at the reception afterwards. Yes, it was a little stiff, a little awkward at times, but it meant that Samuel had Parents at last. And you could see from the way he beamed, how important this was to him.

****

YOM HASHOAH

You have to look hard to see them. They are there and not there at the same time, they are in a place and no place, between the shadows and the other shadows. But sometimes you can see them. Sitting patiently, most of them. Or standing at the edges. Some of them look a little scruffy, dressed as though for a long journey or maybe having just finished one. Some are a bit smarter. There are mothers with small children on their laps, old people with sticks but they stand there, erect, and they are listening.

They are all listening. They are listening as we read the list of Names, as we do every year on the Holocaust Memorial Day – from the big book with the names and the forenames and as far as is known where they came from, when and where they were born, and where they went to – though this is also not always clear; For some it says *'Alterstransport Theresienstadt'* and for some it says 'Riga' or 'Minsk' or 'Auschwitz' or sometimes 'The East' or sometimes just '*Verschollen*' which means that no-one will ever know. For some it says *'Freitod'* - but this is an interesting word, an embarrassed euphemism and I don't know what it really means. They died for free? They chose to die of their own free will? Or maybe just that they chose for themselves how and where to die – alone or as a pair, they picked the time as best they could, they took maybe a pill with a glass of wine and sat there or lay there, maybe even holding hands together until they could leave this world behind them together.

Anyway, we don't read it all out, it would take far too long, even as it is one needs around thirty-six hours to get through the list and people take turns and those sitting in the tent keep flasks of coffee for those who come at 2 in the morning, and the policemen stand guard, but it is there in the book for anyone to read who might want to. Often of course we read a surname and then also read "*Geboren* something" which means someone had a maiden name and then fell in love and married and had a married name too, and often of course there is a whole string with the same surname, because these are lives we are reading out, not just names, abbreviated lives and abbreviated records but lives where people fell in love and married and built up families and had siblings and parents and grandparents.

Then.

Sometimes there is a very faint stir as someone leans forward, sometimes one of them moves with a sort of gesture of recognition and you wonder whether they have just heard their own name read aloud. The children especially seem to listen more carefully as we get to certain letters.

They come every year and they know the routine; and we take turns to stand on the little podium by the microphone on the pavement and read the names into the darkness and there, between the place and the no place, between the shadows and the other shadows, they listen.

Still, it's nice to be remembered, isn't it?

****

OUR FATHER, WHO ART IN HELL....

He had not been a good father. I think it is fair to say that and even though the events described lie in the past and one should not normally speak ill of the dead, I think it fair to say he had not been a good father. Perhaps he had been good in other ways, ways I will never hear and never know. I hope so, for his sake. But what I did hear and what I did know was pretty horrible.

Let us call his children John and Jane, names that mean nothing much and will not identify him, or them.

He had been, amongst other things, a rather dogmatic vegetarian. Well, not all vegetarians are such wonderful people. Some do it, they say, because they love animals and don't want to have them hurt. Adolf Hitler was a vegetarian; he loved animals and did not want them to suffer, but he did not love People and he saw no reason why they should not suffer, and as for the *Untermenschen* - they did not even count as People. Had they counted as Animals, maybe he would have been nicer to them. It is strange how the world allowed one man to ruin and destroy so many other lives, just because of his own neurotic inability to love people. Rather than isolate him in a mental ward - they gave him total power and then obeyed him even when they knew it was pointless and wrong. Strange. But it is often so, that the victims of abuse honour their abuser, the one who limits their freedoms and destroys their lives. They feel unable to say "No" to him and not just because they fear a Secret Police or similar. It seems that, having accepted a bad situation, they feel compelled to respect it and to retain it. "I have given my oath to the *Führer*" they will say afterwards. "It is a matter of Honour." Whereby they mean, they sacrifice their real honour, they submit to dishonour, because of some notion of loyalty to an abstract ideal far removed from the reality in front of their eyes. Or they say "I was following the Party's instructions" as though an abstract organisation of anonymous grey leaders who all fear each other can know better than you do what you want and what you need and how you feel.

You cannot pick your parents but you do pick your partner and you could - in theory - leave that partner if they are abusive or unreliable and unfaithful. But so many people stick with the abusive partner for years, allowing their dignity and their rights to be destroyed in the name of - whatever. "For the sake of the children" is often used as a good excuse. "It's not that bad really" they might say, or "It's not really him, it's the drink talking" or even "Well, I married him so I suppose I have to put up with it."

But the children are not free to leave, not for a while, and they need protection from the abuser, not someone who maintains the system far longer than they should, who tolerates the abuser and lets themselves be abused and so becomes the wrong kind of role model.

The mother of John and Jane was dead now but she had spent years, decades of her life allowing herself to be beaten, to be shouted at, screamed at, humiliated, raped, to be treated as a punchball - all in front of the children. And she had tolerated the man who did this to her, she had gone neither to the police nor to a doctor. In the end she had gone, still silent, to the grave.

I don't think I want to write down, not even here, not even now, what he had done to John and Jane. A rabbi, like any counsellor who listens calmly to the stories that are played out in humanity and in families, hears things that stay in the mind for years, things that are hard to digest, hard to wash away. (It is dangerous to believe that you can wash them away, especially with alcohol; The alcohol eventually washes from the body, but the stories stay in the mind.)

And now he was dying. This is often the only consolation for any victim of any injustice, to know that the perpetrator is also mortal and will also die and leave his or her power behind. Judaism does not believe in a Hell like the medieval Christian images of pits of fire and little demons with long forks and an eternity of pain.... but there are times when I almost wish we did, for it seems unfair to allow the Really Evil to get away with just vanishing, being snuffed out, with not enjoying "the *Olam HaBa*", the "Coming World" - a rabbinic concept that states that those who deserve it move on to another plane of existence whereas those who do not deserve that simply end, simply go...... In the Bible there are merely references to a grey boredom in *Sheol,* which is barely described but seems very like a boring provincial town on a rainy Sunday. One has no desire to rush there, to enjoy any paradisical orgies.....

John and Jane had been brought up with this twisted idea that "it is written" that they should respect their parents. But the parents had either shown little inclination to demand respect for themselves, or to show respect for others, and so they had grown up with a twisted guilt that was clearly continuing the corrosion inside them. But now they needed advice, and quickly, for the bastard did not have long to go and there was a funeral to organise. Both had left home and left town years ago, though they could not leave their family or their childhood or their guilt behind so easily. Now they had come together to the synagogue to see me. I made time, we made time, we sat and we talked and I made a few notes and I felt the bile and the anger rising inside me but I kept a calm face and a calm voice, for these were two human beings facing an enormous paradox and an enormous challenge - the challenge of how to bid a final departure to someone they were bound to yet hated. I cannot write 'a Farewell' for that would imply they wished him a wellness, a 'Fare thee well';

Not can I write 'a Goodbye' for this would mean they would want 'God to be with you'. No, they wanted a respectful but definite closure. But how? To make matters even more complicated, there were, it seemed, at least two half-siblings somewhere, for the man had spread himself in his youth, but no-one knew where they were or how to contact them.

Fortunately, you can find almost everything in the Bible. "Turn it this way and that way," said the Rabbis, "for everything is in it" - and they were essentially right. I took down a volume and turned to Genesis chapter 25. I discussed briefly the story of Abraham. Not an easy man. Some people find him a wonderful role model for Faith in God but, to be honest, I see him differently. Never mind. Abraham has had a difficult relationship with his wife, Sarah; at Sarah's urging he has a difficult non-relationship with her maid, Hagar, whom he gets pregnant with Ishmael, whom he later sends away, ill prepared, to live or to die, he does not care which; he manages in old age at last to father a son through Sarah, but with Itzhak it is also a difficult relationship, he is even prepared to murder his son in response to some internal divine command. Both sons leave.

Then there is a third woman, Keturah - whether wife or concubine is not clear and doesn't matter except that six further sons are born, the ones who are always forgotten, people concentrate only on Itzhak and Ishmael - and he sends them away, too, though this time at least with a bit of start-up capital for each one.

And then he dies. He "returns to his ancestors." Which is strange because the first thing we read about him in chapter 12 was that God had told him quite emphatically to leave his ancestral home and to go somewhere else - so whatever it means, this phrase cannot mean he gets buried in a family tomb; no, this "return" has to mean in some other dimension.

And what happens? The text is bare but clear. Both Itzhak and Ishmael, who have not seen each other since childhood, indeed, Itzhak was still a baby at the time Ishmael was expelled, come together to bury him. They bury him next to his wife, Itzhak's mother but not Ishmael's mother. The other six sons neither come nor send condolences. And then - we learn that Ishmael has built up a life for himself elsewhere, has founded his own family and is hopefully, in spite of everything, a better father than his own was.

Biblical texts are fascinating always for what they do <u>not</u> say. The rabbis delight in looking for gaps in the narrative and trying to fill them with their own ideas, with '*Midrash*', but this is an exercise we can all play. The text does not say that they grieved; The text does not say that they wept; The text does not even say that they were reconciled with each other or perceived in each other another victim of abuse who shared their own pain and fear and insecurity. No, it just says they performed their filial duty, they came, they buried him, and they went off again to get on with their own lives.

Ishmael by this time had established his own family; Itzhak would take longer to get around to this, he needs twenty years before he fathers a set of twins. Each had been damaged in different ways. One had seen his mother given a loaf of bread and a skin of water and thrown out into the desert with him, to suffer hunger and thirst and nearly die; the other had been taken from his mother, tied up and saw his father hold a knife over his throat. Different traumas, but each of them had good reason to hate the old bastard. And they probably did. They didn't send messages or invitations to their unknown half-siblings. But they came and did the funeral. That's all.

John and Jane were grateful. This ancient story gave them the structure they needed. They could do what had to be done, they could assuage this portion of the guilt at least, they could clear their consciences. "It doesn't say "Love your father and mother" in the Ten Commandments," I said. "The word is "*Kaved*" - to honour, respect them for the fact that they are and have been your parents and brought you into the world. But '*Kaved*' also means a weight, something heavy, a burden. You honour someone by carrying a burden for them, by carrying them as a burden, in a way, the burden they form by just being there. But there are times when you can put the burden down where it belongs, and rest your aching muscles."

It was a quiet funeral. The man had left few friends and many of those who had known him had waited long years for this moment but were not then in a position to come and gloat. I didn't talk to John and Jane about the *Yahrzeit* rituals, about remembering the deceased every year on the anniversary and honouring their memory. I reckoned they had done their duty the once and that was enough. It was already more than he had really deserved. And they won't easily forget him anyway. Though there will the wording on the stone to think about later. "Beloved Husband of...?" "Beloved Father, deeply missed?" I doubt it. KISS - "Keep It Simple, Stupid!" Name, Hebrew Name, Date. That's enough. I wondered to myself what had made him that way and what his own father had been like, but neither John nor Jane had ever known these grandparents.

When people convert we welcome them into the Covenant between God and Abraham, we even call them a Son or Daughter of Abraham. Few however think about what this implies. It pays to read between the lines, for this is where the real story will always be found.

****

ASHES TO ASHES, DUST TO DUST

God, we read, made the Heavens and the Earth. The Heavens - well, Mankind is beginning to fill them with all sorts of orbiting rubbish and debris. The Earth, he filled a long time ago. You can look at a field, any field here, and if you are a tourist on a country stroll you will see the green grass and the wild flowers; If you are a farmer you will see the weeds and the clumps where the soil is richer and whether there is the potential for grains or root crops or pasture; If you are a land surveyor you will see the hedges and the fences and the gates and the possibility of getting planning permission and what sort of value that might add; And if you are a rabbi - you will wonder what lies below the surface.

The field in question was on the outskirts of the town. Actually, I should say it was on what were now the outskirts of the town, for the town had once been little more than a village in the valley near the river but in recent decades, what with the growth in commuting and the new section of *Autobahn* not so far away, it had expanded mightily. What had once, in old postcards, on old maps, been fields and woodland had since been covered with asphalted roads and a small logistical warehouse distribution centre and a medium-sized supermarket with a Garden Centre attached and rows of what the Germans like to call '*Einfamilienhaus*' because it is the dream and aspiration of so many families to save enough for a deposit on a parcel of land, to engage an architect and to build and pay eventually for a house which will be in almost all respects standard and affordable and yet, different from all the others in the row. There will be a low fence at the front and a covered set of steps leading to the door at the front or the side, there will be a car port or maybe even a garage to the side, with a separate gate; there will be a small lawn and a flower bed at the front and maybe another at the back and one day, thinks the owner, one day I shall come here and sit on this little terrace in my folding picnic chair and drink a cool bottle of beer after *Feierabend* and I shall light the grill and invite my friends round who will all admire what I have done and what I have built with my savings and the mortgage, with my hard work and my self-discipline. In the meantime the small children for whom the garden was intended, so that they could play around and jump on a bouncy thingummy or have a red and blue plastic slide, have now grown up into grumpy teenagers who wish they lived in the city rather than out here in the sticks, or they have become students who come home to visit only occasionally, or maybe even the couple have divorced and he has had to buy out her share at great personal sacrifice, so the Family Home stands half empty for a lot of the time and becomes each year a little shabbier, a little less painted or scrubbed, merging a little further into the background, but nevertheless, whatever the story behind it and inside it, it represents stability, solidity, financial security, a tie to the land.

Ah yes, the land. How solid is the land, in terms of both history and geology? The deeper you look into either, the more disturbing things you will find, which is why most people prefer not to look too deeply, either around them or behind them or below them.

So, one day the call came and it was really out of the blue. A builder on one of those big yellow or red 'Baggers', a big-wheeled machine with a hydraulic shovel with large hardened steel teeth had been digging a trench to prepare for yet another row of Family Homes. The second chap standing by, directing where the piles of spoil should be put - you see these guys, with their yellow plastic helmets, how they wave or shout or gesticulate so that the guy with the protective earphones in the enclosed cab and pulling the levers will nevertheless know what to do - had suddenly indicated he should stop. In the big shovel was a pile of bones.

There are procedures for this sort of thing. Of course. It is almost a daily occurrence. Routine. Maybe in more innocent parts of the world or on desert islands a digger can dig to his heart's content and build sandcastles and pools, but here - here there is always the chance of an unexploded bomb or a shell or a piece of tank, there is always the chance of some scraps of military equipment, a rusted helmet, a bundle of rotted uniform, some twisted aluminium from a plane that dived steep and deep. Decades after the war officially ended there are still thousands of missing soldiers and airmen from all sides, there are still hundreds of unregistered, unknown former subsidiary labour camps or mass graves, stopping points of death marches, bits of secret underground factories, old scraps of bunker.

The landscape changes, lakes dry out, new roads are built, quarries are dug, pipelines are laid. There are still many men who earn their living by studying old aerial photographs to see where a row of craters indicated that one day or one night so many years ago some shit-scared young man in a rattling tin box held up by hope and dodging the shrapnel had let fall a 'stick' of bombs. If he had survived the return flight he may have been de-briefed back at his airbase by an Intelligence Officer, and reported where he had been and what he had done (though he might not have said that he had dropped his bombs a minute too early before target because he could no longer control his bowels or his trembling hands), maybe an aerial reconnaissance plane at high altitude had checked out the site later, had taken one of those amazingly-sharp black-and-white photos you can buy in books now, that show how almost four hundred holes had been blasted uselessly into an empty field at enormous expense and loss, maybe killing a couple of the Reich's cows, whilst perhaps two or three had hit the railway sidings at the top of the picture. So now, they study these pictures and try to see if there is a gap in the row, whether between the fourth and the sixth craters there should have been a fifth, and this gap indicates the site of a bomb that, having been manufactured at great expense and transported to the base and loaded in the aeroplane and flown at great risk all the way to the target area, did not bother even to explode. How ungrateful. Of course if the one that was dud was number one or number six in the sequence, then you would not know where it might be, for so many bombs went wide, there were high winds and planes that could not stay still for more than a few seconds without swerving away from searchlights or night fighters or flak shells, but nevertheless these men do their work seriously now and compare the old photos with modern maps and plot what can be identified and sometimes they go out and search with metal detectors and probes and other times they must simply wait until they get a call from a building site. Then measures need to be taken, an area must be evacuated, the '*Dienst*' would be called in, those special army units formed of men who know how to scrape away the clay and unscrew the tip or drill through the metal case and remove the fuse, unless the whole thing is so deformed or so rusted that nothing can be done except to control an explosion over seventy years too late.

This is the procedure for bombs dropped from the air. For some of them, at least, because of course many crews never made it back and maybe still lie undiscovered and undisturbed in the mud or the marsh or the sea..... But no-one could ever count the billions of artillery shells or the shells from tanks and mortars that were sent on their way in the heat of battle, when both sides were more concerned about survival than registering every hit on a map, and some slithered into the mud and just stayed there, waiting, waiting for someone to stumble upon them decades later. Hopefully not a curious child who would play with this exotic piece of metal, so redolent of the presumed heroism of war, not understanding the risk. And hopefully whoever was digging would feel their spade hit the side and not the tip.

Each of these things were designed to kill and each still can, given the opportunity by an unwary finder. The world's surface is still littered with hidden mines......

And then there are the people. Now, people are, as we know, composed of flesh and bone and - so long as they are alive - they possess a life force that allows them to move about and to think. But when this life-force has been knocked out of them or shot out of them or starved out of them, there remain just the flesh and bones - oh, and perhaps a few bits of uniform with metal studs or buckles. The flesh goes very quickly; Depending upon how damp the soil is or how acidic the bones can follow too. Or they can remain for a while, even for a few hundred years, browned, stained, blackened, never white. Chemical reactions take place. A person is reduced to a piece of upper jawbone and a row of teeth still smiling up as an archaeologist brushes the protective soil away. A metal helmet or a water canister shows the man had been a soldier. Or a total lack of anything else indicates they were probably a prisoner, not even properly clothed. Sometimes you can find, if you are an expert in these matters, bones with signs of wounds, skulls with bullet holes. Sometimes you might find bones which, from their size and shape, used to hold together a female body or a child's body and so it is a fairly safe presumption that this was not a former battlefield but a place where people were killed without fighting back. Sometimes you find a deposit of ash below the turf, with small bone fragments and teeth within it. Anything is possible and those whose job it is to look at fields and wonder what might lie beneath them are used to all sorts of surprises, however many photos and maps and battle charts and memoirs and casualty lists they have consulted beforehand.

What can one do? After all, the dead are long dead and the need for more rows of family houses is great and once planning permission has been granted to turn a field into an estate, a '*Siedlung*', nobody wants to be held up for long by a few old bones. And yet..... there is still a vague sense of pietism, a vague sense that "Something ought to be done", that we should somehow apologise to the dead, not because they are dead, it is far too late for that, but because they have been disturbed. Soldiers or airmen can be exhumed and possibly even identified and, in the presence of a Bundeswehr chaplain or the military attaché from the British or Canadian or Russian embassy, formally reburied in a military cemetery under yet another low white stone. But civilians? You cannot tell from a bone whether this was a forced labourer from Romania or the Ukraine or Denmark or Belgium or Poland. You cannot tell from a bone whether this person had been on a Death March from Place A to Place B or from Place C to Place D, and where they had been born and where they had grown up and fallen in love and dreamed their dreams and learned their skills, before one day they were taken off to some camp to be worked to death and then - if that hadn't worked - walked to death.

Bones are anonymous. You cannot submit each one to a DNA test. It is only in the Book of Ezekiel that they might come back together again. But you can at least bury them again, together, in a special place with a hedge around it and with a marker stone and a bronze plaque. Somewhere fairly far away, so that the town may continue to grow and it will not defile someone's future garden or get in the way of their car port or their grill or reduce the value of the plot. And then you can ask a local pastor to come and say something and, if possible, especially if there is a vague possibility that some of these bones had conceivably belonged to someone of the Hebraic ethnicity, a local Rabbi who will also go there and put on his robes and stand at some recently-turned piece of ground and take out his prayer book and say some words that will blow away in the wind like the lives and hopes of those whose bones have been found. Of course, things could be more complicated if it were certain that the people had been Jewish, which is why this possibility is rarely stressed. For then someone might demand that the remains not be moved. But there were certainly enough other victims at the time. And the Jews were mostly far away by this period. "In the East".

Maybe a photo will be taken for the local paper, or maybe not. This sort of stuff does not sell papers nor attract advertisers. Maybe a Local History Society will have dug into the archives rather than into the earth, maybe they will put a picture on their website. The town's Tourist Office will not, this much is for sure. Within eight months the first houses will be ready for their owners and the Bagger will be digging somewhere else.

Just wait for the phone to ring........

****

TEN EYES FOR TEN EYES

On the whole, looking back, I have had it easy as a Rabbi. I mean, I have had fights, I have experienced frustration and anger, I have had to watch my contracts with congregations being broken and accept lies being spread about me by the people who had done this, so as to justify their actions to the memberships. I have had to watch what I have worked hard to build up being neglected or even actively destroyed by a successor. I have been let down by ambitious colleagues. This has happened so often that eventually I just lost the interest in working with such people any more. I decided that I can continue to serve God without having to serve a Synagogue Board. That was a major revelation, and a healthy one. The slight matter of paying the rent and the health insurance - well, these are practical issues, not theological ones - unless your theology is based on the premise that, whatever happens, God will provide.

But we who grew up and worked after the *Shoah* know - even if only from what we read, what we heard - that God did not always provide.

Some rabbis in those days had to lead their communities out of the shtetl and to the killing fields where they had to dig and prepare their own graves. How ironic that the children of Abraham should be forced to do this, when Abraham himself was able to purchase a pre-prepared grave for his wife for a mere sum of money? When the only thing Abraham's servants had to dig were life-saving wells? But what did those rabbis feel like, what did they think, as they led their flocks? Then there were rabbis who had to share an enclosed freight wagon with their communities, to share the cramped conditions, the stink, the lack of sanitary facilities, the lack of privacy, to share the atmosphere of increased tension and fear as the hours went by and the wheels rolled and jolted across the tracks. Did they attempt one last sermon? Did they try to explain to those in their wagons what was happening, what they thought God's plan was? I doubt it. Or did they stand in silence, wrapped in their own thoughts, maybe praying, maybe defiantly refusing to pray? From one week to the next their status and their security was taken from them by an invading army of strangers in grey uniforms and now everything around them was turning from grey to black.... to the blackness of the earth, to the blackness of the smoke, to the blackness of their despair. Could they still be spiritual leaders in these circumstances and what did they have to say and who would be prepared to listen? Some did, and there are stories of those who kept people's spirits raised even in the huts with their rows of bunks. But I am sure that not all managed that.

No, however much I may grumble about what I have experienced as a rabbi, I have been spared challenges like those. Shortly before I was ordained I read of one of those horrific mass murders when, on the night after a successful happy wedding, the boyfriend of one of the sisters of the bride went round the house and slit the throats of the bride's sisters and parents..... The unfortunate bride herself would have learned of this tragedy on waking up at her honeymoon hotel after her wedding night. A phone call. "Thank goodness I don't have to officiate at THAT one," I thought - where would one start to try to make any meaning, any consolation, out of such a brutal and senseless murder of almost an entire family and just at the moment of their greatest happiness? But it happens and God alone - presumably - knows why. Not me. Not we. We all have to die but sometimes an entire family is wiped out in a motorway crash on their way to their holiday, sometimes a young couple are killed on their honeymoon, sometimes a pregnant woman dies and the baby with her..... sometimes the death is somehow even more tragic than it needs to be, if I can put it that way; it seems even more unfair, it seems even worse planning by The Boss. The death is then also a form of punishment for the bereaved, a hammer blow, unexpected and removing not just a person but a whole series of hopes.

These sort of thoughts went swiftly through my mind as I saw on the television news a brief report of a tragic, brutal, senseless mass murder in America. A man had shot his wife, his daughters and son and then himself. But they were British and it was the intention for their funeral to be held in Britain. "Well, at least it won't be me having to handle THAT one," I thought.

It is an old, old classic: How do you make God laugh? You tell Him your plans..... It was next morning that the phone went in my office. A vicar, from a village up in the Pennines. Poor chap. He had been suddenly confronted with the need to find a Rabbi within driving distance and there are very few of us around, so we are hard to find. He had a difficult funeral to arrange. A family. The father had been Jewish and so he needed a rabbi who would co-officiate with him. And yes – it was the same case. Ironically, I had heard of the village, but only because it was close to an interesting old railway line. I had never been there, but had at least a vague idea where it was.

So gradually the information trickled out in various calls over the next few days. The wife, the mother, had come from this village where her family had lived and farmed - sheep - for generations. She had been the clever one who left the village and went off to university where she had met the man of her life – her truncated life, as it turned out, the father of her children, the children who would not survive them. He was also a bright chap, charming, optimistic, who had done some strange business deals and amassed a fair fortune over the years, partly in this country, partly in the States. Except that –

nobody seemed to know exactly what it was that he did. "Something with shares" was the nearest any of these village people could understand. He had been a pleasant son-in-law and there had been a wedding in this little church, in this little mossy grey-stone granite village church and later even some christenings. But for the past two and a half years or so they had lived in Texas. There had been less and less contact. No summer visits. Fewer letters, fewer calls. Something did not seem to be going well but nobody knew what.

And now this. I thought it incredibly brave of the wife's parents, but they had insisted that the family should be buried together - despite everything. In the churchyard at the church where they had married and where the children, their grandchildren, had been baptised. I know the Church has rules about suicides and murderers but somehow this vicar - a very impressive man, calm, quiet, reserved but determined - had arranged that this would not be a major problem. They would lie together in a row on the other side of the walled enclosure from the rest of the graves - but still inside the cemetery. All he needed was someone to say "the Jewish prayers". We, too, have our rules normally about where to bury a suicide and so forth but thank goodness the times are more tolerant and in any case it was not my problem to make any decision. I was simply being asked to go there, to stand there, to "show presence", in fact to be honest I was mainly to be there to act as some form of visible symbol of the Jewish God who would accept this Jewish soul despite all that had happened. I can get pretty uncomfortable when this pressure is put on me to "play God", but in this case I felt different. The situation was bad enough as it was without me playing conscience games. But how Jewish had - he - been, really? Clearly not committed enough to seek a Jewish wife or to encourage his wife to convert, clearly not interested enough to raise his kids Jewishly - in America there are many communities which will accept the children of a Jewish father into their religion schools, into their youth camps but it seemed this had not been the case. However - and this was a major mystery - from the police report it was clear that, shortly before this horror had happened, he had driven to a local small-town synagogue to talk to a rabbi. But the rabbi had not been there. A janitor had explained to him - it was in his statement - that the rabbi only came weekends and that the place was closed and no, he could not open up the prayer room, not without permission. Was this the final straw? Was this the last attempt to seek guidance, consolation, counsel? Nobody would ever really know. But it was, somehow, significant. I wonder what that rabbi felt when he got the news? I never thought to ask who it was but of course many smaller congregations out in the sticks have to make do with part-time help, indeed I have to do the same with the smaller neighbouring synagogues.

On the whole I was passive, waiting for information to come to me. It was not yet known when the bodies would be released, when they could be flown over. But I promised to do my best to clear a day for this. It seemed he had not had much family left - both parents had died, the mother only a year previously; the father had survived the camps and come to England only after the war. Alone. There was a sister, in London, I was given her number and called. It was not an easy call. She was, even now, still in shock. "Hello, I am sorry to trouble you, I am the rabbi who has been asked to officiate at your brother's..." - She was the one who had been Jewish, had married a Jewish man, had had two Jewish children of her own. There was clearly a long history and most of it unhappy. She did not feel she was her brother's keeper. She did not feel she wanted to come to a church for the funeral service. Her brother had not even come to their mother's funeral. She was in deep grief for her two nieces and her nephew, even though they were not Jewish, she had had no real relationship with their mother but she felt it awful that the children should have had to suffer like this, to become victims.

I asked if there were any other people I should contact - but there were no other family, her father had lost everyone, her mother had had one sister, their aunt, who had died of cancer five years previously. She did not know of any former schoolfriends or colleagues. Between the lines there was clearly a lot that was not being said, a lot I was not being told, and there was nobody else I could ask. It did not look as though there would be anyone else Jewish there at all, and I saw no point in trying to assemble a minyan of pensioners prepared to ride out in a minibus just so that I could say '*Kaddish*' - I could do it better on my own. So in due course the Reverend called to say that it could be next Tuesday if this was all right with me? - and it was - and since the family wanted it at 9.30 in the morning would I care to come over the day before and he and his wife could put me up? This was incredibly generous and helpful but at the same time meant the whole thing would drag on further - but I accepted and was later glad that I did. It gave us both time to talk together, to measure each other up, to exchange information, to plan. It was a good three hours' drive, the last two in the early evening along those beautiful winding country roads with high dry-stone walls and overlooked by glooming peaks, through small villages. The vicarage was comfortable and the Reverend's quiet wife had made a vegetarian dinner for me and I had time to look around the village a bit and get a vague feel for the place from which this girl had come, this girl who became a woman who would die at her husband's hand in a car outside a small town in Texas. With her children watching in horror until their daddy turned the gun on them, too. After dinner at a big wooden plank of a table we sat in armchairs with a whiskey in our hands and he told me a bit about the family and what he knew - he had come here after the wedding but had done the last two of the christenings. Knew her parents and siblings, of course. We discussed, as colleagues, the various rituals we were expected to perform and whether they truly worked and whether we believed in them. I explained how and why I could not officiate at a mixed-faith wedding like the one that had been held here – the wedding ceremonies are very different between Judaism and Christianity, the marriage is not a sacrament, and so forth – and he understood, but he understood also how things are different with a funeral, when the emotions are different, the spiritual needs are different, the whole situation is different, for each individual is actually being placed in a separate grave, not being brought together into a joint life, not sharing a marriage bed. What sort of future eternal life awaits, and whether they will be together, who can say? In the New Testament (it's in Mark 12 and parallels) Jesus gets asked, even challenged by some of his Pharisee colleagues what his opinion is on the posthumous status of married people and his response had been quite clear; For him, the death of either partner automatically annulled the marriage bonds, leaving the surviving widow or widower free to remarry without guilt. "In heaven there are no husbands and wives." Presumably at this church the Reverend's predecessor had stood by and read the words, "Do you take This Woman, to be Your Wife, until Death do you part?" and the man had nodded and scraped his feet and said "Yes", with nobody present ever thinking about how that death might ever come, when and where, and how it would bring them together.

I had the easier task, I knew, and I would be able to drive off afterwards as well whilst he would have to stay with the mourning village which had lost one of their prettiest and cleverest daughters. There must have been many a man there who had been in love with her too, when she was younger, and who would be thinking, "If only she had married Me and not that murderous Jewish bastard." I would understand that feeling but of course, each of us makes our own decisions in life. There would be older people who had watched her grow up and play with their own children at the village school.

We Jews are a minority. We know this and we get used to it. Nevertheless, that morning there were over forty people in that church and I was the only Jew. The Reverend spoke wonderfully, absolutely wonderfully, and I was in awe of him. Not too much, not too little. He spoke of the need to understand that we cannot understand everything, he spoke of the need for compassion for those who do what we cannot comprehend, he spoke of the layers of fear and despair that can drive a person to behave out of character. He did not mention any of the facts that had appeared in the papers over the past week, the news of business deals and gangsters and threats and police investigations and possibly a corrupt politician - anyone who wanted to know this could get the newspapers at the village store. But he spoke of Love that brought people together and held them together even in difficult, nay impossible situations. And he commended them all - them ALL, he stressed this - into the hands of a compassionate God.

I, in my turn, had relatively little to say - but this we had agreed beforehand and I was very grateful for that. I had made a few notes but did not use them. I spoke of the commandments and of sin but also of atonement and the concept in Judaism that death can cancel out any moral debts and burdens one may still be carrying. And I explained that I would say the Jewish prayers not in the church but at the graveside. Technically this is no different, one could argue, after all, it is for the Christians consecrated ground, but although I have often spoken in churches or even read a psalm or two, I feel uncomfortable reciting a prayer when that Jewish man with the bleeding wounds and the arms stretched out to take his weight, the one who also felt alone and abandoned at the end, is hanging up on the wall behind me.

Incredibly, the Pennine skies were not weeping on this day in the way they so often do; a blustery cold wind blew but the sky was mostly blue. Five open graves lay in a row. Five coffins were carried by bearers, grim-faced and dressed in formal black. Three large, two smaller ones. The mother was buried first, then the children, to her left, in order of age, I was told. I had of course only seen photographs, pretty kids, smiling faces. One a teenager. Then, on her right, the fifth coffin was let down and lowered into the earth. Grave-digging is an art, and I have great respect for anyone who can prepare a deep oblong hole with straight sides and vertical sides and a flat base. It is, I am sure, not easy, and to do it five times in a row and ensure that the earth from one does not fill the adjacent one must be even more difficult. Those rabbis who had to lead their flocks to dig their own graves did not at least have to worry about whether the hole was geometrically exact. Though - what must it be like to look into the hole you have just dug and to know that this is to be your eternal home?

We have a very helpful prayer book especially for funerals, with some useful readings. We have the '*Kaddish*', we have the '*El Maleh Rachamim*', to the God of Mercy, for whose blessing we ask, on behalf of those no longer able even to mumble from a transcription. We have the ritual of taking a shovel and throwing some lumps of hard Pennine soil onto the lid of the coffin with a "Thwunk, Thwunk, Thwunk" sound that somehow resonates through every heart and every mind of those standing around with bowed heads. The sound of finality. We come from the soil and we return to the soil, that is why the first man is *Adam* because he comes from the *Adamah,* the earth. Soil and Soul, that's all we are, dust and destiny, and when the soul has left it is only the material that remains to be put where it can once more decay into its component parts and join the earth again.

In Hebrew a cemetery is called a House of Life, a '*Beit Chayim*'. No-one really knows why though there are several explanations. Those lying there are in fact not there, they have gone to eternal life. But here is where one buries the lives they had and maybe also the lives they would have led had they had longer to live them. Five lives had ended and five coffins came into the cold embrace of that soil. That was all we could do, for them and for us, for the dead and for the living. To accompany their bodies for those last few yards.

It felt like a collective sigh went round those assembled when the Reverend raised his arms and pronounced the benediction. He had asked me to do the same, in Hebrew, at the end and with some misgivings I did so. But the need had been met, the need for "a Jewish rabbi" to say "the Jewish prayers" at the burial of a family. Later on, at the church hall or at the pub or over garden gates, people would talk about the strange fellow who came with a hat on and who said those strange words. And hopefully they would have found it as something helpful, something positive.

We had already agreed that once the burial was over I would drive back - there was, after all, a lengthy drive ahead of me and other calls upon my time. There was one journalist from a local paper - we had been afraid, the Reverend and I, that a camera crew might turn up unannounced - I gave him a card so he could at least spell my name right but for the rest said there was nothing I wanted to add, no statement to make. I got out of my gown in the vestry. One of the men from the undertaker's also needed my card so they could write. There would be a fee to be paid. To the congregation.

It was a long drive back, though the weather was bright and clear, and I stopped twice at cafés for a coffee and a pee and a little time just to sit and think. I found my right arm was shaking a bit, my neck was aching, there was still too much tension inside me, one has to get it out before driving further. Back at the synagogue there were some calls to make, some post to deal with, the usual class at 4pm, but my mind kept going back to that grey-stone enclosure and the Pennines brooding above them. It is surely no coincidence that God chose a mountain for the revelation - even if the rabbis in their *midrashim* try to make out Sinai was only a small one; Just looking at a mountain makes you feel small, insignificant, aware of the way it sweeps up into the endless sky....

I have never been back to that area since, though it is an attractive part of the country. I suppose by now the grass will have grown tall over the row of graves. All five of them in a row. I was never called back for the setting of a tombstone or any anniversary commemoration, thank goodness. But one thing sticks in my mind even now, so many years later. It was a remark from the Reverend. Just a passing remark, as we sipped our whiskey. There were so many things that neither of us could understand about what had happened, and so many things we did not understand about the information that had come trickling out from official sources. He was also puzzled, he said, that when the bodies had been flown back to Britain, he had been told by the Coroner's representative that their eyes had all been removed. Why? Where were they? Where are they? What had those eyes last seen? What information do they hold? Who would decide, or instruct, that the eyes should be removed from the helpless corpses?

So often I am asked, "Why does Judaism demand 'An Eye for an Eye'?" And I have to explain that we don't, and try to explain the context for that legal statement of limitations. But someone, somewhere, an official with the power to do so, has kept ten eyes, presumably in jars.

I wonder what they see.

****

THE WEDDING TO END ALL WEDDINGS

As a Rabbi one is called upon to "officiate" (an amazing, officious word) at a variety of life-cycle events briefly referred to in the trade as "hatch, match and despatch" - birth, marriage and burial - though nowadays one could add "detach" for 'divorce' to the list. A wedding is a *Simchah,* a joyous occasion, a time for celebration and happiness. So they say. Personally, I prefer a good funeral to a bad wedding any day. At least with a funeral you know the main character will stay buried; with a wedding, there is no guarantee that the main characters will stay married. Before a funeral people are preparing for a brief ceremony of farewell, maybe long-awaited, maybe sudden and unexpected, sometimes truly tragic, sometimes a relief after a long decline, there is a wide range of possibilities since the deceased could be anywhere between new-born and, say, a hundred and five. Some of the dead are - still - truly loved, some were just tolerated, in some cases they have outlived all their contemporaries or the heirs are simply glad to see them go before the costs of the Care Home consume the entire capital. Of course it is never as simple as that, there is usually a wide variety of emotions, from those who feel truly bereaved and bereft, and those who appear out of a sense of duty, to represent 'the firm' or 'the club' or whatever, but who had no personal knowledge of the person in the coffin. To lose a parent is different to losing a grandparent, or a sibling, or a schoolmate, or a spouse, or a former lover. But a Funeral is finite, it is planned, it happens, it is done, it is part of the grieving process, the mourning, the attainment of Closure.

But - What is a Wedding all about? Who is celebrating what? Sometimes I have had to tell a new and nervous young couple to calm down, relax, close their eyes and just let the day go past. Their work will start when the wedding is past, when they have to work on building their marriage, whereas the Wedding Day is actually a day when the families will do most of the organising and make most of the decisions - and pay the bills. Maybe at a second marriage with more maturity, more life experience and older parents one can do things differently, but if you are in your early twenties and this is your first 'Big Day' then, I tell them, there is really no point in arguing with your mother or your future mother-in-law about the length of the dress, the colour of the serviettes, the types of flowers, the menu, what the DJ should play.... Just smile prettily and let them get on with it, it will all be a blur for you anyway on the day, you will eat hardly anything at the dinner, you will barely notice who has come...... You will eventually get off to some blessed peace in a hotel bedroom somewhere and that's when married life officially starts. Of course, nowadays it is rare to find a couple who are still virgins, but strangely the fact that they may have got to know each other physically and intimately already does not necessarily make it any easier once there is a gold ring on the finger and a commitment has been publicly made.

There are different customs which express different feelings. Even within Judaism and certainly within the Bible. Is the father of a bride happy, not that his daughter is happy but that at last he has got rid of another daughter, safely shuffled her off into the care of someone else? Look how Rivka, Rebecca is asked by her brother Laban if she wants to go off with a stranger who has turned up with several camels loaded with wealth, to marry an unknown son of an unknown but elderly rich chap who has no other heirs. She seems desperate to get away without any further delay. May one be permitted a slight touch of cynicism?

Later Jacob will work for seven years to be able to purchase at the appropriate price the woman he has fallen in love with. Seven years? That's a long time for an engagement, with perhaps the fear that at any moment some other, wealthier suitor could turn up. Then the bitterness of discovering he had been cheated by his new father-in-law (and brother-in-law) and palmed off with the older but second-best daughter, Leah. So now he has to work another seven years for Rachel - but at least this time demands his return payment in advance - there is no mention of a big wedding feast for this second wedding, however. It would have been interesting to have been an ear on the wall there.... With concubines such as Bilhah or Zilpah, or Hagar, it was much easier, they were just 'acquired'. We have many other occasions when it states "A took B to wife" but there is little information on weddings; David seemed to prefer pre-married wives and one wonders whether Solomon could even remember the names of his thousand wives. Kings married for political reasons, to make alliances. It was a practical matter. None of the characters in the New Testament gets married at all, though there is a wedding feast where the wine runs out.

Naturally an important part of the product quality was that one bought a Virgin - I have read the account by a British soldier I knew of an Arab wedding he attended in Sinai in 1943. The male guests sat in a circle in a large tent, the young girl was led in, maybe thirteen years old, sat down, the groom approached her, stuck his finger into her, (I don't think I need to describe where), displayed the bloodstained finger to all the guests, then handed over ten fifty-Piastre notes to her father. Then the guests began to eat the roasted sheep and rice, following which a belly strip-dancer performed in such a manner that fighting broke out with knives and whips and cudgels and the party ended with two dead and several badly wounded. Now THAT was a wedding party..... The groom came to work next day with glazed eyes and explained he had had five hours of non-stop sex.

Of course, Weddings were different in the days of parallel polygamy and not, as now, serial polygamy - that is, one could have several wives at the same time, not one after the other. And that is not even counting those people in every generation who work on the principle that they may have four wives, at least one of whom ought to be their own..... Back in the 1960's when a Moslem railwayman in London got run over at work the magistrates had to decide which of his three wives was the Senior Wife - or Widow - and therefore entitled to the compensation! Even so, traditional Judaism sees the wedding as the official signing and sealing of a contract between two parties "according to the Law of Moses and Israel" and these are essentially the parents of the bride and groom, not the bride and groom themselves! The groom promises in writing to support the wife with specific sums and to cover specific needs for nourishment, clothing, shelter, protection - and the rabbis added later a lot more about her emotional and sexual needs as well - and guarantees financial protection should he die or divorce her - there is a bride price to be paid and some of this capital is clearly deposited in the wife's name, she has first claim on his estate should he disappear. I don't suppose I need to go into too much detail here, but it shows how seriously the matter was taken; in the olden days a slave was a slave, a prostitute was a prostitute, a captured woman was booty, but a wife was a wife and she had status, she had her own servants, her own tent or part of the tent, whatever. Love? Romance? Don't make me laugh. How would a man dare to make pregnant a woman he really loved, knowing in advance just how dangerous this could be for her? As Jacob found out to his cost when the new inexperienced midwife was unable to save both the beloved mother and the child and Jacob, with his long experience of helping ewes and nanny goats give birth, had to pull the baby out with his own right hand.... as Rachel (which, ironically, means 'Ewe') expired in agony and exhaustion....

But there are many misapprehensions about weddings. Is it a public affair or a private one or a bit of both? A bit of both, actually - traditionally the vows and blessings were made with witnesses, in public, whereas the couple then had to come together in private, in '*Yichud*', in unity, either to consummate the marriage - the first time they would be together without chaperones - or at least to relax together after the strain. Maybe to have something to eat if they have been fasting on the day, for the wedding day is considered to be like dying as a single person and being reborn as a married one. Technically the marriage is not considered complete until all three major components have been accomplished - the handing over of the bride price (nowadays a symbolic ring), the signing of the legal contract document (the *Ketubah*) and the *Yichud,* the consummation when, as it says in Genesis 2, they 'become one flesh'. I once had an argument with a couple who wanted the entire ceremony to be videoed - this in the days when video cameras were large and needed tripods and cables everywhere - the WHOLE lot. So that relatives could watch it all later. I am a flexible chap and I try to meet the desires of my congregants but I said "I have no problem with the filming of the public sections, the processions in and out, the singing of the blessings, the fitting of the rings, the drinking from the wine cup, the breaking of the glass, the signing of the *Ketubah* - but when I address you quietly, under the chuppah, just you two and me there, then I will speak quietly because this bit is private, it's just between me and you." 'No," they cried, "we want EVERYTHING to be videoed!" We went back and forth a bit until at length I conceded. "All right," I said, "Then we can video Everything. But there are just two conditions; Firstly, this has to include the wedding night, which is a significant part of the ceremony, and secondly, I need a copy so as to check that the consummation really took place." They were suitably horrified. "But Rabbi! That's PRIVATE!" "Aha," I said, "My point exactly." That was one debate I won. Nowadays, whatever one says, half the guests are holding up their mobile phones anyway, filming non-stop. But people get all sorts of silly ideas when it comes to weddings; I had to officiate once when the groom landed on the lawn by the canopy from a helicopter... a vicar told me he had been asked to officiate once underwater in a diving suit and had refused.... they went elsewhere and presumably found someone who was indeed prepared to get wet. 'Gimmick Weddings', they are called in the trade. And who really needs to start their married life with a gimmick?

Of course, it sometimes happens that families will get deeply into debt over the costs of the wedding and have no money left to start off their marriage together....

Well, I have a private "rule of thumb" that goes something like, "The bigger the wedding, the shorter the marriage". The reason is that when there is true love a modest ceremony will suffice, just the couple and at most a few close family and friends, whereas if someone is busily and loudly trying to make a point then the chances are that somewhere, somehow, something is not quite right. Either they want to cover for the fact that the bride is pregnant, or that the father of the bride is having problems with his business, or that the groom is known to be bisexual and had an affair with the Best Man, or that the two pairs of parents, the '*Machatonim*' cannot stand each other, or...... who knows? One is merely a little cynical, a little suspicious. After all, back in Genesis 29 Laban wanted with excessive food and drink to hide the fact that the groom Jacob really wanted the other sister as his bride!

I know I am not the first to have this concern. In the past many communities had what they called 'Sumptuary Laws', local regulations applied by the rabbi or the community council to limit how much could be spent on certain celebrations. To stop things getting out of hand. A limit as to how many musicians should be hired, how many courses should be served at the banquet, a maximum, a top limit.... They were concerned as to avoiding getting the non-Jewish neighbours jealous, or suspicious as to where the wealth had come from, but also of putting to shame poorer families and orphan brides who could not match that level of needless outlay and extravagance. ('Needless' because you do not need it for a wedding ceremony.) Even hundreds of years before that a famous rabbi had insisted on being given a cheap funeral in a simple coffin so as to set an example to all that one really did not need anything fancier and more expensive.

Well, the Shapiros were planning a Big Wedding for their Harvey, that much was for sure. I did not know the family at all, really; It was one of those weddings where the groom's family belonged to one of the "Orthodox" shuls in town whereas the bride's mother had converted through our community and was not therefore "kosher enough" for the other synagogues. So we at the Reform synagogue would be responsible for the wedding, but no way would it be held in our synagogue building! Oh no! That would be too obvious, on the embossed invitations, that would be too embarrassing, that would be 'giving in'! There was a large Country Club some half an hour away, a former Manor House or something, one of those places that has been turned into a 'Venue' for conferences, celebrations, classical concerts, dirty but discreet weekends and the like. Grey stone, a portico, sash windows, manicured pale green lawns (never 'grass green' for some reason in the brochures)..... And gradually it became clear there was to be a full kosher catering (enormously expensive) and a jazz band and a string quartet (that pleased me) and a disc jockey and an additional marquee and Lord knows what else besides.

Janet was out of her class, that was for sure, and her parents, modest people, he was a grocer and she was a nurse, had no real idea what was going on but had been assured that they would not have to pay for it - a great relief. Traditionally of course the bride's parents have to stump up for most of the unnecessary expense. So much is spent on temporary, short-lived things that will disappear or fade or be consumed within hours... decorations that will be dismantled afterwards, flowers that will dry out in the sun, serviettes and *kippot* to match the colour of the bride's lingerie (or have I got that bit wrong?)....

We have a rule that, since I am employed full-time by the congregation, I only 'officiate' for members of the congregation, so when Harvey and Janet first made an appointment to come and see me I gently mentioned this and could see that Harvey was uncomfortable with the idea of being a member of our congregation, but I was "gentle but firm" and gave him the application form. Of course, he would leave after the first year at most, maybe even after the first quarter's subscription payment, but it's the principle of the thing. However, although we discussed this and that about the details, how I would use a Reform *Ketubah* document which is egalitarian and allows the bride to say something as well and speaks more of mutual love and respect and less of the financial value of the bride dependent on whether she is a virgin or a widow or divorcée, and he accepted that there would be two rings and so forth, I could not get him to agree to hold a rehearsal at the synagogue, which is normally a good opportunity to meet all concerned and show them where they ought to walk or sit or stand as bridesmaids, as parents, 'Best Man' and so forth; nor did they want an '*Aufruf*' to the Torah reading on the Shabbat beforehand - it was painfully obvious that the only reason I had been invited to officiate was because as far as I was concerned Janet was Jewish whereas for the Orthodox rabbi she was not. For him it would be a 'mixed marriage'. One gets a lot of such issues in a community and one never really gets used to it, though one of my beloved teachers taught that "Sometimes it is a *mitzvah* to let yourself be used." Yes, it can be uncomfortable and yes, it is always an implied insult but, what the heck, it shows that we have a vital function to fulfil, to be the safety valve, the alternative, to break the monopoly of the other congregation. So I put up with it. Grit your teeth, put your head down and carry on. It's often the only way.

There are two main alternatives when it comes to the Civil Ceremony. Britain is theoretically a society built upon laws and precedents and the rule is that anyone is entitled to get married in any way they want, the State really doesn't care whether it's in an Anglican Cathedral or a ceremony performed for the Flying Spaghetti Monster or using Star Trek Vulcan rituals - BUT - there has to be a civil wedding ceremony with a Registrar first, otherwise it does not count, the couple are not officially married, there will be no relevant tax allowances and no widow's pension and all that. So either the couple go to get married at the Registrar's Office a day or two beforehand and show me the signed certificate, before I am allowed to commence the religious ceremony, or - and this is a major privilege based on some snappy politics generations ago - the synagogue can appoint a responsible person to act as the Registrar's representative, to hold and bring the big heavy Register and fill in with their special indelible ink all the relevant details and this can be signed by those concerned. The actual certificate will be issued later by the office, signed and stamped. On this occasion Harvey and Janet decided to combine the ceremonies on the same afternoon, which is fine but meant that they had to invite Raymond along as well - he is one of the wardens, an accountant and a very solemn person indeed.

I will spare us all the details of various other minor negotiations that followed; issues about photographers and video-cameramen and bridesmaids and bridal flower-scatterers and the prayerbooks and whether there was a *kiddush* cup they would like to use and whether the Best Man knew his Hebrew name and so forth. Actually, this was Harvey's second wedding and it seemed that a part of the splurge and the glitter and the glamour was to ensure that nobody might think that his second wife was going to be in any way inferior or less favoured than the first. Except, of course, in terms of her Jewish identity - and that of any future offspring. So much for the religious aspects of this oh-so-happy day. (Oh, and I had checked that he had obtained and given a '*Get*', a Jewish divorce document too.)

Came the day, and I drove down to the Country Hotel. Although I had offered him a lift, Raymond decided to take his own car so he could get away afterwards, he had no desire to spend an entire nice Sunday afternoon in his suit and a marquee when it was a good time for gardening. I would have to stay at least until the Grace After Meals with the special extra *Sheva Berachot*, the Seven Blessings for the Groom and Bride. I have a routine, what to pack in my 'wedding case' - gown, *tallit*, a white *kippah*, a small bottle of kosher wine in case they forget, a spare ring in case one gets lost (! - this was the advice from one of my teachers - it can be anything, a curtain ring, a plastic bit of bling, anything that can be used on the day as a temporary replacement until the right one turns up - I have never needed it yet but feel better for having it), the *Ketubah* rolled up and wrapped, a good-quality black rollerball pen, prayer book). Once parked I looked for the girl - it is almost always a girl - in her competent grey skirt and white blouse (also apparently a uniform) who would represent The Management and would be my liaison person. These people seem to be cloned but they are so invaluable. Somebody has to check where the chairs are to be set out, and the canopy, and the little table for me to put things on, and the reading desk where Raymond could open his Register, and ensure that a nice glass with a long stem that will easily and crunchily break is wrapped up in a serviette, and so forth. Somebody has to tell the waiters when to start their rounds and, keeping an eye out for my nod, when to tell them to stop. Somebody has to ensure the broken glass will be removed at the end. This and so much more is her job.

The musicians are tuning up (though I often don't know why they bother) and one or two cameramen are playing around, checking through viewfinders, looking for angles, the way the sun's rays will hit. Guests are arriving, mingling with loud chatter and champagne glasses. Waiters start their rounds with trays of fiddly nibbles. When we do weddings at the synagogue I know where everything is, which room (often my Study or the Library) the couple will retreat to afterwards, where the *Siddurim* are, where the *Bentschers* – the Grace After Meals booklets are, which way they will process, and all that; in a new venue, which I see for the first time less than half an hour before we are due to start, one has to work quickly to work out where to stand, where to put the things down, where to put the case, how to distribute any books and so forth. Sometimes there is a box of little printed service booklets. Someone who looks still sober has to be asked to stand by the entrance and ensure that all guests get a booklet, that all the males get one of the *kippot* printed with "The wedding of A and B' and the date. It happens often enough that the *kippot* last longer than the marriage, which can be embarrassing.

Experience helps in these last-minute preparations. Where is the Bride? Thank goodness, yes, she is here, nervous, fabulous dress (all wedding dresses are fabulous and the Rabbis said that there are occasions when it is permitted to make a little white lie, for the sake of peace, and one example they give is that you must ALWAYS tell a bride that she is beautiful!), nervous parents, gum-chewing bridesmaid, they can go and sit over Here, please. The groom, the groom, where in heaven's name is the groom, are here, yes, he looks a little tired, the Best Man too, check with the BM if he has the boxes with the rings? Yes, good, one problem less. Do they need another slip of paper with their Hebrew names written down to copy? Come to that, do I have the slip of paper with the names of the Witnesses? Yes, thank goodness.

There is nothing really special about all this, it is all a part of the job. An engine driver or a pilot will perform his routine checks before starting. A handyman will check he has everything in his toolbox and the right overalls on. A bus driver will check the fuel, the tyres, the lights, his cash box, the destination blind and route number display. It is just a part of the preparations for doing your job in a competent, professional way.

The job? To be as much as anything else a Master of Ceremonies, to call the audience - oops, the wedding guests to order, politely, to explain to them what is going to happen and when to stand and please no flash and so forth and to turn their mobile phones off, to put Harvey standing Here and his Best Man Here and his father There and this old lady, his grandmother, should have a chair brought forwards, please? Thank you, and today there will be no brief *Minchah* service, no Afternoon Prayers, but straight into the ceremony, a nod to the musicians, a nod to the lady in the grey skirt who nods to the Bridal group standing nervously behind a curtain somewhere and off we go...... First two little girls scattering flower petals over the carpet from little baskets, fortunately this time neither of them falls over her white buckled shoes and starts to cry, needing to be scooped up and 'hushed' by an embarrassed mother, they cannot be over four years old.....

Raymond acted as *Gabbay* for me, handing me the things I needed as I needed them, the wine cup, the *Ketubah*, the rings, Harvey said "Yes" at the right moment and repeated the betrothal and marriage formula after me, Janet did the same, there was some hubbub from the audience who clearly had little concept of the official solemnity of the occasion (something illustrated as much by their clothing, I often wonder why many female guests seem to dress at weddings in order to distract the most strong-willed of grooms from his bride), no babies cried for long. I addressed the couple - quietly - about the significance of the step they were taking, their promise to build up a "House amongst the People of Israel" and "according to the Law of Moses and Israel", I read the *Ketubah* in its Hebrew and English (so much easier than the un-pointed Aramaic of traditional texts) and they signed first the Register under Raymond's guidance and then the *Ketubah* under mine, pointing to where their signatures should go, and eventually all was done.

With a flourish Harvey stamped on the glass. Although I often try to explain that this is actually a sad moment, a moment of reflection on loss and tragedy and the destructions our people have suffered, whatever I say, people always roar "*Mazal Tov*!" the moment the glass crunches. The couple turned and processed down between the rows of chairs, being photographed, greeted, and more.

Whew. All had gone well. I thanked Raymond who packed his things away, I packed my own things away and took off the *tallit* and then the gown, which can get really hot on a summer afternoon. From now on, once I had put all into my case, I was Just In The Way, an official guest who had to stand around, a glass of orange juice in my hand, smiling, nodding, accepting gracefully several compliments ("That was great, Rabbi!") and a few quieter ones from non-Jewish guests who explained carefully how this was their first experience of a Jewish service. Hardly typical, of course, but there we go. The jazz band started up and by the time the bride and groom reappeared to greet the guests quite a few were already tipsy. There is a nice and very relevant 'lightbulb joke' - "How many Wedding Photographers does it take to change a light bulb?" Answer: "Just one more! Just one more! Just one more!" These guys usually think they are being paid by the minute, by the hour. Years ago I had to explain firmly that I was not going to do the whole ceremony again for the sake of the video cameraman getting a different angle.....

As 'MC' one has to judge the moment to wander over to the family standing in a row in This sequence and then That sequence and then the Other sequence with Uncle Joe in the Middle and then Cousin Zipporah, you should be at the front! and politely suggest they should draw this phase to a close and move to the dinner table. The guests will have had time to check out on some big board or through place labels where they are meant to be sitting, the caterer also has his years of experience, the Children's Table with its pre-pubescent suited and frocked lovelies all high on excitement and mutual dislike and embarrassment will get plenty of fish fingers and chips and ketchup, for the rest of us there are several courses to play with and maybe even eat some. Poached salmon. Coleslaw. Melon. Dried-out kosher chocolate cake. Red wine, white wine, fizzy water. Coffee and chocolate mints. The conversations in the background rise and swell and reverberate and drown all attempts to hold a conversation with the person across the round table. But before it all starts I have to go to the Top Table (thank goodness I am not sitting at it this time, placed at the far end usually) and call for silence and solemnly pronounce the blessings for wine and bread and break the large-size challah and present chunks to the happy couple, and the parents, and why is that women in the green hat staring daggers at me? As I sit and toy with my Starter I realise that somehow, from the corner of my eye, I had been aware of a frosty look from her direction several times during the ceremony, rather than a jolly smile.

People think one is happy with a Free Meal but in fact one can spend anything up to five hours waiting for the opportunity to complete one's duties, recite the *Birchat HaMazon*, the Grace After Meals and leave the wedding party to whatever orgiastic bacchanalia they have prepared - certainly it is better for all concerned if the Rabbi is not there at some later stages of the revels. And once again, though I call for silence, and blow into the microphone to ensure that at least it can go "Swoosshhh" and urge people to take a booklet, and request "the Gentlemen please to cover their heads" and announce that we are going to start on Page One and "Please join in if you wish", the guests just chatter and chatter all the way through the Hebrew. If in exasperation I suddenly switch to English for a paragraph they will, amazingly, shut up for the duration, then burst into chatter again when I return to the Hebrew. Why, why am I bothering? Who is concerned for the spiritual welfare of this new couple, who cares if God will bless them, who is concerned about the desire to hear once more the sound of children playing and singing in the ruined city of Jerusalem, who is grateful for the wide and fruitful land we have been given? Not one......

But it is done, I have stayed till the end of the meal, sung till the end of the Grace, finished with the *Sheva Berachot* again, this time there were three nervous guys who had agreed to stumble each through one of the shorter ones while I handled the rest... I have done my duty and with a few smiles and handshakes I can take my leave and get back to the car. No, wait, it is a good half hour back, maybe a quick call first. Oh, and a thank you to the waiters and the waitresses and the girl in the grey skirt who is supervising everything so efficiently.

By the time I get home it will be 8 o'clock at least and I will be exhausted, my shirt still sweaty. But at least not surrounded by people I don't know, for whom I have no small talk and, thanks to the noise, little chance to make it anyway. The string quartet won't come on till the evening. A pity. Working musicians, Lord help them,

Next day, Monday, back in the office. A phone call is

switched through. It is Harvey Shapiro! "Hello," I begin, cheerily. "*Mazal tov* again! How are you all this bright morning?" I am vaguely expecting a Thank You and feel I have deserved one, but Harvey is using a different tone of voice. "Rabbi, my mother is furious at you, you really ought to apologise to her! You ruined the whole wedding!"

I am taken aback. "Excuse me, I'm sorry, I don't understand. Did I say something wrong?"

"No, that's just the point, you didn't talk to her at all and she is very hurt. Very hurt, Rabbi." Only a nice Jewish boy can say those words about his mother with that burden of guilt-inducing pathos.

I am flabbergasted. "I'm sorry, but can you explain? I certainly don't recall insulting anybody, I certainly didn't mean to, what am I meant to have done?"

And then it comes out. That woman in the green hat. The one who had refused to meet with me beforehand, the one who had put her foot down and said 'No rehearsal', the one who despised me as not being a "real rabbi" - SHE had been the mother and because nobody had introduced her to me, nor had she come forward to introduce herself, I had simply forgotten about her in the haze of preparations! Forgotten that she was meant to be there! And - in my favour, to be fair to me - she was presumably Harvey's mother but the man who was presumably Harvey's father had brought along the current wife, "Mrs. Shapiro Mark 2" and so when I had shaken hands with "Mr. and Mrs." it had never crossed my mind that there might be someone else there that day with a close family interest to either of the couple! Since the family were not members of our congregation I had simply no idea of the complex family constellation and Harvey had done nothing to enlighten me. The lady, watching her son marry a second time and to a most Unsuitable girl, pushed to one side by her successor, might have had good grounds by her lights to be a bit bitter - but not at Me!

So I was the BAD Rabbi. The careless, incompetent one!

But somehow, I didn't care.

Oh, by the way – before I forget – Harvey and Janet - they split up four months later. It seems he had got someone else pregnant..... maybe a week before the wedding, maybe a week after, for all I know even during it. I don't think, somehow .I'll be asked to officiate at his third wedding.

And I reckon I will somehow live with that.

****

LIKE PUTTI IN MY HANDS

It is amazing how many classical paintings and frescoes seem to have Putti in them - little naked toddlers flying about or gazing wistfully upwards from odd corners or behind trees. I don't think it's a discreet form of child pornography, even though all the little boys have very visible tiny penises (no testicles, of course) and any little female children seem to have some evanescent covering or shawl covering any potential naughtiness. I wonder, in fact, whether it is a form of memorial to all the small children who died so young and yet, for their families, are still somehow there, as little angels, in the background? A form of comfort for whoever commissioned the painting that the dead are still visible, close to God, as cadet-angels or something similar? They died pure and pre-pubescent, untainted....

The thought comes again when I am confronted with one of those innumerable tragedies. SIDS it is called - Sudden Infant Death Syndrome - and we have a funeral to organise that should not really be necessary. But the baby was sleeping quietly in his Carrycot when they strapped it onto the back seat of the car and when they got to their destination barely a quarter of an hour later he was blue and dead..... Nobody can understand how it happened, nobody can understand what went wrong, the child was not left in the cold, not left in a hot airless car, not in a draught, not dropped, not allowed to put something in its mouth - no, it just went quietly to sleep and did not wake up. It stopped breathing. A silent and sudden form of heartbreak.

The parents have come to see me. Red-eyed and very subdued still. He is a doctor at one of the big hospitals, so he knows a little about these things. This was their first child, a daughter. We have two choices for the funeral; the cemetery near where they live, over in a small town in the next valley, or our Jewish cemetery. He would like it to be in our cemetery because he doesn't want to pass the grave every time he drives to work; she however wants it near their home so she can go to visit more easily. This needs to be sorted out between them, I cannot really apply any pressure either way. In Judaism it is the individual grave which is holy, not the cemetery as such, that is a more recent idea and there is no law against burying someone Jewish in a cemetery that does not belong to a Jewish organisation but to a church, to a municipality, to the military, wherever.

Where is the baby? At the municipal mortuary. There was a post-mortem, of course, people always want to know if a baby that dies suddenly had been hit or throttled or shaken or maltreated in some way, usually not out of sadism but just to stop it crying endlessly. Why do they want to know? Just to punish the parents further? But this was just one of those unexplained and inexplicable cases where whatever physical instincts that the body uses to keep breathing had paused for a while, for a fatal while.

Our Jewish undertaker Alec is a nice chap and I trust him, even though I know he gets a lot of pressure and hassle from a few other people in the town. His limousine is a little shabby, but he has a good heart. I call him. Explain the situation. He will collect the child and - we have now decided between us - bring it to the next town across the hill, in the next Dale. Here, too, is a section for Infants. We fix a date and a time, not far away. Now that the decision is made there is no need for further delay. But it will be a quiet funeral, no cortège, no other family even invited.

And so it is. A blustery Thursday morning. I am there by 10am, we had arranged 10.30 so I sit in the car with some classical music on the radio and try to keep calm. The limousine pulls up next to me at the car park. There is no need for a hearse, not for a coffin the size of a shoe box. Alec is driving it himself, not one of his men. We walk together to the top corner of the cemetery where, under a tree, a small hole has been prepared. Alec, who has been carrying the little plywood box next to his chest, under a black cloth, kneels to place it in the hole, struggles a bit to get up, then stands to one side. Father and mother step forward and look down. There is little to say. No eulogy, no list of good deeds, no list of people to mention. Just a few standard prayers. This little scrap of humanity came, slept, and left.

And left behind a bigger hole, bigger by far, than the one it has now filled.

****

HALF THERE

It is clear that she loves him, and loves him deeply. She comes to him, sits with him, stays with him, whole days and maybe nights. She caresses his head, she strokes his cheeks, she places the tip of a finger on his lips.

Does he love her? It is hard to say. It is hard to say anything, in fact, because his eyes are vacant and his head is either in a metal clamp when he sits or allowed to roll back when he lies. He does not seem to make any attempt at speech, not even a whistly shriek, not even a "Ngaaah, ngaah" with no diction but at least a sign of an effort to communicate. He sits there and he lies there and he stares into nothingness and he makes no move, no twitch, does not try to communicate by winking and blinking in a certain sequence or pointing to letters on a chart. In fact, if he were not still the colour of someone who is alive, and were it not for the charts hung at the edge of the bed, and the tubes in his arms, and the tube from his bladder, one would assume he were dead. But no, he is alive, half alive, at least. Some organs continue to pump or to filter or to transpirate and so, technically, for the purposes of the Clinic Administration and the statisticians at the Health Office and the people charged with meeting the monthly bills for treatment, he is alive.

But not for anyone else. Apart from her.

She loves him still. In a way this is touching and inspiring. In a way it is worrying. When will she give up, when will she let go, when will she reach a stage of acceptance, when will she stop coming every day she can to play music cassettes to him, his favourite music, to which he makes no response, to tell him in as jolly a voice as she can manage what has happened at her job or what her sister has just done, to which he makes no response, to ask if he likes the curtain open? - to which he makes no response. When will she find the courage inside herself to leave him?

It was a Christmas when it happened and he was the innocent party. A few years ago, already. He was driving at the legal speed and he was sober and it was another car that came shooting out of a side road with a driver who was not quite so sober and smashed into his side of the car. She, sitting next to him, was thrown out, spent two weeks in plaster, and was then released. Her parents had come to visit her and they had told her that he had been badly injured but the doctors said he would live. Well, in a way they were right. Half right. He, caught in the mangled metalwork, needed three firemen with acetylene torches and axes to dismember the framework of the saloon car wrapped around him - or what was left of him - and he was then taken with a lot of sirens and blue lights to intensive care where, as the saying goes, he was "stabilised".

"Stabilised". It sounds quite good, in fact. "How is he? Oh, he's stable." Effectively it means he is not getting any worse but then not really getting any better either. Since nobody really knows how the human body works and even doctors and surgeons only know what they have been taught by experts who don't know either - they are also taught to bluff when necessary, as it so often is - the general rule of thumb is to keep someone "stabilised" for as long as possible in the hope that eventually the body will heal itself. We all know this, but we all deny it. "You have a cold? Go to bed for a day or two. Let it get better. You have a digestive problem, an irregular heartbeat, a deep coughing in the lungs, breathlessness, a strange pain in an indefinable spot? Well, take some pills, take some medicines, keep warm, lie down, stay as stable as you can - and hopefully you will get better. If you don't, then all we can really suggest are more pills, more medicines and - most important of all - more time." The medical profession largely comprises people who have learned the value of a white coat, a paternal or maternal voice, a calm manner and a stethoscope over their necks. But unless they are the kind of surgeons who do active invasive surgery, who slice somebody open in order to cut bits out, stitch bits together or glue broken bones together, most of the treatment consists of "keeping the patient stable and letting Nature take its course." Of course I am being a bit unfair here, I admit it. But only a bit. And the doctors I know and to whom I have spoken will largely confirm that the remedies they can offer are still largely hit and miss, even if, over the decades and with much research and progress, some more 'hits' are being registered with certain conditions. Medicine is a magic art filled with mysteries, dressed up as a science. No two human bodies are exactly the same and so no treatment or dosage can be equally effective for each one. You may be able to work out What has happened but not Why, why now, why to this person and not that one? There can be identical twins with the same DNA and yet one will develop a tumour, or liver failure, or a blood clot, the other not. Sometimes as a doctor you hit lucky and are praised for your skill, sometimes you have to shake your head and offer the family your condolences, "it was too far gone, there was nothing more we could do."

The doctors here had managed this very well, for three years and a bit, in fact. That is how long Steven had been lying in this bed, occasionally being turned, occasionally being lifted, occasionally being washed, occasionally being raised into a semi-upright position... I had not been aware at all, nobody had told me, nobody had felt it was my business and in a way they were right for there was nothing I could really do, either. The practice of "visiting the sick", "*Bikkur Cholim*", is considered to be a *mitzvah*, a moral duty which also brings you in due course merit and reward because those who are sick, by definition, spend a lot of time by themselves in their sick beds, in their wards or their rooms, they cannot get out to meet people and are left with their loneliness and their worries and their pains. Sometimes all they need is a brief visit so that they do not feel forgotten. Sometimes they need help, someone who can arrange for them what they themselves cannot do - to write a letter, to make a call, to contact an office, to postpone a bill - if you are stuck in a hospital ward somewhere for several weeks, who will tell the Electricity Board not to cut off the current? Who will tell the bank that you have not forgotten the credit card bill but are unable to deal with it personally right now? Not everyone has family, or family living close by, and hospital social workers are busy people with many claims on their time, and you can feel helpless and worried when isolated from the world - and feelings of helplessness and worry do not help with "stabilisation".

Sometimes the sick, having been confronted (perhaps unexpectedly or for the first time) with their morbidity and mortality, want to discuss things they have been thinking over during the long sleepless nights. Why did this happen? Why did it happen to Me? Will I get better? What if I don't? How will I live after I get better from this? What should I be thinking about, in case I do NOT get better from this? Then one can, as a Rabbi and not just as a fellow Jew, perhaps proffer some insights, even give some advice, even maybe help with some arrangements, bring in a form, bring in a prayer book, help restore contact with long-lost family members.....

But all this presupposes that the patient is conscious and is aware that you are there. What if they are not? Of course, nobody really knows where someone is when they are in a coma, say, halfway between this world and the next one, their body breathing here - or being helped to breathe - and being hydrated and cared for, while their life, their soul, their living being is - somewhere else. It has become the custom nowadays to talk to coma patients on the assumption that they might, after all, hear you, to play music to them, to touch them and stroke their arms and squeeze their hands - it can't hurt, people say, and maybe, just maybe, inside that lump with its regular mechanised breathing, a person is aware that someone is reaching out to them. You never know. I recall one congregant who told me that, after three months suspended between here and wherever, when "nature had taken its course" and her consciousness returned and she could breathe by herself again, she had no recollection of any of her family or nurses or any other visitors (including me) talking to her, but she did recall her grandmother sitting by her bedside the whole time. The grandmother of course had been "away from here" for many years, but I had no problem in believing her tale. Sometimes one is only half alive, half here and half there, and people who care can be trying to reach out to you from both sides, to encourage you, to strengthen you. Why not?

But when the patient is deeply unconscious when you visit, you feel utterly helpless. Sometimes one goes simply so that the family can later be told "the Rabbi was here" and that may comfort them; or so that you can make your own assessment of the situation and leave a visiting card to be put in the patient's file. Sometimes it is an intensive ward and sometimes an extensive one, or a ward where the patients are mostly geriatric and hardly here mentally anyway, or where palliative care keeps the patients drugged to the extent that they cannot feel pain but in consequence little else either. Who knows where each and every one of us might end up at some time, how our lives will play out, how it will be for us in a few more decades - or less? When and how will the End come?

The problem here is that the End for Steven has been postponed, but not in any positive way. The Catholics have a term, 'limbo', for a sort of nowhere-space between the worlds where the souls that are not yet ready for admittance have to wait until the time is right. Everything remains 'on hold'. Steven is in limbo. His soul does not seem to be quite Here, but neither has it left entirely and gone There.

The other problem is Margarete who clearly cannot let go. Steven's parents live down south, somewhere in Bayern, and they come once a month to visit but only briefly, for there is nothing more that they can say or do and if the weather is bad they skip the visit and they themselves are not getting any younger either. There is a brother in Canada, he has been twice but soon saw that as far as he was concerned his brother was already dead, just breathing. Without the technology the breathing would have stopped years ago and everybody would have been able to return to a life without Steven, with some grief, some regrets but also time and energy to move onward. This way - they still have a Steven in their lives, but one with whom they cannot talk, cannot share memories, cannot discuss his likes and dislikes, they cannot bring him food for he is nourished through tubes, he cannot smell flowers or read cards......

It was Margarete who had called the office of the Gemeinde and asked for the rabbi to come and say a prayer...... she isn't Jewish, but he is... and she felt that on his birthday it would be nice for a rabbi to recite some foreign blessings that might help. That might help? Well, I suppose that is what we all do all the time, we do things that "might help", it is all a matter of faith, we cannot guarantee that a ritual WILL help, just as a doctor cannot guarantee that an operation will help, one does what one can and one hopes the patient's body will react in the hoped-for way......

We had fixed a time, I had taken a taxi there, met at the entrance, she had walked me along light-filled corridors with large windows and views of the trees outside, the flower beds, other white-painted buildings scattered in what was probably a purposeful way if one could understand the purpose. Maybe there is a reason for one block to be the power plant and one the kitchens and one a hostel for the nursing staff...... The hospital is indeed situated in an attractive spot, outside the city, but that doesn't really help if one cannot see it. Steven lies on a big bed in a separate room. Tubes run into him and through him and out of him. He is motionless, all the time I am there with Margarete. There is no reaction when I greet him, speak to him or, taking the bookmark, read to him from the prayer book.

But Margarete smiles and looks relieved. We sit there for an hour while she tells me about Steven, about his family, about the accident, about the music cassettes she brings, about the books she reads aloud to him, about how she looks at him each moment to see if there is a smile, a blink, a reaction of any sort. She tells me that she loves him still. She is maybe thirty and I cannot help but wonder what sort of one-sided love this would be, or what she gets from it. A woman her age, attractive, intelligent, educated, caring, should be thinking ahead, seeking a partner, arranging a family, not tying herself for life to a body without a soul. Where is the boundary between 'praiseworthy' and 'foolish', when does self-sacrifice become human sacrifice? It is not Steven's fault, of course, but she would get more companionship from a cat, or a rabbit, or even a hamster. Something that would twitch its whiskers and look at her and pounce upon the food she put out for it. That would tremble when you stroked it.

There is much debate, as always, about the right to die and the right to let someone die and the right to help someone die or the right to help someone help themself die.... Steven may be an extreme case, but he is the question personified. No, he cannot give educated informed permission; no, he cannot sign any forms; no, he cannot, himself, open the bottle of pills and swallow them. He cannot be said to be "of sound mind", indeed most of these severe neurological trauma cases will never be of sound mind again. But when people talk loudly about "the sanctity of life" I wish I could bring them and show them some of these people who, for whatever reason, are only half alive. I have met people whose minds were alive while their bodies were half dead or more, and I have met people whose bodies were alive while their minds were simply absent and not reacting.

Time has passed. I have done what little I can, not for him, but for her. For the good name of the community to indicate that someone is prepared to take the time to come. But that's about all. A Nursing Sister comes in, she indicates that there will be things to do, to maintain some level of hygiene. Best not to be around.

I may leave, with a clear conscience, having achieved little but at least having done my best. Outside it is a short walk to the bus stop and I have already checked when the next one is due, they run only every half hour here. Back to the city, where people rush around, filling their busy lives, worried about never having enough time. Never thinking how to define the term "enough".

Each day more people are injured, badly, in some stupid accident. Some die. Maybe they are the fortunate ones, they go to their destiny. But I know other places like this, too, and have visited some of them, where the people are put who are not alive but not dead, who sit or lie sightless, wordless, being fed, half here, half there, half wherever, half gone.

****

THE MARKS OF CAIN

Poor Cain! The victim whom nobody cares about - except me! God had created death and dying and vulnerability, God had created loss and grief, but nobody had considered the consequences, nobody had been able to teach him what to expect when he hit out at his brother. With only his fist, be it noted, for the text makes no mention of a weapon. How old were they? Was this gift from his first harvest, Hevel's from his first flock of new-born lambs? Where are the parents and how do they react at their loss? They have no reason to love this stern unforgiving God either, after they have been expelled into the cruel world. Now they are "in the field". Eve at least had thanked God for helping her get pregnant and to give birth – the first time. She thanks God, not Adam. Adam is silent. She names both her sons, her husband has nothing to add. She doesn't thank God for Hevel. His very name means "Vapour' or "Breath" or "Nothing really substantial at all"....

Adam remains also silent in Genesis Chapter 4, passive with his second son. He does not raise his sons to be believers, to show gratitude. The initiative to bring God, his Grandpa, a present, an offering, seems to come from Cain alone and Hevel just imitates him. True, Hevel brings "of the best" of his animals, but how could Cain know which is the "best" of whatever turnips, carrots, cabbages, carrots, grain he has to bring, the fruit of the earth that his Grandfather has cursed? Could it even be that he wants God to lift the curse? (In the end it will only be his distant descendant Noah who will see the curse washed away, eight or nine generations further on.) Is he trying to make a direct approach to his grandfather, behind his father's back? Is this the first time he ever approaches God? We cannot know; In a way it does not matter, in a way it does. Why does it not matter? Because this is not a true story in terms of science and evolution and palaeontology. It is Myth, symbolism. Why does it nevertheless matter? Because there are still people who do not understand this, who assume that every word is the truth, the whole truth and nothing but the truth, who are simply unaware of the gaps in the story and what the Bible does NOT say..... and who see Cain as the archetypal murderer. Which he is not. He is as much a victim as anyone else. His famous response to God's furious question – "How should I know? Am I the "*Shomer*', the guardian of my Brother?" is wholly legitimate. When has anybody taught him any concept of Family, of fraternal responsibility, why has his grandfather rejected his gifts but accepted his brother's, if the brother's gifts were so much more desirable then surely the recipient was responsible for keeping an eye out? And so forth. He does not so much neglect responsibility as to point out that he doesn't bear any. There have been no precedents, no warnings, no guidance, no education, no explanation. This God's first question to Adam (not his wife – it's in the second person singular!) had been "Where are you?" and now his question is "Where is your brother?" God seems, if anything, rather careless at this stage, placing two dangerous trees in the garden, only warning about one of them, not keeping the Snake well away, and now this….

The best argument against the concept of 'Intelligent Design' is often those who believe in it.

Cain will be expelled eastwards – how strange that it is always towards the East that the Jews are sent? East of Eden....To Babylon, to Poland..... "*Kedem*" in the Hebrew and the Jews have made the word into a metaphor for progress, "*Kadimah*!" - "Forwards!" Which it wasn't, always. Not a sunrise – for Jews, our sun often set in the East. But he will get his revenge against God. He who has been condemned to be alone and a homeless wanderer will have a son and he will found a city and he will name the city after his son Chanoch (the name means 'Dedication' or 'Training, Education' - how symbolic!). He will in this way show his parents and his solitary grandfather how one should and could respect a son, how to integrate him into the family narrative, give him pride and a home and a sense of identity and so found a dynasty. Adam and his wife will have to start again and this time Seth (once more it is the mother who names him as a 'replacement' for Hevel) grows up alone but healthy and founds the dynasty that continues through the next chapters. God, who a few verses earlier had been terrified that Adam and his wife might eat of the Tree of Life and become immortal themselves, has also revealed the weakness of an Eternal Being when confronted with the mortality that this God himself had created. All he can do as a punishment is to remind the offenders of their own mortality - their sin will last only a limited period, in Judaism, not be passed on to succeeding generations, as in Christianity - and God cannot change the naughtiness, cannot eliminate it, cannot reverse it, only banish it. The way we, too, handle rubbish - we throw it away somewhere where we cannot see it anymore. (Or at least, we think so...)

But Cain is not just a piece of rubbish. Cain is the first person ever to be born, Hevel the first ever to die. Where IS he now? Is God's question merely rhetorical or does God also need to find out? Hevel is always named "his brother" as though he never has an own identity, just as in Chapter 3 "the Woman" is so often "his Wife" and not Chava, Eve herself. What role does the younger brother play? Is he always deliberately annoying his older one, imitating his actions, fighting for the recognition that the first-born had always thought was his by right? Is Hevel grinning at Cain when Cain tries to speak to him? He had not himself tried to initiate any conversation with Cain. What else can we think of that might explain why Cain lost his temper and hit out when words failed him?

One could ask, that if the body lay on the ground and the bloods cried out to God - Where is Hevel's skeleton now? Was God the only one to hear the bloods crying out?

The question God asks remains unanswered. It actually resonates for each of us, for it will apply in due course to each of us, too. Where IS Hevel, now? Is he waiting in Heaven, with Membership Card No. 1? Will we all get a chance to meet him at some point and ask him how it was, back then? And come to that – and just as importantly - Where is Cain, our Brother?

****

THOSE WHO WAIT

This happened to a colleague, not to me, but the story burns inside. A colleague one respects, trusts and believes, not one who tends to exaggeration and excessive fantasy. The facts may be slightly different to the way I can present them here, but the outline is clear.

One day the call comes to visit an elderly lady in the Home where she now lives but where she does not expect or intend to live much longer. Such calls come. But this lady wishes to unburden herself of a secret which weighs heavily upon her, and when one is carrying a heavy burden on the spirit it is harder for this spirit to free itself and rise up when it should.

"I had an abortion once," she says. This is not necessarily what one expects to hear but then, what is it that one can expect? Everyone who lives has a life, and a life is never simple, and there are all sorts of complications and contradictions and conflicts which can arise, and the time may come - when one has time - to reflect on these and to try to sort out what can still be sorted, to arrange what can be arranged, to atone for what may be atoned, and simply to unburden oneself of the rest, to cast out the pain and the shame and let someone else listen to what comes out, pick it up, and wash the mess away. Old ladies were once young ladies and young ladies - even if they are not 'ladies' but only girls - have always done foolish things, such as listening to and believing the things young men and young boys say to them and promise them. Throughout history the same stories replicate and repeat.

But always a little different. Otherwise, History would

not be interesting and the Future less unpredictable. This lady - let us give her the name Lydia - survived in Poland because, although she was Jewish, she had blonde hair. On such minor factors so much can depend. And as a blonde girl who spoke Polish and went to university she was able to hide herself in the open - often the best place to hide - and she even became the lover of an SS officer, which gave her different guarantees - and raised the stakes. For she also had a boyfriend, a Polish Jew, with dark hair, and for some time she was able to continue meeting him from time to time, hidden, hurried, flustered and tense meetings, with snatched seconds of love and tenderness - and then one day she discovered that she was pregnant, and this was at an inconvenient time, for her protector had been away for almost a month and if Germans know anything it is how to count.

And so she had taken yet further risks and found a woman prepared to help, and although there was surely so much more that could be said about what happened in those dreadful months and years, suffice it to say that Lydia was now a gracious lady of a certain age and almost no accent, lying in a bed in a Home for the Elderly, looking back over the years she had been privileged to keep when all her friends and families were having their own years taken from them.

Including the child who never got even one day.

And yet. There was more to say. As there is, if one sits and listens. And what she said was this. For some time she did not see her boyfriend, could not, and indeed after that she did not then see him again. In the chaos of the war and then the war after the war (which few people know about) there was no way of finding out whether he was even, against all odds, still alive. Until one day, some years later, she learned that he was not.

And how did she learn this? Not through a letter from the Red Cross, not through access to a yellowed list in an archive, not through accounts from fellow partisans describing his last heroic seconds, not by finding a neighbour or a relative. She found out because he appeared to her in a dream, and he was holding on his lap a young child, and he said to her - in the dream - "Do not worry, I am here with our daughter, waiting."

The colleague did not tell me if Lydia has moved on yet, or whether her lover and her daughter are waiting still. But that's all right. I don't really need to know. The main thing is - She knows. Or knew.

The main thing is - Someone is waiting. Always.

For us, too.

****

GONE, BUT NOT FORGOTTEN

One day she was there and one day she was not. She had gone. Vanished. Disappeared. The Police could not help because it was the Police who had taken her, and these police were not the sort of police who set up a hunt for missing persons but the sort of police who hunt persons so that they become missing.

Unfortunately, there are Police like that in the world. And the most drastic and brutal breaches of all human rights and all forms of justice are almost always perpetrated under regimes dedicated to increasing law and order. Men in uniforms see it as their divine duty to beat with sticks and rubber truncheons anyone who has the temerity to walk on the streets without a uniform. The unstated theory is that the fact that they do not wear uniforms is an unmistakeable sign that they are ideologically opposed to uniformity and hence to authority - and hence they have deserved whatever comes to them. But whatever comes to them should come in secret, and so they are taken away in unmarked vans and brought to police cells in underground bunkers and there they are beaten and raped and humiliated and tortured until they either die or wish to die. But it is very rarely that they ever come back. It is even rarer that their families or loved ones ever learn anything about where they were, or where what is left of them are.

Much has been reported but little has been documented. A significant difference. There were pregnant young women who were kept alive with a bag over their head until they had given birth to a baby that they never saw and never held but that was given to a family of officials for adoption, and then the mother of course could be disposed of.... There were the things, the unspeakable things done with drills and pincers and electrodes and such simple, innocent things as buckets of water. But that was, of course, all a long time ago, and no-one cares any more.....

Well, not quite. There are some who care, but their voice is not loud enough and year by year they are fewer. They are the mothers and the fathers and the brothers and the sisters and the husbands and the wives and even the children of those who went one day to work and never came back, who went one day to the shop and never came back, who went one day to the school or the library or to a meeting at the university and never came back, but vanished instead into the air that is so thin that no sound can be heard...... more of a vacuum, a black hole, a less-than-nothingness.

One mother was fighting. An '*Eshet Chayil*' - the word can mean 'a competent housewife' but also 'a fighting woman'. And this woman was a fighter and for over twenty-five years she had fought to find out what had happened to her daughter, who had gone out one day, in her miniskirt and colourful top and swinging hair, a biscuit from the biscuit tin in her hand, to meet a friend - and had never come back. Had never been seen. Had - Vanished. Disappeared. Vapourised. Like tens of thousands of others, most of whom had committed no crime under even the most repressive of legal systems, but whose names had been found in the address book of someone who had been arrested....

They were difficult times. Back then. Over there. It seemed that Law and Order were under threat and the only sensible response that the Authorities, the Government could think of was to make as many people as possible disappear, so that they could not cause any more trouble. By existing. Like children who hope that by closing their eyes the monster will go away, like murderers who hope that by killing all the witnesses there will be no-one who will ever report, never betray....

Margarete would not forget her daughter. And she was the kind of woman who, having fled tyranny once before in her youth, and having lost her parents to vicious dictators, saw no reason why she should flee tyrants again in her old age, and lose her children too. This is no small matter, for the men who can make some people disappear because they are inconvenient can, of course, make others disappear the same way. And those who help them. It takes more than guts - for guts can be spilt over the operating table with a rotating saw. It takes more than spirit - for even spirit can be dulled by weeks of solitary hunger in a dark cell. It takes these, yes, but it takes more, much more. It takes a Belief, a belief in a God, a belief in a justice, a belief in a world where such things should not happen, where a parent's worst nightmare - the loss of a child - should not occur just because some policeman, charged with protecting the public, decides to prey upon it instead. And when there is no grave, no body, no proof, no date, no knowledge, no nothing. When the child has "been disappeared".

The "dis" words are almost always negative. Can you though be Dismissed and Missed at the same time? Dis-appoint. Dis-connect. Dis-grace..... Maybe not distil or distinguish? To distract rather than attract. To disgust rather than - well, gust as such no longer exists in English apart from 'gustatory pleasure', but it's obvious what the word implies... a lack of pleasure, indeed a dis-pleasure.

So what is it to 'dis-appear'? It sounds almost harmless, the way a magician makes a rabbit or a pigeon or a ball disappear - but you know it is still there, somewhere, and has not really suffered. But Lissa had not disappeared; she had been forced into a police van - that much, at least, someone had been brave enough to report afterwards - and she had been driven away, and her captors - guardians of law and order - had then done with her whatever they pleased, because the Law did not exist once you were in its hands.

Lissa had been named after her aunt, Margarete's sister, who had also disappeared - but that had been some years earlier, in another time, in another country, another continent. And Margarete had been helpless then, but she did not want to give in now. She had gone to the police station, she had demanded - yes, demanded - to see the Chief of Police, something only a person very desperate or very foolish or very, very angry would do. She had written letters to newspapers and to politicians. She had made common cause with other women who were also prepared to take the risk of standing, still, in mourning, outside the Parliament building. None of this had helped - at least, none of this had helped Lissa. But she had probably been beyond helping within a few hours, at most a few days of her 'disappearance'. It had helped Margarete, and it had helped the women who had suffered with her, and - who knows? - maybe it had helped in that someone else did not disappear, maybe some policeman changed his mind, maybe some politician picked up the phone and called a halt. The country's image was suffering, for even hardened businessmen, who care not a jot for human rights but only for the chance to make a sale and a profit, must have second thoughts when it seems that the potential customers themselves are being killed before they have had a chance to make a purchase.

It has happened several times in history that a country's leadership for some reason decides to persecute everyone who is creative, intelligent and of a different opinion. Whether it be a Church or a Party based on a specific ideology, if these people are allowed to get the upper hand, within a few years the country is lacking almost anyone with intelligence and creativity; they have either left or died, there remain only the cunning and the stupid, and it can take such a country two or three generations to restore itself.

There came a time when Margarete had to admit to what she already knew, had already long known. There came a time when she had to say out loud what her soul was constantly repeating silently. There came a time when she had to say Goodbye to Lissa, to her pretty, vivacious, intelligent daughter, who was no more and who never would be more. And that was when someone made an appointment and brought her to me. She was on a visit here - to see some lawyers, some politicians, some newspaper journalists. And one of the lawyers had suggested to her, that she come and see a rabbi.

Why a Rabbi? For a long time, being Jewish had not been very important to Margarete - at least, not in any positive sense. She had, it was true, lost her family and her homeland because of being Jewish, but that had hardly been a good reason to sink herself deeply into spirituality and Jewish tradition. In a Catholic country it was just one more reason to be different and therefore potentially vulnerable. The Synagogues appeared to be for the comfortable middle-class, whilst she had been a poor refugee fighter who had worked her way up from the bottom. But now, when a ritual was needed, when some form of liturgical acknowledgement of her loss was required, it was old memories that had surfaced.

She came, accompanied, into my study. Bent in body but upright in spirit - that much was clear from her eyes alone. A proud woman, a fighter. One who would look politicians and policemen in the eye. Rabbis too. One who would only respect those prepared to look back. A truth for a truth, not a lie for a lie.

It is hard to know where to start. Especially when one has bouncy, youthful, active children of one's own, for whom one always fears, of course - for all parents fear - but not in the same way as Margarete had had to fear for her children. Much of her story had already been told to me, there was even a small bundle of press cuttings. She took the chair I offered, the young lawyer and a journalist with her sat on each side. Sometimes small-talk is simply too small to be worthwhile. So I simply welcomed her, said I had read something about her fight, had heard from the group that had invited her over, and asked what I could do to help?

It is not so unusual to have a ceremony for someone who has no known grave. This situation applied earlier to those travellers lost at sea or devoured by wild beasts or murdered by bandits, and nowadays one can call millions of victims to mind who have no known grave, not even counting those lost in aviation or shipping disasters or in battle. But a person's Name remains important, even if there is no Place. Even if there is no stone, no plaque, no inscription, no text, one can recite a Name and conjure up a.... a something, a temporary presence, an awareness, a remembering. So we talked and we arranged to meet a few days later - she was only visiting for a short time in any case but one needed time to invite any other supporters and sympathisers, 'indirect mourners' for she was the only direct one - and when the time came we met, a small group of about a dozen, in a simple room. Most of those present were not Jewish but were there for her, and indirectly for Lissa. Lissa was mentioned. A poem was read. A statement was read. Margarete sat, silent, head bowed but alert, part of her lost in thought, part of her listening intently. There is a prayer, the '*El maleh rachamim*', that urges God to find the lost and the dead a place of rest, a place of refuge - a form of return to the Garden of Eden but this time, one hopes, all the snakes are banned. And then there is, as always, *Kaddish* - the prayer that is no prayer, just a praising of God in an ancient and incomprehensible language, not even Hebrew - but it has become the prayer for all seasons, for all solemn occasions, for all acts of remembrance.

Wherever she is, however she died, Lissa is no more -

on this earth. And with only one elderly and ageing mother to carry the memories of a pretty teenager, there will not be long before even this mental image is extinguished. But sometimes it is worth lighting a small lamp - even if it makes the rest of the world seem darker, even if the shadows seem more threatening. Sometimes one has to light the lamp, the candle, the flame - just Because. That's all. Just Because.

It is an empty gesture, but it is a gesture. A gesture against the emptiness that is left, when someone disappears.

****

THE SPY WHO WENT INTO THE COLD

The building was pastel green and pastel pink and creamy white, it stood back from the road, not quite in the woods but also not quite a part of the city. Out towards Spandau, the S-Bahn line there had been reopened shortly before and so I took the train and walked the last bit when we got the call.

The call? The usual call, or at least one that became fairly frequent. Someone who had had nothing much to do with the Jewish community for most of their lifetime had now decided that, since the end was approaching, it was time to talk to a rabbi. Usually, as in this case too, it was a non-Jewish spouse or daughter or so who would make the call, very nervous, not quite sure what to say and to whom and how to address them and whether it would cost, but aware that a visit was desired, was required, if at all possible.

I think my first conscious contact with Berlin, still as a schoolboy, was through John le Carré's famous espionage thriller 'The Spy Who Came in From the Cold'. Later I also read 'A Small Town in Germany', about events in Bonn when this was the actual capital of the republican rump of the Reich and Berlin was a savage isolated island of intrigue and threat between mistrustful former allies. I myself visited Berlin only once - for a conference - during the time the infamous Wall still stood and I recall still how we had to fly at a certain level that, we were told, guaranteed much air turbulence and how one afternoon, like visiting a Zoo, we privileged foreigners went to 'visit the East', through the Friedrichstrasse checkpoint. The House of Tears, as it was also called. I recall the greyness of everything, the alloy coins, the newsprint of the newspapers, the general atmosphere of the buildings. Fifty shades of grey at a time when this meant anything but erotic. Small, crowded cream trams running through grey streets. It was a tiny taste of life in a divided city in a divided country in a divided continent in a divided world. I had no idea I might later come to live and work here, maybe if I had I would have made more notes, taken more pictures. Years later I met the former British military commander of West Berlin who told me and showed me where they had planned their Last Stand should the Soviet tanks come roaring in, as they threatened to do for several decades. Which row of houses, which deep-set road, would act as the *de facto* tank traps. The only problem being that if the Soviet forces had reached that point it would mean that their own base, supplies, resources and - importantly - families would already be in 'enemy' hands. A strange form of Cold War preparation. But there it was, for almost thirty years - two generations almost - from 1961 to 1989 a wall and more than a wall, an Attitude combined with barbed wire, minefields, searchlights and more separated one suburb from another, went down the middle of streets, cut off a church from its graveyard, cut off family members from each other. For almost thirty years Germans shot other Germans who were trying, illegally, to flee Germany to get to Germany. One really wonders how we can claim any sense of intellectual or moral superiority over beasts or even bacteria. And the way that history repeats itself was also more than ironic; If a Jew wanted to leave Germany in the 1930's they were classed as a 'fugitive' and had to pay an enforced 'Reichsfluchtsteuer', a tax to the government for daring to want to leave even if that government wanted you to leave and made this very clear. In the DDR anyone who expressed a desire to leave was also threatening to "flee" the country and could be imprisoned in order to ensure his freedom from foreign temptations, or - cynically, sold to the West for a substantial sum of money, even though the government had made it known that his art, his songs, his music, his writings were unwanted in a Socialist paradise for farmers and labourers - which had space for a few amenable academics but no room for intellectuals.

Life was one big party in the DDR and it was this one big

Party that decided everything. West Berlin was an island in a hostile sea filled with sharks who smiled with icy bureaucratic politeness at you when they were forced by international protocols to let you through but took their time and made it plain they were only doing their duty. It was said that West Berlin was unique because, whichever direction you went to, you came to the East....

In the novels - based apparently on le Carré's own experiences - the conflict between the two main parties is carried on underground, silently, secretly; each side tries to gather information about the other without being clear what use this information will ever be, each side tries to prevent the other from gaining information about itself, or devotes vast efforts to seeking any member of its own side who might be leaking information to the other side. Complex and sophisticated systems are created and used together with networks of informants. It all seems like one deadly chess game but an advanced version where the Board has been expanded to include not only Knights and Bishops but also Traitors who can play for either colour depending on whim - thus adding a certain unpredictable spice to the game - and Police pieces who are placed in the players' pockets but who can be brought out to invade the board, say, once in each game for each side and arrest and remove any piece at any time of either colour for no given reason.

This is all background for those who did not need to know. Behind the films and the novels there were of course other complex and sophisticated systems known as People and these formed networks and were engaged in the game that was no game, a game that carried such high risks for such apparent trivialities, scraps of information. Some out of a sense of loyalty or disloyalty to one side, some out of anger, some out of fear, some out of a desire for money, some - I suppose most, really - out of a mixture of motivations. And someone in some obscure anonymous office "ran" such networks. And this chap, I learned, had been one such. It had been his task for a part of his career to recruit people who could observe, or take surreptitious photographs, or use their ears, and at times and places at which one could meet, either on this side or on that side; this was of course also possible before the Wall was built but even afterwards it was possible for those who had a piece of card that gave them diplomatic immunity from some of the nastiest tricks played by the border guards and their superiors, the '*Organe*'..... and then there were dead-letter boxes for scraps of paper, there were hurried telephone calls, there were defensive chains whereby a piece of information went from A to B to C before being passed on to D and so anyone coming across it along the line would not find out too easily who A was. Modern forms of Chinese Whispers. It sounds exciting and brave but most of the time, I gather, it was deadly dull with a sense of sourness in the stomach and constant tension in the arteries. Bureaucrats gathering information on other bureaucrats. How often has one, as an adolescent, wondered what was inside the room behind the lighted curtain where one's distant and unknowing Beloved lives what is actually a totally normal and unremarkable life?

In this unremarkable pastel block of flats there lived a family and one member was about to leave for "another place" and he had wanted to talk to a Rabbi, any rabbi, before he went because he somehow assumed that a Rabbi would be able to help him in his preparations for this one-way journey. Sometimes people feel that they have to give a sort of Confession, even though it is the Catholics who place this demand or offer before the dying, not we Jews. But if someone can get a bit of peace of mind, can get rid of a few worries, a few regrets, a few sorrows so as to make their passing easier, well - one sits and listens and nods and makes some comment that may indeed help. Or not, as the case may be.

He did not want to talk much of his job, I suppose he had learned over decades never to talk about his job, maybe indeed he had been picked for this job by his superiors precisely because he was known to be a man who would not talk about it. Even his wife, nervous, tense, worried, constantly stroking her right arm with her left hand, mumbling, knew little. She of course was not Jewish, just a girl he had met locally while stationed here so that he had decided to stay. Their daughter also not. Ash-blonde, a smoker. Ill at ease. Confronting what was to come, trying to be brave. It was too late to deny any more and now, suddenly, this desire on his part to contact a religion strange to both of them.

We talked. It turned out they had left it late, for whatever reason, though who knows what the timetable says in a case like this? He was weak and could not talk much but his wife sat at his bedside and talked for him and he nodded and occasionally wheezed an interjection or a query. The main issue was whether he could have a Jewish funeral, this man who had travelled so far from his roots, who had hidden himself amongst the anonymous citizens of a strange city, the outsider in so many ways, as an American, as a member of the Occupation Forces, as a Jew, as a member of a military agency that was not quite military and not quite civilian, none of the neighbours had ever known what he had done and nor should they, he had been just another guy with a leather briefcase who went off to the office in the mornings and went for walks in the nearby woods at weekends with his wife and little daughter.... But inside him there was still the flicker of a Jewish boy from the Mid-West who had once, a long time ago, gone to synagogue with his own father and had had a *Bar-Mitzvah* and who knew what a *Kaddish* was even if he did not know how to say it.

Time was clearly running short, but we agreed that I could officiate for him, though not at the Jewish community's own cemetery, since he was not a member and this would bring all sorts of additional complications and expenses. Instead, there was a nearby Waldfriedhof, a Forest Cemetery, which they knew, and this was where he would like to lie.

It cannot have been two weeks later that I met with the wife - the widow - and daughter again, this time at the gates to the cemetery, to meet the undertaker and to inspect where the funeral would be the following day. We walked quietly down various winding paths, past various flowering bushes not yet in flower, hiding their identity behind dark green and grey thick leaves. It was that time of year when much was still hidden. How appropriate.

When the man leading us stopped and said "Here" I was taken by surprise - he was pointing to a grave already occupied, a mound of old earth and scrubby bits of grass and a stone that had discoloured but was still readable with a name and dates. How could this be? An error in the plan of the cemetery, a typographical mistake? But no, he explained, this person had lain here in peace for fifteen years and now his time was up. His time on earth had ended fifteen years ago and now his time in the earth was up too, a strange concept. Jewish cemeteries are usually - as far as is allowed by the neighbours - laid "for ever" and we do not gather the bones after a couple of decades and re-use the plot, but the ethos of this place was nature and recycling, of lying under grass rather than granite chippings, of returning to the soil and then letting someone else have a turn, of not hanging on to your place - unless, of course, someone was prepared to pay extra. So we looked around, noted where a bench was, a litter basket, a pathway, a large tree with low overhanging branches, this was a mature cemetery now, and we agreed it was a perfect place and they were comforted in this knowledge.

Next morning at 11.30 we met at the same gates and walked the same paths. There was an elderly couple who were introduced to me as neighbours and six or seven older fellows there as well, solemn types, the way they stood made one think of former military, they kept their faces down and did not speak much but they filed along with us and, lo and behold, where we had been the previous afternoon there was now a fresh, clean grave with straight edges and no sign of any previous occupant or memorial. In went the coffin, in went the soil, I read the prayers in Hebrew and Aramaic but also added translations in German since it was obvious there would be nothing understood otherwise.

It is hard to deliver a eulogy about someone whom one had never known and who had, moreover, kept his life a secret even from his family, even from the neighbours - about the other chaps I was less sure - so one had to be content with vague pleasantries, of a devoted husband and father, of a man who had worked hard for his principles all his life, adding a sentence about how he had wanted to return to his roots and to his religion towards the end. Nothing controversial, no betrayal of State secrets.

It was over, we walked back to the gates, shook hands. I could not come back to the flat, I had appointments at the office, and they understood, and it was probably a relief because they would not have known what to talk about in any case, but had felt they ought to invite me. No, let them go and drink a coffee and talk about old times if they wish. I could walk the other way, to the S-Bahn, and back into town and the rest of my day. Job well done.

Le Carré's classic ends enigmatically when the chief character chooses to accept death over life. It's a choice we all have to make, eventually, under whatever circumstances. Crossing over, not only from East to West but from Here to There. From the cool but sunny surface, into the cold soil.

****

THE LIAR

"My wife and I have decided on a trial separation," he told me, with almost a smile.

"No, we haven't," she said.

We were sitting at a table in a café, an outside table where one could talk fairly openly. Just we three. Between us a plate of sandwiches and cakes, a coffee pot, cream jug, sugar bowl, frippery linen serviettes, all the appurtenances of a nice Cream Tea or whatever, a social activity. But what was going on here, both on the surface and under the surface, was not very social. He repeated himself.

"My wife and I have agreed on a trial separation," he said.

"But I haven't!" she said, keeping her voice down because of those at neighbouring tables but nevertheless with a tone that indicated her determination to express her own point of view.

"My wife and I have agreed on a trial separation," he said again. This was crazy. I had known this couple for several years, I had visited them many times, stayed over in their guest room on occasion, I knew their children, I knew a lot of their backgrounds, we had worked together and planned together for this man with his smile was one of my employers and this conversation had come as an almost complete shock. Almost complete, for I had heard that there were some vague 'difficulties' and he had sent an e-mail advising me that "things may soon be different" but without being specific and I had suggested, informally, casually, that maybe we ought to meet up for a chat. She had agreed straight away, he had dithered a bit but all right, we had fixed a day, he had picked me up at the station and here we were, talking. Talking but not, it seemed, listening.

"My wife and I have decided on a trial separation," he said again, as though he was reading from a script inside his head.

She sighed, exasperated. "Look, I don't know what you mean. I have not agreed. It is <u>your</u> idea."

One of the biggest problems of our profession is that you get too close to people. The people you work with in a congregation or in a wider community are not just "clients" or "customers" you meet over a shop counter or on the other side of a desk in an office or lying temporarily in some side ward. You visit them in their homes, you meet their other family members, their pets, you see their tastes in decoration, you learn about their hobbies and their travels, you hear their anecdotes of years or decades of togetherness, you see the family photos. It is true that one needs to maintain a professional distance of sorts and it is true that you are there only because, technically, you are employed to be there, you are paid to listen to them, to advise them, to counsel them, to comfort them, but this is something easily pushed into the background since nobody would expect you to send a bill afterwards, like a lawyer, itemising and charging for each minute of conversation, each telephone call, each mail or letter. Plus VAT. No, you are "there for them" and they are people who might seek your help, your advice, your assistance and to do this properly you need to know them to some extent. To what extent? It all depends. There are probably very few professions where one sits with a cup of tea in an armchair while a woman explains to you her husband's problems with premature ejaculation. (And you wonder why she is telling you this?) Or where an elderly man says in a foreign accent he does not believe in the "superstitious rubbish" you are peddling, he doesn't believe in a God and all that stuff, but he still wants you somehow to give him helpful answers in the name of this God in whom he does not believe but his father did.

Most psychiatrists and psychologists and counsellors and therapists and 'professional coaches' and so forth have visiting hours, you book a slot with them, you visit their practice, you sit in the waiting room then enter their neutral room and sit in one of their neutral chairs with a neutral lampstand and a neutral pot plant and you talk about what is bothering you and they sit there and nod and grunt and occasionally make a note or ask a question and then they indicate that your time is up and you thank them and you get up and you go, possibly making a note in your diary for the next appointment and possibly handing over a payment. The relationship is clear or, at least, the chances of some 'transference' across boundaries are kept to a minimum based on decades of experience of risks, of professional ethics, of design and training, even the layout of the room or the presence in an outer office of a receptionist. But we, we go into their homes, their living rooms, their kitchens, we sit even at their bedsides when necessary. The boundaries are much harder to define. They are there, but they are diffuse, semi-concealed. The neutrality is compromised.

Ironically, it is at such times that one of the parties concerned may pull the Joker and re-impose that relationship with its strict divisions between employer and employed, between the impatient patient and the counsellor who himself needs counsel, between the one who pays the salary and the one who has to prostitute themself when necessary, so as to earn it. It can make for a very uncomfortable time, it can lead to catastrophic misunderstandings, it can lead to an abuse of position from either side. There is much said and written about counsellors and teachers and those in authority who misuse their power, and much less about the other way around. But believe me, it can be much nastier.

Eventually the time came to point out politely that I would need to get back to the station, leaving this conversation apparently open-ended. I shook her hand, trying to give it a comforting squeeze. I climbed into his car. He closed his door, started the engine and, even before we had driven off, told me, "I'd like to introduce you to my new girlfriend."

Oh shit. Oh shit oh shit oh shit oh shit oh shit. So THIS was what was behind his statement, his hints, his stubbornness and obduracy, his insecure smile. "Thank you but no," I said. I refrained from any '*Mazal Tov*!' I was still in shock and did not want to ask more, but he volunteered it all anyway as we drove towards the station. "She's wonderful, I met her through my work, she has beautiful eyes, you would love her." A precarious assumption. He mentioned a name which I shall refrain from repeating. "Does she know you're married?" I asked, cautiously. "Oh yes, but that doesn't matter to her," he said. This man, a leader in a Jewish community, seemed to think that this sentence made some sort of sense! Where does one start untangling the moral complexities and contradictions there, the ambiguities? I once had an acquaintance, someone who should have known better, who said that since his new paramour was not herself married, what he was doing "did not count as adultery"! The implication being that he could put his own marriage at risk but at least deserved credit for not destroying hers, or that bigamy was somehow on the menu as an acceptable life form.

I stayed silent, seething inside, waiting for what I thought might come next. Alas, I was right. "She is very interested in Judaism," he went on. "'Actually, that's how we met, she wanted to ask me all about it. I'd like you to arrange a conversion for her."

"I cannot talk about that now," I said. "I think there's a lot to sort out before we get that far." I knew nothing of any background, of what had been perhaps going wrong - for him at least - in their marriage, of why he had been open to this new piece of low-hanging fruit, of any other symptoms of a mid-life crisis or any other. (I love the term 'mid-life crisis', it implies you are still only half-way through your life-span; A sign of arrogant optimism or optimistic arrogance. But what it means is that you start acting like a teenager again and so are starting the process of maturation from its beginning once more.) This couple with their home, their children, how could he just sit there with the cakes and sandwiches and put it all at risk by lying to me in the presence of his wife? What was going on?

It got worse though because I was, of course, in his car, in his territory, trapped, unable to get out until we reached the station car park. I had to sit there while he took a turn off to the left and drove slowly along one of the streets. "That's where she lives," he said, pointing to a nondescript block of flats. He sounded excited, like a teenager who has spent hours at dusk hanging around outside in the street, waiting for a light to be switched on at a certain window. A middle-aged Romeo lingering beneath a specific balcony. "I could introduce you to her! I have already told her such a lot about you."

Oh no oh no oh no. "I'm sorry," I said, not being sorry at all, "But no, I must get the train. Another time, maybe." Please God, never? Would he get over this, this infatuation, this destructive and self-destructive obsession? And: "Does your wife know about her?"

"Of course not," he said, with almost a touch of pride in his voice, "and she must never find out. I am telling you this in absolute confidence, right, so you must make sure you never tell her anything." This is a nasty trick. We don't have the privacy of the Confessional in Judaism but some professional standards of discretion are (rightly) expected of us as Rabbis and now he was, very deliberately, the bugger, placing me into that shark-infested, stormy minefield of an ocean that was opening up between them. Now, thanks to his demand, if I told her, I was betraying him; if I didn't tell her, I was betraying her. The bastard.

What can I say? Something had broken, the sense of trust between us. He didn't seem to have noticed yet, he was still in his pastel clouds of new adolescence. I was privy now to a secret that, as I learned over coming weeks, even other Board members did not know about. I managed to catch the train, change at the junction, get home some hours later with a sick, depressed feeling in my stomach, with a stiff soreness in my shoulders, with a grey cloud in my head, with a sense of foreboding that from now on it could only get worse.

And it did. To cut the long, miserable story short, some weeks later the new couple were seen holding hands. Someone told his wife. He assumed (wrongly) it was me. The boundaries were re-established in the form of a registered letter that advised me that I had several weeks of notice but that the employment contract would be terminated immediately after that and that, in the meantime, I need not make any reappearances. No more coffee, cake and sandwiches and frilly serviettes, no more car rides to the station - this I could live without. I was however upset that she had been upset that I had not informed her - I had been correct in that it had been a real no-win situation. I refused to take this lying down, but it was all too late, the damage had been done, the hurts had been inflicted. Even the other Board members refused to take any responsibility. They had been lied to too, but did not want to admit it.

It is in the nature of Liars that they go on lying. To their partners, to their friends, to their colleagues, to their rabbis. To God. And most of all to themselves. There is, I feel, a reason why men carry their '*Schwanz*' in front of them. It is so that, wherever they are and with whomever they are, all they can do, their whole lives long, is to follow it. Whatever the costs to all around. I no longer work for his community, but I keep in touch with a few people and I know that the lying continues, even now.

One day his time will come, as it does to us all. A 'trial separation' from his new lady love who has, incidentally, since been converted by a less-scrupulous colleague so that they could celebrate all the hypocritical holiness of a wedding ceremony. I have told one of the people there that, when it happens, I am prepared to come and officiate at his funeral – for nothing. I would even pay my own travel expenses. But only on condition that I be permitted to dance upon the grave once the ceremony is over. It doesn't work so well in German, but on his headstone there should really stand: "Here lies So-and-So. As usual."

****

OUR RABBI THE THIEF

Or:

THE SUMMER HOUSE

What's this? In the file, between two pieces of photocopied paper, lay a banknote. A big one. Dark red. Five hundred Euros. I picked it up carefully between two fingers and put it to one side, on the desk. "That shouldn't be here," I said and continued looking through the papers.

Next to me sat the Chairman of the congregation. A small place in the former East Germany. Some years ago, it appears, he founded a Jewish Congregation, mainly with recent immigrants from what one quaintly calls the 'Former Soviet Union' whereby it is unclear whether it was formerly a Union or formerly a union of Soviets. He had applied for funding to the State and explained that since he had a Jewish community to run he was entitled to State funding. They in turn had pointed out that there was already a Jewish community in this town. He had responded that it was the wrong kind of Jewish community and therefore he needed to establish an alternative one which would have the same rights to State funding as the existing one. They had demanded evidence of the existence of his community, documents to establish the number of members and so forth. He had countered that it was unthinkable in the modern day and age to give a list of Jews to the State for any reason. They had responded that the past was the past but that if he wanted to claim that his community had two hundred members, then they would like to see some evidence of this. He had countered that this was unfair because they had, to his certain knowledge, never made the same demand upon the existing official Jewish community which had, he could prove, far fewer members than those for whom they claimed State subventions.... and so it went on.

It boiled down to a chronic state of conflict, trench warfare, with occasional advances by one side blocked by the other or driven backwards in a counter-offensive. Lawyers profited and journalists sometimes, just sometimes dared to mention it, but usually their editors would sit on the stories and refuse to provide any publicity to these quarrels "for fear of stimulating antisemitism." As if antisemitism needs fuel, or causes, or even any Jews! Each side wanted to get or to keep as much of the State subsidy for the local Jewish communities as possible. Not for the sake of God, not for the sake of Judaism, not for the sake of increased Jewish activity or education or religious services or for more Jewish social welfare or more subsidies for inter-faith work or Jewish culture, no, just Because. Two testosterone heroes, neither of whom showed much interest in religious observance or theology, fighting each other for the right to represent the Jews of the city. And to be recognised as such, and subsidised as such, by the Powers That Be. The fight went up to the State Court and the State Department of Religious Affairs, the *Landeskultusministerium*. The officials, some of whom had no understanding of religion at all since they had grown up in the non-religious German Democratic Republic, who understood Party structures but not Church ones and certainly not Jewish ones, were usually out of their depth and also worried about putting a foot wrong and upsetting whichever group had the loudest voice.

What was needed now, both sides eventually decided, was proof of their Membership, which had to be submitted to the local Court for registration and acceptance. Since any division of the spoils would be proportionate, per head, then the more members, the better. (Or, if necessary, members with two heads could be signed up? Certainly there was an incentive to include under the rubric 'membership' anyone and everyone even remotely related to Judaism, with a Jewish grandfather, or already deceased, or even the family pet if necessary.) But someone would have to check the papers before they were submitted to the court. And that was my task, today, as the *'Amtsrabbiner'*, the 'Rabbi in charge' (a laughable title). The Chairman had invited me to his house, sat me at a dark table next to a dark sideboard, placed a cup of tea and some heavy Russian biscuits by me and given me the file. With the various bits of paper. The membership forms, the copies of birth certificates (mostly in Russian or Ukrainian), notarial statements and - wherever he considered it necessary - a banknote.

The challenge was so blatant that it annoyed me. I had some sympathy with a small Liberal community attempting to establish itself in the face of determined opposition from a secular community of immigrants that claimed to be 'Orthodox', but not for tactics like these. Of course I knew why he was doing it, and he knew that I knew. I knew also that this would not be his own personal donation to the community, these banknotes would themselves have come from communal funds, a form of investment in the hope of further growth. Some years ago I had heard of a chap in Western Germany, in the Rheinland, who had asked ten old Russian pensioners to sign up to his community at, say, an 'Honorarium' of ten Euros a week, and he had then gone to the local civic authority and demanded fifty Euros per head per week to run a congregation.... Good business if you can find it. Later I came across a Chairman who paid themself substantial sums to lead services - as a chairman the role was honorary but as a prayer leader one could legitimately expect payment, and generous payment at that, and if musical accompaniment was required, then their mother could also be paid for helping on the piano. Things that would be wholly honorary in England, performed for love of the activity, are paid here – if you can access the funding. So Religion becomes a matter of accessing funding, not the divine.

There is much that it is important to know but it is hard to explain to those not involved. Nevertheless, an excursus is necessary here for, after years of experience, I have learned that nobody outside Germany understands Jewish life inside Germany, or how it is organised and funded and led. Now is an opportunity to explain why these banknotes lay before my nose and what was going on.

The relationship between Germans and Jews has always been complex and especially when it comes to German States (of which there used to be many until 1870, and then several in succession ruled by the Kaiser, by a weak and fragmented Parliament that had fled to Weimar, by the National Socialist Democratic Workers' Party, by a succession of military administrators of different Occupied Territories, and then by a Bundesrepublik in one part and a puppet government in the other, each one dependent on their main sponsor, whether this be the USA or the Soviet Union... and then following the events of 1990 there was a painfully-recombined sewn-together patchwork Bundesrepublik which does not quite know how to relate to its own past..... a past which perforce ought to include coming to terms with concepts like Alsace-Lorraine, Saarland, Kurland, East Prussia, Danzig Free State and Corridor, Silesia and more...

'Germany' is a concept beloved by drunken Germans who do not know any German history, who know nothing of conflicts between the Northern and Southern German Bund and for dominance between Prussia and Austria, or the fights with Denmark over Schleswig-Holstein in 1866 or the Treaty of Westphalia of 1648 and following treaties in 1655 which enabled a pragmatic compromise that stated, effectively, "If the ruler of some local principality is Catholic, then that principality is Catholic, and if he is Protestant, then that principality is Protestant, and anyone who doesn't like it is welcome to leave..."; Amazingly, three hundred years later the same basic principle was put into effect, that anyone living in the Rhineland or Niedersachsen or Bavaria, whatever their religion and culture, was considered a Democrat because these were parts of the Bundesrepublik Deutschland and anyone living in Thüringen or Brandenburg or Mecklenburg was a good Communist, because these were parts of the German Democratic Republic, the only difference being that after a while the rulers of the latter decided that they could no longer allow those who wished to leave to do so for the former, for their country was being bled dry of labour and skills....... In the same way in the Jewish communities now we have a rule of thumb that if the Chairman thinks the community should be Orthodox, then it is so and if he or she thinks it could be Liberal, then it is so....

What we see here repeated again and again is an emphasis on the Collective over the Individual, a feeling that one should adhere to the rules of the Collective - whatever they might be, whoever set them - rather than developing your own. Of course, respect for communal rules is important - but we have seen what can happen when obedience is blind. And here individuality was deliberately discouraged, because it would be hard for the (non-Jewish) officials to understand and define what was what.

And what we also see is that this principle was applied by the State to Religion too. Religion is not a personal matter in Germany, it is a matter of concern to the State. It can affect what Kindergarten you may send your children to, in what hospital you may work, where you might be buried. The State will decide which religious festivals are classed as public holidays and which not. There are close links for historical and political reasons between the State(s) and the official State

Churches which are classed as quasi-governmental bodies with the right to extract taxes from their members. Many years ago, Gilbert and Sullivan wrote a piece (in '*Iolanthe*') in which a soldier explains British parliamentary politics thus: That everybody born is automatically either a Liberal or a Conservative; well, the assumption for decades in Germany was that you were either a Protestant ('*evangelisch*') or a Roman Catholic (*'katholisch'*). There was the additional possibility of being one of the 'Old Catholic' unreformed believers in a pre-1870 paradise, and of course one could (theoretically) be Jewish, though this was often termed '*Mosaisch*' or '*Israelitisch*' so as to avoid the word 'Jew'. On the outer fringes of society were scattered splinter groups of Russian Orthodox or Baptists or whatever and then, after the war with the influx of 'Gastarbeiter' from Yugoslavia, Greece and Turkey, there came various Balkan Christians and – oh horror! – Moslems.

The point was that as a good citizen you had to register at the local civic Registry Office and state your religion, which would be solemnly noted down in your records by the official there and in due course, if you belonged to one of the four 'main groups' a sum would be added to your taxes, deducted at source and transferred to the church or the Jewish community. You could opt out of the tax only by saying that you were no longer a believer in this church or that. Strange, the way the churches allowed what belonged to God to be given first to Caesar for onward transfer and saw no problem in this. It guaranteed them of course a good and steady income, not affected by the actual attendance at church services or the generosity of those who attended them. They were paid by the State rather than directly from their worshippers and members. It was rare until relatively recently that one saw a church in Germany looking shabby and uncared for and poor. The clergy were classed as State Officials *(Beamte)* with a guaranteed pension as long as they kept their mouths shut and obeyed their superiors as any good civil servant should. It is sad to look back now and see for how long these people did indeed keep their mouths shut, but their hands open.

Things have changed a bit, but a lot of the system remains in use. For the Jewish communities, each '*Land*' or federal State has a contract with a '*Landesverband*', a State-recognised association of Jewish communities. There may be very few, there may be a sprinkling, but they are run centrally and paid centrally. The State will allocate to the *Landesverband* each year a specific sum, agreed by the State Parliament, to do with whatever it likes - for nobody will come to check, nobody will audit the accounts, nobody will ask for a financial plan or a budget.

No, the problem is that many Germans still feel a great deal of shame for the number of Jews they (or their ancestors) murdered in the past and so they express this guilt partially by throwing money at those Jews who are here in the present. Whoever they are and wherever they came from and whatever they believe or do. One could even define it thus: They feel guilty about hating Jews and so they remember formally the dead ones, and throw money at the living ones, without actually engaging with them, and transfer their hatred now to the State of Israel instead.

The money flows from this generous State hand and whoever controls the flow, controls Jewish life in the *Land*. If you happen to have a different view of what Judaism should be - tough luck; if you have moved here from America and are used to a different system, to egalitarian or family-oriented services, if you have converted to Judaism through a rabbi in another country, then you can find yourself totally excluded from the local congregation, while still being taxed for its support - since when you arrived and when you were asked your religion you volunteered the information '*Jüdisch*'. Taxation without Representation.

Before the *Shoah,* when Germany was still a modern, civilised country, there were modern, civilised forms of Judaism, for their time; after the *Shoah* the surviving remnants were either wholly ignorant, since they had had no opportunity for Jewish education while in hiding, or they were survivors from camps and marches who had ended up in Germany but actually came from Poland, Hungary, Romania, wherever, and who represented - if anything at all - the Jewish rituals they had learned from their lost families. They may not personally have believed in God anymore, but they knew what a Jewish service should look like and sound like. The men sit here, the women sit there, the cantor stands thus, and the singing is in the Eastern European mode and accent.

There is absolutely nothing wrong with that, so long as it does not become the ONLY show in town, the only synagogue allowed, the only rite officially accepted and subsidised. But that's what happened. One of the major casualties of the time was Jewish Pluralism, the right to be different, to think different and to pray differently. And the influx of ignorant Soviet immigrants, classed as 'refugees' from the collapsing system in which they had grown up, were the heirs to two or more generations of State-imposed atheism and so brought no knowledge, no Jewish documentation, neither they nor their parents had had Jewish marriages, the men were not circumcised, they had never learned to read the prayers..... but they were in their hearts so accustomed to a one-party, authoritarian system and to the concept of submission to what the local 'Big Boss' said that they found this system fully appropriate and absorbed it and were absorbed into it.

For them, and indeed for the first time in history for the

past two thousand years or more, there were now suddenly advantages to be had in being classed as 'Jewish'. One had access to well-funded social welfare organisations which could provide new arrivals in the country with language courses, help in finding accommodation, help with dealing with the necessary bureaucracy, help with child care and summer holiday schemes, help for the elderly and infirm who needed an occasional break in a communal-owned hotel with an appropriate programme, and many other good things too. The only problem was that these organisations were officially called 'Jewish communities' and those who wanted something else, as basic as a synagogue service in which they could take part, or a community newsletter printed in German rather than Russian, found themselves in an excluded minority. Treated, in fact, like Jews had always been - only this time not by the State, but by the State-funded Jewish communities. One of the minor ironies of existence. It is obvious to clear observers that God must have a wonderful, if warped sense of humour. In the 1930's and 1940's the Germans wanted to be freed of the Jews, in the 1950's and 1960's and 1970's and 1980's they yearned to be free of the Russians - then in the 1990's they imported several hundred thousand Russian Jews. Thinking thereby they would somehow replace those who had 'left' in the 1940's, unable to comprehend the differences, the cultural and political and religious differences that the new arrivals represented in comparison with those who had either fled in time westwards or had been 'resettled' eastwards.

Eventually resistance began, small and scattered, as individuals, often those with roots and communal experience elsewhere, expatriate American and English and Israeli Jews, began to protest against this system, began to form their own loose associations, began to define themselves as 'Liberal' or 'Reformed' or 'Progressive' Jews (the labels are usually interchangeable and are never fully defined); the next step was an association of the associations, to enable joint programmes for education, for producing liturgy in translation or new, for joint youth work and so forth. But all this needed funding and who was going to pay? The official congregations - with a few rare exceptions - refused to allow the new groups to use community infrastructure, to borrow a room for a service or a meeting; the Central Council refused for years to accept that these associations even existed until forced to do so by (external) political pressure on the German government..... and so in many towns a new group formed and began to fight for its existence. The local Jews were accustomed not to having to pay subscriptions, and since most were not even on taxable incomes their communities were subsidised for them. They were effectively being paid to be Jewish, rather than having to pay like anywhere else in the world. One can, if one is interested, find online the statistics of community members in specific States, and the amount paid per annum to the '*Landesverband*', and work out what the subsidy per head comes to. But for years Liberal Jews were not only not being subsidised, through their taxes they were subsidising those who refused to share the communal resources with them!

So, this is how I got involved, in several places, supporting a local group of Jews who were effectively rebelling against the system. The system adapted slowly and gradually as individual legal battles were won here or there. But it took time and effort and in the meantime we had battles like this one here, where Community A received several hundred thousand Euros per year, Community B received nothing, went to court, fought its way upward until some non-Jewish judge drew an obvious if incorrect conclusion: "Tell us each how many members you have and we will divide the sum proportionally."

Why incorrect? Because it neglected to take Inertia into

account. By this time Community A might claim, say, 800 members who knew nothing and attended nothing but had been so registered in previous years; and community B might have 100 who had each individually joined and showed interest and commitment, who had bothered to express an opinion and stake a claim. So Community A could say, proudly, "WE represent the majority and WE are Orthodox! But YOU have ONLY one hundred!" whereas the Community B leaders would retort "Oh yeah? So how many of your members ever show up? How many really exist? How many are just the non-Jewish family members of the actual Jewish members, included for now to inflate the statistics? How many still live locally, how many still live at all?" and the Litigation continued.

Plus, the basics of running a community, the rental of a room, the invitation to a clergyman to come and teach and lead services, the travel costs, the accommodation, all cost the same whether the community has 800 or 100 members. There was a need for some 'basic foundation level' to be established.

For now, in this small East German town, I was trying to help the head of what had become the Community B to prove to the local authorities that his congregation really existed, that it held religious services, that it needed access to a cemetery of its own if the other one were closed to it, that things were kosher.

But were they?

So, we come back to this room in this Summer House, with the dark furniture and the files. "I am sorry," I say, "but I cannot stamp and sign all these forms. This one, and this one, and that one, yes, but not this and this." He protests. But I know already what he will say and I have my answer ready. "If we start to fudge things, then we become as bad as the other community and one day, one day all will be revealed and we will be shown to be as dishonest as they are. No, I would rather we took time, asked these people to find more papers, or to go to a *Beit Din* and have their Jewish status confirmed by the rabbinical court, and then I can stamp their forms." He is not happy, I have some sympathy but at the same time my job is twofold, to improve the congregation's reputation and to maintain my own. Neither task is easy. Nor is it well paid. But I cannot afford to pick up those banknotes again and say so.

Over the coming years some good things happen and some strange things too. In the room that we use in the winter one of the members starts to paint the walls with the most amazing murals on religious themes; We are loaned a *Sefer Torah,* a *Torah* scroll, by a congregation in the USA, all arranged through various associations. Once a month I visit and lead services from prayer books which I have 'organised' and afterwards I talk with those who wish some rabbinic advice or guidance, arrange for some people to start conversion classes, a nice meal is prepared for the period after the services and afterwards when we have said blessings and eaten the attendees queue up to receive their travel costs reimbursed. The evening here should not cost them anything, for this funding has been acquired.

But strange things happen too. I am introduced one day at the Summer House (where we hold our services in the open during the summer months) to a man who is described as a Chief Rabbi from somewhere in the Soviet Union. But there is something fishy about him. I am asked by a worshipper about some form of 'Jewish Medicine' which, when I check it out online later, turns out to be a neo-Nazi conspiracy theory based on the premiss that 'the Jews' know how to cure many illnesses and cancers but won't tell the '*Goyim*'..... . One month the prayer books are no longer available, they have been flooded in a cellar when the local river overflowed, I am told. But why were they there? Thank goodness the *Torah* scroll is safe still in its carrying-bag in a wooden case. But it is never used! I am only invited to lead Evening services, never a Morning one.

Then came a call from the State Prosecutor. The Big Chief of Community A had registered a complaint to the police about some membership papers which had been submitted by Community B to the Court to establish its latest figures. It is an interesting question how he got access to private papers submitted to a court, but let that go for now, it is typical but not the most important issue. What was important - and hence his complaint - was that my signature and stamp were on several applications which he considered to be false. Had I indeed signed and stamped such false papers? And if so, why?

It turned out when I looked that these were papers I could confidently say had NOT gone through my hands, with or without a banknote attached by a paper clip. So who could possibly have been responsible for the forgery? Plus - there were two other 'rabbinic' signatures on the papers, copies of which I had sent to me. It is however amazing what one can do with photocopiers these days.

By coincidence I was due to go there again on the coming Shabbat. By e-mail I informed the Chairman that there were problems that I would need to discuss with him beforehand, before the service, and so I would take an earlier train. His immediate response was that there was no need, he would cancel this week's services, explain to everyone that I was ill and could not come and that my contract would be terminated, I was no longer needed! "Oh no," I responded, "I will be there. I will be there."

For security I took with me also a student, someone who had wanted to visit the congregation and the service and who could sit with us and be a witness. We sat together in the Summer House and I asked him, outright, who the other two names were on these papers. One, he said, was an Orthodox rabbi from Germany of whom I had never heard; the other, he said, was a rabbi from North Korea!

He was playing a game with me and it was a dirty game. I could theoretically have marched off straight way, I could have gone straight to the Police. But I knew already - they would not want to get involved. They never do. No, I determined to stay and to lead the service and to let everyone see me and then explain in my sermon that this would unfortunately be my final service with them, that due to circumstances which I could not tolerate I was resigning the position. And that is what I did. He could not stop me, he could not pretend I was not there; I spoke with two other Board members but, being of the Soviet persuasion, they did not wish to say anything against their Chairman. When the service was over, the blessings and the meal and people were departing, I went to the wooden case, took the bag with the scroll out, placed it over my shoulder, and had myself - and the student - driven to the station. By midnight the scroll and I were in Berlin.

Within a few days I had written a full report on the events of the past week and mailed it to leaders of the Progressive Jewish associations in Germany, in Europe and in America and the rabbi of the congregation which had loaned us the scroll. A week later the scroll - these things are precious, valuable, expensive and to be handled with care and respect - was handed to someone who would arrange for it to be returned to America and then to the congregation. And that, I hoped, was it. My links to this community were now cut, but from my side, not his. The State Prosecutor had been informed of the forgery, but it seemed there would be little point in my laying charges. Who would want to get involved? This is the standard problem. It is always considered to be "an internal Jewish matter". Once I was thrown out of a congregation because I had begun to question whether the chairman was in fact Jewish. It turned out he wasn't and thanks to an independent journalist a national scandal was created - but this did not, of course, lead to my reinstatement!

Every now and then, out of curiosity, I checked out the community's website. Everything seemed to be going bloomingly. A wide range of activities were advertised including *Shabbat* morning services with *Torah* reading. Which could not, of course, be true, since the *Torah* scroll had been removed. But it seemed that nobody had even noticed. I had carried the bag so casually over my shoulder that nobody seemed to have registered what I was taking. So one day, after almost a year, out of a sense of mischievousness, I wrote the fellow an e-mail. "Shalom, How are things going in the community? And by the way, how is the scroll?"

He called ten minutes later. In panic, in outrage. "It has been stolen!! It has been stolen!! Our wonderful, valuable *Sefer Torah*!!"

"Calm down," I said, "Don't worry, it has not been stolen, it is back in America. It was on loan and I have returned it to the owner." Hah! And I added that, since I was the Amtsrabbiner, the rabbi who had brought it to the congregation, acting as the courier and the custodian, I had considered it my duty to take it back when it became clear that the congregation was faking my signature and my stamp, and I had done my best to ensure it was returned quickly to the one who had placed it on loan, and my only question was how his community had been apparently offering services with *Torah* readings for the past months?

Hah! Again.

But – Two days later there came a letter. One of those legal letters in grey, windowed envelopes and a printed franking. Inside was a polite invitation to present myself at a certain time at the Bundeskriminalamt, the Federal Prosecutor's Offices, to explain why I should not be charged with the theft of a *Torah* Scroll valued at such-and-such. My heavens! At last, at last, at last, someone was taking accusations of criminal behaviour within the Jewish communities seriously!

Fortunately I had been paying substantial annual sums for legal insurance (although even so there were costs not reimbursed) and within a short while I had found a lawyer, explained the situation to him, shown him copies of all the relevant e-mails, and on the appointed day he came with me to the big 1950's building where these poor chaps have to work. Do soulless buildings suck the souls from the officials who work there, or do the soulless bureaucrats turn all their offices, corridors, stairwells and facades into some sort of bland, blank infinite greyness? I know that I could not survive for long in such an office, I would need my own personal marks here, the kettle, tea bags, mug, packet of biscuits, a flowerpot, some posters, desk toys, anything, anything to show that I was an individual and not just an automaton. But let that be. Maybe there are specific rules. These people have to turn up to work, whether or not the sun is shining through the dusty windows, then sit themselves at these characterless work surfaces and switch on their monitors and keyboards and do whatever they are told to do. In this case, to take a statement from a Rabbi concerning an arcane, obscure ritual object which was at the centre of a dispute in another town, indeed in another State. For these were the Federal guys.

First of course I had to explain (and prove) who I was, then what my relationship to the congregation was or, better said, had been, and then why it had ended and then what the scroll actually was, what it was used for, how much it could be valued at, where it came from and how and so forth. Then I handed over the copies of the mails that showed how I had reported to the various associations how I had brought it back to Berlin and how arrangements were made for me to give it to A in Berlin who would pass it to B in Hanover who would ask C to take it on a business trip to New York from where D would take it onwards, and so forth. Thanks to the power and speed of e-mail I had the mails from the congregation who had loaned it, thanking me for its safe return.

The argument centred on who was the Owner and who the Custodian. I was quite prepared to admit that I had taken it, without warning, from the Custodian - '*Besitzer*' in German - but only to return it to the Owner - '*Eigentümer*' in German - and that this had been carried out openly as far as all were concerned apart from this man who, never using the scroll in services, had misused it to claim in public activities which did not in fact take place. But which he wanted to use to 'prove' to the authorities that his community needed and deserved more funding.

Well, since the Owner had written that they had taken possession once more, it was clearly not Theft, and since the Custodian had waited till a year was past to report the item as missing it was clear that the removal had not even been noticed for that time and so it was relatively quickly decided that there were no grounds for pressing charges and the matter should be put to rest. Despite having had to pay a substantial legal bill, for which there was no way I would be reimbursed, I had dealt with the issue and cut my links with this fellow and his banknotes and his faked statistics.

Until I got an e-mail from a friend. Had I looked at the congregation's website recently? No, I hadn't, but did so now. How amazing! On the community's website for all to read is a rubric "Our Rabbi the Thief" and it tells the world that I (with photo) deliberately and criminally came and, like a Moses in reverse, took the *Torah* away from them, stole it for my own nefarious purposes, left them bereft of all Jewish teaching and law, stole their most precious possession.

Should I take out a charge against them, compel them to take this down, demand of them not to repeat such slanderous accusations, such character assassination? There is no point, the lawyer tells me. Whatever I do, nobody can stop the twit from putting onto the website again whatever he wants. Nobody reads it, he says, and we have the documentary evidence, he says, and best leave it alone and ignore it, he says. Well, he is the lawyer and I am the person who would have to pay yet more bills for nothing so, I suppose, I may as well accept this. We know already that no German State lawyer, no German court or judge will intervene again. They are all shit-scared of intervening, they would rather class everything as "an inner-Jewish matter" and close the file. Quickly, before any facts escape.

One consolation is that I suppose I could go there and shoot or stab the bugger in his own synagogue and then, when the police come, tell them calmly "I am sorry, but this is an inner-Jewish matter, you have no jurisdiction here" - whereupon they will retreat in haste and the *Staatsanwalt*, the State Prosecutor, will hurriedly apologise for any disturbance. If a non-Jew threatens a Jew it is classed as Antisemitism, but if a Jew threatens a Jew, it is classed as a religious matter and not for the civil courts, even if it involves criminal negligence, tax fraud, the breaking of laws regarding employment, pension contributions, social security fraud, theft, intimidation, breaking of contracts, sexual or personal abuse, corruption, misuse of taxpayers' money, nepotism and more. Or in this case, libel and false accusations.

We are truly a separate world, a 'Parallel Society', not with its own laws (which is what the right-wingers always worry about when it comes to Moslems and the *Shariah*) - but with its own utter lack of laws - which worries them much less, for some reason. The only consolation is that this fellow's community remains small, remains isolated, is shrinking and that one day he, too, a mere mortal, will join a different set of statistics.

Probably, when he meets the Recording Angel who shall decide upon his subsequent fate, he will present a file with all his good deeds. And a few banknotes clipped between the sheets. But I doubt if it will work there, either.

****

WHERE THERE'S A WILL THERE'S A FAMILY

"What? I did what? I did WHAT?"

I could not believe my ears. The synagogue's Honorary Secretary was telling me on the phone, a little apologetically, that he had received a letter, a complaint from a solicitor representing the family of one of our recently-deceased members. Was it true, the solicitor had felt compelled to ask, that I had stolen and destroyed the Deceased's will?

It was already a difficult situation but now it had become an impossible one. Rodney had led a fairly steady life after some difficult beginnings. To describe all would take too long and in any case a lot depended upon whom one listened to, but it seemed these included a period in the military and a period of 'wandering' as a youth and, according to some sources, he had managed to father three children before he was twenty. A bit careless, it seems, or simply not bothered about the future, after all, there was a war on.... in his case, in Asia, in Korea. Then he went to New Zealand for five years or so and had then returned to Yorkshire and built up a successful business doing one of those things that nobody really understands but keeps several people employed in a bland sort of building on a bland sort of industrial estate. He had married in New Zealand, brought his wife with him, had a child, then they divorced and she went back, with the child, then he remarried someone much younger (as one does, in certain commercial circles) and it was only much later that I, as the new rabbi, came into contact with him, when he was already of pensionable age but still very active, with a twinkle in his eye and a fund of anecdotes on the few occasions we met, usually at the synagogue after a festival service.

But he had made some notable donations to the Building Fund, the Library Fund, the Cemetery Fund and was a popular fellow in the community. The latest wife - let us call her Lydia - was not Jewish and therefore the two children also not, a son and a daughter, both now adult. She seemed to spend a lot of time down south with an aged relative - at least, this was the official version - and to make matters more complicated he was close to his daughter but had fallen out with his son who now lived in Florida and some five years before the son from New Zealand who now lived in England had re-made contact with the father he had barely known and the two had got on well.

With me so far?

When the cancer became known he had asked me for a long talk and I had of course gone and sat with him. This was one of those occasions when Lydia was away again for two weeks, in Eastbourne or somewhere I think he said, and even through his illness she was by no means always present and at his side. But there was a nice large house with a double carport and a garden and many other facilities on the 'Millionaire's Row' that would come to her and the Hon. Treasurer told me in an aside after an Executive meeting that Rodney had promised the synagogue a large donation in his will but didn't want a big fuss making of this. Since the fellow then told a few other people the same thing, each time 'in total confidence' of course, it did not take long for word to get around.

This was, I must stress, not the only reason I made a practice of going round every few days to stay in touch - he was, as I say, quite an entertaining chap in his own way and philosophical, having seen Love, Sex and Death in several forms at a young age and this had influenced his views on life. The last two visits, he was no longer receiving me in the well-sofa'd deep-carpeted lounge but in his king-sized bedroom; once Lydia was there, once not and the live-in carer opened the door for me and, at his request, despite my "No, No!'s" prepared a cup of tea. Regina, a middle-aged woman from Ukraine or somewhere, intelligent and with a nice smile, she held the place together during the man's final illness and the wife's absences - to be fair to her, I think Lydia had real problems with seeing her husband having to use a commode or to have the sheets changed so often or the thick atmosphere in their bedroom, it cannot have been easy for her either. The daughter had young twins of her own, one of whom seemed to be chronically ill with something, the son from the Southern Hemisphere now lived near Hereford but came up every weekend, the other son remained in Florida and did not respond to calls from his sister, oh, things were not quite so easy. When we spoke, he said he regretted this but that each of his family was an adult now and would have to make their own ways through life, just as he had done, and make their own mistakes and make peace their own way. We usually managed not to talk about the illness and more about his early life, how he had met and fallen in love, how later he had fallen out of love but, some years later, had managed to rebuild at least some relationship with the Ex., which was how his son had been able to make contact, and so forth. Religion as such had not played such a major part in his life though he had been a fairly regular attender at the shul, but of course there is nothing like a tumour to make one focus on tomorrow and what it may bring. Or the day after tomorrow....

There were plenty of other things happening at that time, including (amongst others) organisation for a weekend regional conference to be held at a nearby country hotel, our congregation was hosting it and there were a lot of arrangements to sort out, a service to arrange and boxes of prayer books and a scroll to transport and deposit safely in the Manager's office, issues of the catering (fish and vegetarian) and the kitchens, fortunately the actual programme was someone else's responsibility, and also at this time I had one of those really unpleasant fights with the fellow who was the Honorary Secretary, about something so trivial I cannot really recall much about it except that it made life rather difficult and we avoided each other as far as possible.

It was on the Sunday morning of that conference that I got the call. Regina had found him, had called the synagogue's number, had got from the answerphone the Hon. Secretary's number, his wife was at home and had called him at the hotel, he had asked the hotel reception desk to page me (rather than coming to tell me himself in the Breakfast Room) and so I got the news.

I wasn't due to do anything that important till the AGM at 11.30 so set off pretty well straight away and drove back to the house. Regina let me in, she had been crying. Rodney lay there, looking calm. His eyes were open, though not looking at anything. For the first time in my career I leaned forward and gently closed them with my fingers. I called our undertaker's weekend helpline and gave them the information. Regina had a number for Eastbourne and had already called to tell Lydia, I called too, got a man's voice, she had already set off for the station, sorry, he couldn't help further. The son from Hereford, Michael, normally came about 11 on a Sunday morning for Sunday lunch, he was due but would not know yet. The daughter who lived fairly close - I called her. The son in Florida - well, it was still almost the middle of the night there, but I took the chance and dialled the number that was in the little leather book by the telephone. No answer. There wasn't much else I could do now except drink a cup of tea with Regina in the kitchen - she insisted and rightly so, she was also a mourner - and leave my card and then head back to the conference in time for the meeting. I was due to sit on the podium and had a report to deliver. Life and movement politics go on.

That had all been some two weeks ago. Quite a few people had come to the funeral, from the congregation, from the firm, still in existence and now run by a former partner, from the extended family. Lydia of course in black and weeping, Michael in a smart suit and with his partner, the daughter with her husband and the twins. The son from Florida had sent to say he was himself ill and couldn't fly yet but would come the next week. That had not gone down well but could well have been true. None of them of course was Jewish or had had any experience of the rituals and the prayers but I did my best to explain what we were doing and where they should stand and how they should take the little ceremonial shovel and throw some soil onto the coffin as it lay several feet under the surface and before the grave was backfilled. Then back to the house for a catered tea party. Regina had already moved on. There were no shivah services to organise and so that was basically all I had to do for now, spreading condolences and shaking hands as I went, except to mention to Lydia that she should stay in touch as we would organise a stone-setting in due course.

And now - this. The son from Florida had come, for the clearing of effects and the division of the assets. Lydia - the main heiress of course, legally - and her daughter were here and Michael from Hereford had been grudgingly accepted too into the circle and all had looked for the long-anticipated Will. Which could not be found. Rodney's solicitor had said that he knew there had been one, prepared some years ago by his predecessor at the firm, since deceased, but that Rodney had - unusually - not wanted to leave a copy at their office. Every drawer, every cupboard in the house had been turned out, dank mattresses turned over, and the only thing anyone could think of was "The Rabbi was here with him, he must have it. He probably wants all the money for that Jewish synagogue of theirs."

For the Hon. Sec. it was another hammer with which to beat me over the head, as someone incompetent, incapable and potentially criminal and unfit to be their Rabbi, though he never dared say so quite so specifically at meetings, and even the Hon. Treasurer indicated indirectly that he would be happy if I could just happen to find the will and that juicy donation could be arranged. After a period of denial I was quietly advised by a congregant, himself a solicitor, that it might be in my best interests to swear an oath before a Notary that I had never seen or held the missing document in question. Good advice. It would change nothing with my enemies but, should the legal case which was building up go any further, this would help to keep me, personally, and the congregation out of it. When things like this get nasty, they can get very nasty, with the daughter accusing her mother of having an affair while her father was dying, with her brother from Florida accusing everyone of everything, with the son from Hereford pointing out that he was also a legitimate child and his now-elderly mother in Auckland was also entitled and so on and so on. There was talk of Regina having abstracted it, poor lady, but that calmed down. We were best out of it.

As far as I recall it was all sorted out in the end to some extent, but the congregation never got that legacy. I heard rumours that several legal firms did quite nicely out of it. Lydia kept the house of course though I gather she was often down south. Most gathered again a year later for the unveiling of a quite modest stone which gave his name and his dates but did not mention in any way that he was "deeply missed" or "by his loving family". (That had been my suggestion when Lydia came to my office to discuss the stone's preparation, but she had swiftly agreed).

Judaism believes that we all have Free Will and bear responsibility for how we apply it, and that is good. But a missing will can be a much worse problem for all concerned and even for all not concerned. Forget all those jokes about "making a new testament" - and make sure you have made a copy and put it where it can be found when required. Otherwise, while you rest in peace, your family may rest in pieces.

****

A GOAL IN LIFE

I am most definitely not a 'fan' of organised sports. Only twice in my life have I been to a football stadium. The first was as a young boy, when my beloved uncle attempted to infect me with the virus of Football Passion by taking me to a match of his favourite team, which was already (as I later learned) on its inexorable progress downward and out of the League and out of solvency. I recall that it was cold and it was wet and it was noisy and it was crowded and I was surrounded by taller men in damp overcoats and in general it seems that the antibodies were there before the virus itself ever had a chance. And so it was. Never again!

The second time was as a professional. Not a professional footballer - my heavens, how much some of them get paid these days! I say 'get paid' because I am never sure whether the word 'earn' applies. Of course, their professional careers are often short, subject to luck and injury and the sensible ones would stick the lot in a building society account and buy a house and put something into an interest-bearing venture and then they could relax. But most prefer to spend it on booze and blondes, on dregs and drugs and drabs and dragons. But as a Rabbi I once stood in the centre of a football stadium and said what had to be said.

But what had to be said? The story was complex and tragic. On a Saturday afternoon one season several thousand relatively-law-abiding citizens were seeking harmless entertainment and attended a football match. Their team at home playing some foreign team from 'somewhere else'. There remains to this day doubt as to what exactly happened, when, where and by whom but the fact was that suddenly smoke and flames were spreading over one of the stands. It could have been a carelessly-thrown fag, not extinguished, but whatever it was, the wind that day caused the effects to spread with alarming suddenness. Suddenly what was a harmless game turned into a tragedy of screaming and trampling as people tried to get to and then through the exits which are, of course, never designed for this sort of eventuality. In the same way access for those bearing water-hoses and those bearing stretchers is constricted and rendered impossible by the counterflow of terrified fans seeking to save their very lives.

Not all succeeded. The list of casualties was sombre and sobering, and the list of the injured, those who had suffered burns or smoke inhalation or had been crushed and broken ribs and other bones was even longer. Not to mention (nobody ever does mention this, sadly) those who had escaped but were traumatised; Maybe they had been standing next to a mate and they got out but he didn't.... and maybe they were blaming themselves, maybe they should have stayed, helped, gone back for someone? Useless questions, pointless questions, but the questions that people always ask themselves after such an incident when they have survived but others have not. I do not know and never asked how many uncles had taken their young nephews to that match or whether and how everyone found everyone they were so desperately looking for, calling for, in the dazed crowds outside. Not all were there to be found. I do know that some families lost several members that day.

The news quickly hit the radio, the television with endless repetition of the same film clip of billowing smoke clouds and little figures running in different directions, the players paused and looked on helplessly, and then the local and the national papers came out too and at first I read it and thought merely "Well, at least I hope none of our people were involved." Fool that I was. Whether or not pious, observant Jews are allowed to attend a football match on a Saturday is not even a moot point, but it turned out, alas, that three of "*Unsere*", our folk, were among the casualties. The civic authorities and the club and the league and others were keen to put together a Memorial Event for the occasion, a little while after the fuss had died down, the smoke had cleared, most of the damaged stand had been demolished.....

Ironically I was not involved in the funerals for they were actually members of a different congregation, my colleague there had to handle that, but I was called upon as a 'representative of Judaism' when the civic organisers were seeking to fill a podium with appropriate people (all men, incidentally, in suits or robes) who would have to mediate somehow between the feelings of the living, the memories of the dead and the absence, so it seemed, of any protective deities. It was felt relevant and appropriate that a Rabbi should stand there together with a Catholic Priest, a Protestant Minister, a Free Church Minister and an Imam. Football is, after all, a great leveller of societies, at least in those cities - such as Glasgow (Rangers and Celtic) or Liverpool (Liverpool and Everton) - where one does not have hostile competing Protestant and Catholic teams whose supporters are prepared to murder each other to the appropriate threatening chants in the name of honest sport.

What I have learned at such events - communal joint memorials - is that it almost barely matters what you say; What matters is that you are there, that you turn up. It matters that some organiser thinks to invite a Jewish representative, and it matters that you find the time - in this case on a Saturday afternoon again - to go. You put on a dark robe if it is summer, a warm coat and hat if it is winter, you sit in the row on the platform or you stand at the microphone and people realise that this truly is a city of many religions, many ethnic groups, many languages, but that at heart all are human beings who are prepared to come together to play, or to watch sports. Due to bad acoustics or dodgy microphones or loudspeakers that overlap each other it is usually the case that a half can either barely hear you or they can hear you but not understand what you are saying. If, of course, one then sings a prayer in Hebrew - the '*Kaddish*' or the '*El Maleh Rachamim*' - then even fewer would have a clue, but the same applies to the Moslem chap with his Qur'an chant or the Hindu cleric with his moaning, chanting wail, sometimes accompanied by a little squeeze-box, or any of the others - we are there to be there, to represent visibly an invisible deity, to say with our voices something which all present at least understand is meant to be comforting. And so they will be comforted. After all, what a mother says to a crying baby - is it meant to be understood literally? Or just as a soothing background noise to help settle alarmed or angry emotions?

Fortunately, it was not raining. The wind was soft. The acoustics seemed, from where I was standing, to be effective. The stands were crowded once again. A sombre crowd, no banners, no chants, no attempts to annoy and provoke the fans of the opposing team. The media in a mass - maybe this is why they are called 'mass media', for they always seem to stand together and record together? The first shock had, as is often the case, been replaced by anger and the search for a cause or, if necessary, a scapegoat. Of course, Nobody was responsible, as he so usually is in cases where an elderly wooden construction catches fire in a place where many people gather and smoking is not prohibited. Of course, there was to be an official Enquiry and of course Lessons Would Be Learned and all that. Fire precautions, quicker response times, better communications, more regular Inspections and so forth. It took a few years, in fact, before someone - a survivor - began to query why the Club's chairman had suffered several mysterious fires at his industrial premises in the previous decades. But that was all hushed up in due course, presumably so as not to disturb the Memory of the Dead. Better by far to assume that These Things Happen and not to try to pin the blame on any local worthy. It is ironic that the most hard-bitten secular businessmen still use the term 'Act of

God' to explain why they do not wish to (oh, sorry, do not need to) pay insurance claims.

The civic dignitaries in their chains of office; the local MP's, eager to show how much they empathise with their voting fodder; the Chairman of the Club and some of his minions, representatives of the other team of that day as well, the League, whoever, all had given up their Saturday to drive here and stand stiffly and express in clipped phrases the same message over and again, "our hearts go out," "a great tragedy", "sport will never be the same again" and so forth. There have been several major catastrophes at football stadia over the decades and, historically speaking, this was one of the relatively smaller ones, but for a provincial city not used to such events the shock went deep and stayed there for many years.

Strictly speaking one could see it as a misuse of God's name to use God as a sort of Club Mascot, prevailed upon to calm the feelings that had been aroused, to comfort the mourners and of course to help the Club get over this disaster and to go on to a glorious long-term future. But there is a civic duty to represent different population groups however bizarre their beliefs might be and so I and the other representatives of a Deity who, at least as far as we Jews are concerned, never wanted human beings as burnt sacrifices, not even as sacrifices to red ink in the accounts or to insurance policies, chanted our chants and bowed our heads and made the right moves before it was time to file off back to the room where we had donned our gowns and left our bags, to shake hands, to thank each other for being there, to express our sorrow once more and to put the ceremony safely to bed.

I have never been back. The stand has been rebuilt, the club still exists, people still attend the matches - never as many as the promoters would wish, of course - and the headlines are long past.

Those who died, died; Those who lost loved ones, have themselves been forced to move on. But never, ever try to tell someone "It's only a game". It's much more than that. Sometimes, it is even a matter of life and death.

****

OEDIPUS SCHMOEDIPUS

It was one of those things that turned out so much differently to how anyone had expected. One of those things that teach you never to make firm plans unless you have a back-up plan as well and a lot of flexibility. It was, indeed, a lesson for many of us.

Jürgen had been adopted as a child, or better said, he had been given up for adoption. He had been told this at some point, I never quite found out how old he was when he got the news, which must be rather stunning; to discover that your mother and father are not in fact your mother and father, that your real mother did not want to or could not keep you and that nobody knows who your real father is or was, maybe not even she. I wonder how I would react to that? You are not an orphan because your mother, your real mother, the woman who gave you birth, was alive enough to sign some forms. Whether your father even knew he had become a father - who knows?

I got to know him when, aged 18 and part-way through his university studies, he decided he wanted to become Jewish. In many respects a routine case, he was old enough to make his own decisions, had done some reading, had made some enquiries, had made his decision. So now he had to attend my regular classes and come to Sabbath and Festival services and show that he meant it seriously. But he was a serious kind of chap. Didn't laugh much or smile much. Friendly, but somehow focussed more inwards than outwards. He was studying Theology, his foster parents - as he now had to call them - had raised him as a churchgoing lad. But now - well, we had a couple of deep talks about his motivation. He had even at one point wondered about becoming a Pfarrer but then discovered that due to what he had learned of his own origins he had problems with a God who had abandoned his own son on the cross. Now he was even wondering whether, in due course, to become a rabbi....? That worried me and we talked briefly. Most sensible seminaries will accept converts, but only after they have lived a number of years, typically three or five, as 'normal members of the community'; there are of course a few not-sensible seminaries, some of them online, which will take a student before they have even completed the conversion..... How can one teach a congregation about Jewish life if you have not yet experienced it yourself?

Such people sometimes convert to Judaism because, I suppose, they are looking for a different father figure, a better one. He took it seriously, attended all the classes and services, didn't ask a lot of questions when we had group discussions but absorbed a lot of information, he was after all a bright chap and trained to study. And during the course he met at the synagogue Julia, a divorced woman with two not-quite-teenage daughters, and they seemed to get on well and one day they made an appointment and came to see me. They knew they would have to wait until after the conversion was completed, and all the paperwork had been sorted out, and they knew that she was, as she put it, blushing slightly, "almost old enough to be his mother", in fact they were only about 13 or 14 years apart, but they would like to consider becoming a married couple. He looked happy and more relaxed than I think I had ever seen him before. It seemed a bit like a fairy story. The girls, too, would get another father figure. Maybe a better one.

He passed the Beit Din with ease, impressing my colleagues with his seriousness and his knowledge, with his Hebrew reading skills and with the fact that he was already planning a Jewish wedding and taking on family commitments - he, who had not known his own natural father, would become in turn the step-father for the girls. Julia sat nervously outside during the interview but was invited into the room afterwards and came out radiant with joy. A new start for her, and a new start for him. Those who knew them got a good feeling, were happy for them all. I went round to the house a couple of times, to chat and to discuss ideas, and saw that the girls felt at ease with him and he with them, close but not 'too close' - it may seem unfair, even paranoid, but when a young man of 20 or 21 moves in with a woman who has daughters aged 12 and 11 one cannot sometimes help wondering where the real attraction lies. But there was no sense of that here. You don't need to ask, that would be clumsy and foolish. You can just see who drapes herself over a chair and how they sit at a table together, how relaxed and natural they are. No Lolitas with lollipops.

It was time for him to become truly an Adult at last, to leave the shadow of his childhood and his origins or, indeed, to confront it. The way I heard it, he had decided soon after the Beit Din to contact the Social Services Department and enquire for details of his birth-mother. Since he was over eighteen, he could legally do this. Whether any of the details in the old file would still be relevant, whether she had changed her name or moved to another country, whether she was even still alive, nobody could know, but this gave him a beginning for his search and he followed the trail doggedly for three months, helped by modern technology and social networks - and he found her. Not that many kilometres away.

So, somehow he had got in touch with his mother. Now what? I think he actually planned to invite her to his wedding. They set up a meeting, They met. It turned out - I never met her in the flesh but once when he told me about his search, resolving the ghosts from his past, he showed me proudly a photo of them together in some café, taken presumably for them by someone from the next table - that she was, surprise surprise, an attractive woman, only fifteen years older than he was, still in her prime, and single. If he was 21 at this point, then she was about 35, 36. But looked quite glamorous. Maybe a bit surprised to find she had a son of 21 who was a very bright young graduate who had become Jewish and engaged, but Life is full of surprises.

This is one of the biggest understatements one can make. The next development was rather shattering. A few months later, Jürgen had been to see his mother a few times, she had come to visit once, came a call from Julia. Jürgen had left. He had not only left, he had gone to move in with his mother. They had – she could hardly bring herself to say it – fallen in love........ and the wedding was off. Of course.

What a business. I did not in fact see him again. Jürgen, who had been so interested, so committed, such a regular, moved off to the next town to live with his mother. But not the way so many young people do. His membership of the congregation lapsed. Julia was heartbroken and also moved away a year or so later when she had had time to find another job. Ironically, she worked as a psychologist. I don't know what the girls learned from this. His foster parents were bewildered by all this; they were quiet churchgoers, Protestants I think, who had invested a lot of their lives in Jürgen and had had enough problems with the thought of his becoming Jewish but had accepted this. I had only met them once, when I had urged him to bring them to a service and show them what he was doing at his weekends, to show we had no secrecy, we were not a cult kidnapping and brainwashing.... As it turned out, the day they came there had been some fuss about something-or-other and apart from shaking hands at the *Kiddush* and saying '*Shabbat Shalom*' and 'pleased to meet you' I had been rather distracted and had not had chance to talk to them properly. Julia was of course in touch with them. Now - They could understand, rationally, the idea of their son looking for his real roots, when the time was right. But this – this they had not thought of, not counted on. Nobody had.

Let us spare ourselves the obvious jokes. In any case, even if he was now a Jewish boy, she wasn't a Jewish mother. He was clearly yearning for the love he had not got from her for twenty years, and was catching up in a big way. She - well, who knows? Did she have other family, her own parents, ex-husbands, other children given away? I never asked and never found out. There is no law to stop a man of twenty-one living in the same flat as his mother. Enough young adults - and not-so-young adults - like to live at 'Hotel Papa' or 'Hotel Mama'. But not quite like he.

For me - Had it all been a waste of time? In a way. I had spent time and effort on arranging a conversion for a man who had then dropped his religion soon after acquiring it; I had spent a little time preparing for a wedding that was then cancelled. I had spent some time counselling a heartbroken woman and some rather bemused children and then they left anyway.

But - well, I learned a lot too. Mother love is one thing, and the command to love your father and mother is also an important one. Like all these commandments, though, a lot depends on how you interpret them.

****

TURNING A PAGE

"Where they burn books, they will burn people" said Heinrich Heine, and he was right. His writings were also banned for a while. In 1933 there was a major, infamous burning of books in Berlin where, of all people, university students went through the libraries to extract 'forbidden' literature, unclean and immoral writings that would endanger the purity of the nation. Not just Marxism and suchlike but the books of socialists and realists and romanticists and of course anything written by anyone who had the faintest touch of Jewish ink in their pens. I don't know if they burned Hardy's 'Jude the Obscure' but if it was obscure enough to them, then they probably did.

But normally we don't think in quite such terms. Apparently even within Judaism there were occasions when the books of major thinkers (defined as "those who think differently from others") such as Rabbi Moshe ben Maimon were burned as being a bad influence because they could lead to intellectual laziness, students could just look up his answers in his '*Mishneh Torah*' rather than wading through the dozens of varieties of question in the Talmud.

But all that was a long, long time ago.....

So it was a shock when a mob publicly burned a novel in front of the City Hall. Truly a shock, an attack on the values that we claim we hold - freedom of speech for all who say what we want to hear, freedom of thought for all who think as we do, freedom of belief for all who believe something that we can at least tolerate.

The English are good at not reading books, but they tend to respect them. Almost everyone can name a few specific famous authors without having read any of their books - Chaucer, Shakespeare, Dickens, Jane Austen, Stephen King, whoever. To burn a book seems wrong and a shudder went through society. Further, for a country based upon a comfortable form of Christianity which was founded to work closely with the monarchy and thereby combine providing what belongs to God with what Caesar is also entitled to, the pomp of authority and the knowledge of being always right, to be confronted with another religion - Islam in this case - which actually believes in the concept of Blasphemy and Sin was a further shock. It is all so, so, ungentlemanly; so un-English.

It is not, in fact, easy to burn a book. Many a fanatic has discovered this, to their embarrassment. You can scorch it and make the outside of the pages darken but a book that is closed forms a compact and poorly-combustible whole, protected from the necessary oxygen, unless thrown into a fire already blazing merrily and at a high temperature. Fahrenheit 451, if I recall correctly. (It's about 240°C by the way). I presume Ray Bradbury did his research properly. I was not there at the time - and I do not like mobs at the best of times, whatever their reason for coming together, and especially not angry mobs such as when a train has just been announced as cancelled - but in this case, I learned later, the chap who had come, himself burning with outrage, determined to create a public scene, had had to nail the book to a bit of wood and pour lighter fluid or something similar over it before he could get it to burn as an incendiary incident. He was bloody lucky not to go up with it, becoming a holy martyr to wholly stupid indignation. But the principle is the thing. Most 'spontaneous' riots need to be well planned. Whenever one sees on television a film showing how a mob burns the flag of some country it currently despises, one needs to pause and think "How many of these people just happened to have an American or Israeli or Danish flag at home, ready to be brought out for the occasion?" And then, "In that case, who DID arrange for one to be available at just the right moment?"

On occasion they will still burn people as well as books in an attempt to drive an idea from the world. Fire is also considered cleansing, purifying, and ash is much easier to deal with than real people, as many a mass murderer has found out. It removes most of the evidence very effectively, reduces the space required, eliminates organic decay and consequent smell from any remains...

To be positive, the riot was not followed by others in which the majority local population burned down all the local mosques and raped and massacred all the local religious minorities in revenge. This might happen in other countries - alas, it often does - but it did not happen in this proud Northern city. Instead, what happened was that the Bishop called together a committee meeting to discuss the matter. And to underscore the essential British principles of pluralism and tolerance even if there had been some lack of mutual understanding, he invited representatives of the Moslem population and also myself as Rabbi to represent, as one so often quaintly puts it, "the oldest of the brother religions".

This terminology is often used along, for the sake of balance perhaps, with "sister religions". I am never quite sure how to take it. On the one hand it is much better than having one's religion described as a damned and vile spawn of Beelzebub that should be burned out of every crack in which it has sought refuge; On the other hand - well, what do we know about Brothers in even a biblical context? From the very beginning, about rivalry and competitiveness and mutual betrayals? Beware of naivety and wishy-washiness. Then again, Judaism is often described as "the oldest of the three monotheistic religions" and therefore I am asked frequently to speak first when on some interfaith podium. Also well meant, also an acknowledgement that the Hebrew Bible came before the New Testament which in turn came before the Qur'an. No argument there. But the problem is, Judaism has renewed itself and reinvented itself so many times since the Biblical period, as it adapted to an existence without a Temple, without a Priesthood, without a Homeland, without a Monarchy, as it absorbed the fact of living solely in Diaspora, solely in Exile, as it developed more abstract texts to replace the animal and material sacrifices..... Having (usually successfully) absorbed so many other ideas from surrounding cultures, it then absorbed the idea of nationalism and of acquiring its own nation state. It took a while - too long - to achieve this and there are many still who choke on the idea of the Jews having their own country - wherever that might be, for attempts were also made to consider bits of South America (in Argentina), East Africa (in Uganda), the Caucasus (Birobidzan) or even Silesia in Western Poland (in 1946) for a Jewish republic - because they would rather deal with an historic biblical civilisation that is more easily compartmentalised and, being dead, keeps its mouth shut and does not interfere in world politics. So, the Judaism I represent is NOT the old version but an updated one. The Christianity we meet and discuss with can also come from a broad spectrum of degrees of belief but is also mostly quite distant from First Century concepts, it has become organised and urbanised. (How fortunate that the Pope does not bless an 'Urbi and Orgy' each year; indeed, by mentioning the 'orb' as a synonym for the Earth he is acknowledging that the Earth is indeed a ball and not a disc and has a specific place in the planetary systems - something which his own predecessors denied for centuries.)

Yet now - when both Judaism and Christianity have grown older and milder (I so wish I could add "wiser") and have attempted to establish a relationship of guarded mutual acceptance, based upon a combined and miserable experience of European wars between representatives of different religions that have led to millions of deaths, of centuries of oppression of free thinkers and scientists and philosophers, now that Christianity has to a large extent grown out of that attitude of arrogant intolerances, it - and we - are confronted with another monotheistic religion that in some basic respects is still stuck a few centuries before us in its ongoing development. This is, I know, a dodgy thing to say but - these things take time. Maybe centuries. In Europe we still have the first two or three generations at most of those who came from a dominant majority culture in other continents, who have little understanding of what happened in Europe over the past millennium and how Europeans have got simply tired of it and want to move on, and not be dragged back into such divisions and such conflicts. They come often from rural and not urban backgrounds - just like most English people did two centuries ago; they come from countries with an homogenous majority dominant expression of religion - just as most English people did two centuries ago. They come from a society where the Patriarch still rules the family and women have little to say - just as most English people did two centuries ago. It is important to keep making these parallels because it helps provide an historical context. No English politician should ever say that it is "unthinkable" that people burn books in the public square and accuse the author of Blasphemy, when several market squares in Oxford and elsewhere still bear the charred marks of where scholars were burned alive for daring to translate the Bible..... where the countryside is littered with the magnificent ruins of former monasteries and abbeys demolished by government decree, where many old manor houses still have a 'priest's hole' to hide a terrified cleric from the secret police of the day, when people look up to a man who had several of his wives executed and picked a fight with the Pope and executed any of his friends and counsellors who disagreed with setting up an own breakaway church as a government department as a jovial symbol of broad-shouldered smiling English robustness who enjoyed his roast beef and ale. Good King Hal!

Bloody hell. And don't get me started on the Puritans or the

Civil War. The English, like so many other peoples, get through life by ignoring their own history as much as possible, perhaps picking out odd bits for pageants or plays or naughty drinking songs. The rest is consigned to the darkest of the Dark Ages. Not even illuminated by the Enlightenment.

No, nothing is "unthinkable". But we can at least - and should - say that we have by common consent consigned such attitudes to the past. With the exception of Northern Ireland, we have accepted living in a country where Anglican and Catholic churches stand at different ends of the same road, with Methodist and Baptist and Congregational chapels standing here and there, with a compulsory system of non-religious Religious Education in the schools, with a monarch who is symbolically the head of a State Church but does not interfere in it theologically to excuse their own dalliances. There is still the odd prejudiced person here and there, but now one can be elected to Parliament or hold a government job without being an Anglican (this was not always the case), one can take an oath on different forms of Scriptures, the key word is "Tolerance" and this tolerance is, as so often, based on an essential ignorance of what one is tolerating but a blithe assumption that, oh well, with a smile and a shrug and if necessary a cup of tea, it will all work out really.

And the great thing is that this works surprisingly well - until someone stands up and refuses to tolerate something. Until they stand up and shout "Blasphemy!"

Blasphemy is a very difficult subject to deal with because it is subjective. It is the accusation made by people who believe that they believe in God. Can one understand this sentence? It is fundamental to any attempt at understanding this existential problem. There are people - a very few - who really believe in God. If they are Jews or Christians or

Moslems they may have very different concepts of God in terms of divine power, divine love, divine mercy, divine justice, divine punishments. At interfaith meetings now we put (deliberately and importantly) a great deal of effort into finding common denominators, in expressing gratified surprise that our partners in debate also have concepts of prayer, of holy days, of pilgrimage, of charity, of purity, of morality, of the importance of family, and so forth. It does not help - at this basic level - to dwell too much upon the differences, as to whether God demands from us sacrifices, human sacrifices, total submission, acceptance of a self-sacrificing and self-sacrificed Son, a specific Prophet; When we speak of the value of "Family" do we include issues of monogamy versus polygamy, open marriage versus adultery, the possibility or prohibition of divorce, pre-marital sexuality, the age of marriage, the age of consent, the arranged or enforced marriages, the rights of the bride and the wife, the sanctity of the embryo versus the right to abortion, the rights of the husband over the wife or wives, the issue of whether the clergy could or should have families of their own, the prohibitions on incest which vary from one group to another? Or do we just say "Family" and smile happily at the mutual agreement, the nodding heads, the feeling of relief that we have found something that we can agree about in common? But of course, by definition someone from another faith community who has a different opinion on any of these or other topics is technically deviating from what WE consider to be the True Way.

Theoretically, the biggest problem of all for Catholics is that there are still Protestants. After five hundred years of Counter-Reformation opposition to all these schismatic tendencies which deny unified, centralised and legitimate absolute Papal authority, somehow these renegades are still there, with their churches, seminaries, prayer books, rituals, episcopates and federations of different denominations within the same confessional framework. Theoretically, the biggest problem for Protestants is that, five hundred or more years after their pioneers fought and suffered in Bohemia, Germany, Switzerland, Holland and England for the Reformation of their religion and a return to the Biblical texts which all ought to be able to understand, there are still Catholics, blind and obdurate to reason, who seek their salvation through an elderly father-figure in Rome who plays obscure political games and denies them a lot of what they yearn for, who refuse to accept modern translations of their liturgy and their biblical texts, who let others tell them what to read, what to teach and how to vote. Theoretically - yes.

But practically their biggest problems here are paying for the upkeep of their church buildings and the roof repairs which are necessary, and finding the new clergy they need in an increasingly-secular society. There are Church Primary Schools and there are Catholic Secondary Schools and there are all sorts of institutions, mostly in crumbling, darkened outdated city-centre buildings and so the Church authorities have better things to do than squabble about abstract theological issues of Communion and so forth. Oh, a few do it, but then, there are always a few, aren't there?

The Free Churches are not much better. Dissenters have largely stopped dissenting and have been absorbed into the mass. Nonconformists have conformed for decades. Recent influxes of different Christians from Eastern Europe after the war have introduced Polish Catholics and Ukrainian Orthodox and other rites into the mix of this vibrant city as well. In the meantime, we Jews have dwindled almost to vanishing point and yet we are still looked up to somehow as "the elder brother".

So, there are some people who <u>actually</u> believe in this God but there are many, many more, by far the majority, who <u>believe</u> that they believe in God. Maybe they believe in the Church - their Church, of course - with its structures and hierarchies and traditions and rituals and aesthetics, its pioneers and personalities, its melodies and maladies and its own form of madness, living in one reality but in total denial of other realities. Maybe they believe in the power of rituals or specific phrases in the Liturgy. But do they really believe in God? If they did, I feel, then they should accept EITHER that God is merciful and will overlook the mistakes that they and, more importantly, others make, that God will look with grace upon human weaknesses and intellectual fallibilities; OR if they believe in a stern, vengeful, wrathful, punishing God, then they should be prepared for God to smite down all the evildoers, all the slanderers, adulterers, heretics and those who lead others astray. These are the people who should suffer divine retribution in the form of illness and plague and all-consuming cancers, whose places of false worship should be destroyed by earthquake or lightning, whose families should drown in the floods while the righteous survive to triumph over them. But the point is, If you believe in a God who could do either of these, then one should be able to stand back and let God show whichever divine attributes one expects.

By definition, Anyone who takes a different viewpoint to your own is Wrong, is a Heretic or even a Blasphemer and therefore, if this theory or assumption is correct, it should be possible to demonstrate it by historical events. And yet, one of the inconsistencies of religious faith is that it is so often the Good who suffer, the innocent who, like Job, are made the playthings of powers beyond their control, that when natural catastrophes occur they do not distinguish between the clearly guilty and the clearly innocent but bury or burn or drown all impartially... Dare one say even this without being accused of Blasphemy?

But there are so many so-called Believers who seem to feel that the God they believe they believe in is incapable of punishing the sinners and that they must therefore take this task upon themselves. They simply do NOT believe that God has the interest or the power to do what God should be doing. These are the people who believe in an all-powerful God who is somehow not powerful enough to do what has to be done without their (eagerly-offered) voluntary assistance. It is They who must march out as good soldiers of God, soldiers of Christ, soldiers of Allah or whatever, and smite the Foe, most of whom are of course wholly unaware that they are a foe, they are just living their lives as normally and peacefully as they can in their villages and towns, in their buses and cafés and offices and factories and schools and aeroplanes, in their churches and chapels and mosques. Until some fanatic reaches out and affects their lives forever, destroying them or their loved ones, leaving behind scars and wounds and missing limbs and enormous trauma and grief and fear, all in the name of a Just or a Loving God who has somehow forgotten to do this Himself.

It is these who are the most dangerous people. The ones who believe that they believe but, in fact, do not believe and, if they are aware of this, then attempt to cover it with even more action, even more violence. The ones who, rather than waiting for Allah to strike down a blasphemous author, feel that it is their own responsibility to burn his books and to threaten his life.

As I have noted, it does not really do for Europeans to smile in a self-satisfied and superior way and murmur "How primitive!" when people of Asian background, often uneducated, from agricultural villages or from urban slums, act like this. The rest of the Europeans were hardly any better, not so long ago. But that was Then and now is Now and now we have to consider how best to react to the genuine anger and hurt expressed by a large group of the population, who fear that their faith, their religion, their prophets, their very identity are being undermined and denied and publicly humiliated by an author who grew up in their world but has left it to join ours.

But back to work. The first thing I had to do was to read this (literally) damned book. A copy was found. I found it heavy going but - and here I wish to be deliberately vague - I remain convinced to this day I am the only lay person (i.e. not a publisher's proof-reader) who has ever got to the end of it. Most people probably only read the flaps and maybe the first half of the first chapter. I say this because the end is so ironic that it is amazing that nobody ever cited it in any of the reviews or articles about the events. Written in alternate chapters set either in Bollywood or the Arabian desert, seemingly two parallel but never joining narratives, the 'present' chapters starting with an airliner being blown up over the Atlantic and the last chapter ending ironically with a creative artist having to go into hiding in fear of his life - honestly, did nobody else notice this ending? In between thinly-veiled descriptions of a religious seer in a medieval Arabian desert, the names slightly changed but clearly based on other religious mythology. It was not the sort of book I would normally have bought or normally have read, this was definitely classed as 'homework' and was at times very hard going but I stuck to it. At the very least it would be important to be able to see what people were complaining about. Unfortunately, and such is human nature, I am equally convinced that not one of the fanatics who have called for the burning of both the book and its author have ever read it either. It is SO much easier to damn something than to engage with it, explore it, analyse it and then come to a reasoned decision that a certain work is, perhaps, not recommended for children or the weak-hearted or weak-minded....

The day of the meeting came round and I arrived on time, with the book in my briefcase so as not to provoke. The Bishop was of course a nice chap, friendly and calm, Anglican bishops usually are, that's how they rise to their positions, the firebrands and the socially-incompetent are filtered out lower down the scale. The Imams were in traditional Pakistani garb, smart and also polite, aware perhaps that they had to find the right medium between being on the defensive after what had happened, and on the offensive about what had caused it. People sometimes talk about an "accent-free" English but in my experience many immigrants, whether Asian or East European, develop quite thick Yorkshire accents. You speak as you hear. A few other Christian clergy of different denominations sat in the circle, seemingly a little unsure of what their role was, to represent other minorities within the majority, to be tolerant or to set limits to tolerance and if so, how. Nervous smiles all round.

No notes were taken and nothing was recorded, no press were present, we spoke free and we spoke cordially and openly. I have forgotten after so many years most of what was said. But some things stuck in my mind. I asked whether any of those present (apart from myself) had actually read the book, and hardly any had, certainly none of the Moslems. This was hardly a good start, for it meant that nobody could speak with authority about what the fuss was all about...... An Imam explained how terrible it was for a Prophet to be attacked and humiliated and appealed to me to support him; surely it would be unthinkable for our holy people, our Prophets and our God, to be set up for ridicule? But here I had to point out that, in Judaism, this happened all the time. Our holy figures are set up to be criticised within our own tradition. None of them is perfect, all have weaknesses, that in the Midrash tradition the rabbis of old drew up stories about Biblical characters and usually pretty-unflattering ones, describing how these leaders struggled with their own doubts, their own disappointments and defeats.

But this they simply could not comprehend.

I come across this a lot. So many religious people see the universe in terms of black and white, but Judaism sees the shades of grey. Right from the very beginning, right from the first Creation story, the first of two contradictory ones by the way, we find that Judaism posits a transitional period between Night and Day and between Day and Night, that even when land has been made dry and separated from the waters it has to be watered from above or by rivers. It just seems so obvious to us that we cannot understand how others do not see this, but so often they do not. Also, the very word 'Israel' means - when first given to Jacob after his mysterious struggle at the Yabbok - "the one who argues and fights with God" whereas 'Islam', I understand, means "Submission to God". Such totally antithetical approaches to the same idea of a single God. The heathens of old, the polytheistic pagans, were subject to capricious gods who had no real interest in their welfare, who had to be distracted, bribed, entertained so as to provide the humans with what they needed - rain at the right time, fertility, whatever. The humans were nobodies at the mercy of childish, capricious, egotistical deities who perceived humanity just as the source of fun or their daughters as an occasional fuck when, just for fun, one pretended to be a bull or a swan or something. Who made up these myths, and why?

But Jews - no, Jews had a partnership with God, Moses spoke with God face to face and argued against God many times, just as Abraham did and just as so many others have since. No prophet sought the job, all argued against being chosen, before being compelled to accept their fate as a mouthpiece for divine warnings to those who did not want to hear, let alone listen. But for a Jew, should God deviate from God's own path, it is a duty to warn God back, to warn that the people will not accept this, that God has to back off and find another way, a better way to get the message across. It is an amazing relationship, not one of siblings, not one of a child to a parent, and not like a marriage either, but truly like a business partnership in which, maybe, one partner has all the financial resources and capital and the experience but the other knows what is going on on the shop floor and what the markets want. They need each other. The Creator would find existence pretty boring if the Created did not behave and misbehave the way they do. The Created have to acknowledge that they would not exist without at least the tacit consent of the Creator. They have free will and the right to employ it, but responsibly and fairly. Christians who believe in an Original Sin have real problems with this and Moslems - well, here I am less of an authority but it is clear that the way they think, the way they worship, the way they read their texts, the way they weave their philosophies or dive deep into their ecstasies is different to our way. Discussion and doubt are to be discouraged.

This approach does not have to mean inevitably blind fundamentalism, but it does open the door to the possibility. Learning to recite ancient texts in a foreign language in a foreign alphabet and without discussion is one way of training the mind, but it does not teach analysis and comparative approaches and openness to other possibilities.

A printed Rabbinic Bible volume will have not just a generally-agreed text compiled as a composite from various versions in various old manuscripts - (even here there is no total certainty but an ancient academic work by the '*Masoretes*' who compared carefully the various hand-copied scrolls at their disposal) - and adjacent to it a translation or two into Aramaic - for no Rabbi would countenance the idea that his people should not be able to understand the text and the fact that even translations may diverge in what they give is also something that cannot be denied - and then printed below this the commentaries of several worthy learned commentators who lived in different countries and centuries but who nevertheless felt free to comment on and criticise each other, and then commentaries on the commentaries, and then footnotes giving additional sources or comparative rabbinic texts.... No sensible non-fundamentalist rabbi (alas, we do have these others too) would dream of saying "It is written, therefore it MUST be true" without being aware that at least it has been written in different ways and that there were different source texts.

It is to the credit of thorough German scholarship that 'critical texts' of the Hebrew Bible have been prepared which also indicate for specialists who can read the abbreviations and the 'apparatus' the variant manuscripts in various libraries, obscure Codices in the Vatican Archive or in Leningrad (how ironic! What would Lenin say?) and when there are Aramaic or Syriac or Greek parallels or loan words or roots, where there is doubt as to how a text should be reconstructed and translated and explained.....

One result is that in Judaism we often have varying opinions but we are in a system that teaches us to accept that, even though the person with the other opinion is clearly a total fool and an idiot, he is entitled to be a total fool and an idiot, he has the God-given right to be so, to have a different viewpoint, a different tradition, a different melody, a different design of *Tallit,* a different recipe for humous or gefilte fish. Even though it is never as good as yours, or your grandmother's, it is still legitimate, it still counts, it still falls within the parameters of the acceptable. This is an amazing world view that is so hard for others to understand, but which we take for granted. No *Ashkenazi* Jew has killed a Jew for being *Sephardi.* Different *Chasidic* groups follow different *Rebbes* and masters. Orthodox Jews fought and hated *Chasidic* Jews but usually - usually - within defined limits. Orthodox and Reform and Liberal Jews all distrust and disagree with each other. There is agreement on nothing; But there is a general agreement that we do not need total agreement on anything. And as long as we agree on that, things get by.... without bloodshed and usually without burning of texts. It was the Christians who burned the *Talmud,* because they could not tolerate books in which people debated with each other on equal terms, in which more than one Truth was posited, more than one answer to so many questions. The Jews just wrote argumentative commentaries on it. There are many things one can say about the State of Israel, but a 'One Party State' is not one of them!

But how to explain all this to people who are pleasant, intelligent, willing to listen but simply unequipped to cope with such mind-bending concepts? From earliest childhood they have had obedience and submission beaten into them and they cannot understand the idea of disobedience and a refusal to submit being in any way something other than a route to eternal damnation. They cannot understand how casually we take some of the Biblical texts, how we have no problem in saying things like, "Oh, that was THEN, but now, you see, we don't have polygamy anymore, or slavery, or a priesthood... we have moved on, we have progressed and refined our belief and changed some rituals and abandoned others....."

It was a non-meeting of minds. To be expected, really. Syncretism is the new religion for many in Europe, the endless seeking for common denominators, for close parallels, for evidence that we are all alike really under the surface. A mild, vague form of Deism for those who are not even sure if there is a god at all, let alone worry about God's name or nature.... But - the trouble is, it isn't true. There really are people whose socialisation encourages or even compels them to think differently. Those who have grown up in totalitarian states or totalitarian systems have learned not to use parts of their brains, if they wish to survive, they have learned to suppress feelings and opinions and to accept whatever "them up there" throw at them; to dissent is dangerous, possibly fatal. It is hard for those of us who grew up differently to understand, but it is important that we try to do so. For people are NOT all the same and when some think it is all right to murder others for the sake of their false beliefs, a cup of tea is no longer adequate to quench the flames of zealotry. Not even with extra milk.

Just as – in a non-theological field - there are some who feel justified even now in enslaving their workers with inadequate wages and tricky contracts that force them to be self-employed and responsible for all they do, for all their fuel or their breakages, for bearing all their expenses that a more fair-minded and generous employer would have handled as a normal part of the costs of running his operation. The ones who leave employees to decay and die when they are ill or hampered by sick family members, without help or sick pay, who let the Zero-Hours contracts stand even when the weather makes the work impossible for the best-intentioned. "Market Forces" they chant in unison, but cannot accept that labour is also part of a market which can, if it becomes scarce or the workers combine, affect the pricing mechanisms.... Market forces, it seems, exist only to drive the labour costs down and the profits up, not the other way around....

So one must accept that there are sometimes mental gulfs between people, that even if we are biologically and genetically very close to each other, we come from different worlds. In such cases 'a meeting of minds' is more than difficult to arrange. It is almost as though – to change the metaphor – one has two magnets of the same pole, not different ones, and so they not only refuse to meet but actually resist contact with each other.

The meeting ended with smiles and handshakes (although the Moslems did not wish to shake the hand of the female Free Church Minister). A press release would be prepared by the Bishop's Secretary. Nothing had been resolved but at least we had met in the same room, on Cathedral territory, and we left with no blood on the carpet. Maybe, just maybe, some people had been forced today to think through their own beliefs and their own reactions; Maybe, just maybe, some people had been encouraged to consider their place as a minority and migrants in a society which while generally, sometimes grudgingly tolerant, did not know how to define itself except in terms of what it did NOT want; where the boundaries on public behaviour and misbehaviour are. Maybe.

We may have defused one bomb but there are many others lurking beneath the surface, many other preachers who will tell impressionable and naïve young men that it is their religious duty to burn not just the book but the author, maybe the publisher, maybe the bookshops. Is it patronising even to formulate matters in such a way? Wisdom travels at the Speed of Enlightenment. But that is a relative term and cannot be artificially accelerated.

Maybe it is up to God to sort it out now. I hope he has a sense of humour and an inexhaustible amount of tolerance for the way the divine Name is misused by so many triumphalist zealots.

****

NIL NISI BONUM

What I am about to describe never happened, the people concerned never existed and of course nobody was affected by the events which, as non-events, have been expunged from any record. At least, that is the received wisdom. There is only one problem with this approach to life and history which is, that it is not true. Things DO happen, people ARE affected, people DO do things they maybe shouldn't, and which they maybe (hopefully) regret..... and to pretend otherwise is both stupid and dishonest.

The chap was a colleague. Even if his name has been largely removed from all lists of honour, of ordinations and from his congregational records, I want to state this loud and clear. The chap was a colleague. He had chosen a path and he had worked and studied to attain a position. He wasn't a major academic light and I presume he wasn't a saint either, but by various accounts (when it was still possible to talk about him) he had worked reasonably well, displayed some competence and compassion, played only a minor role in Movement politics but was there at the annual conferences and at several, not all of the rabbinic conference meetings I went to. We had the odd chat, but I didn't know him well and we did not seem to share a lot of interests in common.

One in particular.

The scandal, when it broke, was one of those that come from a clear blue sky. Every now and then you will hear on the radio perhaps that "the police have broken up an international ring of child pornographers.... several people have been arrested for questioning here and there and there, the police have confiscated so-and-so-many computers" and so forth. What do you think when you hear such news? Gratitude for a functioning society, for a justice system concerned to maintain morality and punish immorality and protect the innocent? Yes, probably. But what about the idea that people can look into your computer and find Everything there, even the deleted files, even the ones you forgot about? Do you think "What a wonderful world, when police in Belgium can get information on criminals in Greece, Slovakia and Britain"? Do you think "This is the way to break up international rings of swindlers and terrorists"? Or - perhaps - you think "Is nowhere safe anymore, nowhere private?"

The police came to his home at 3am, in classic police style, woke him up, and his wife, and gave him half an hour to dress and so forth while they searched his study and unplugged and packed his computer. At 9 they were at the Synagogue office. Uproar. The synagogue computer has a lot of private information, of course, on membership and members, but it was packed into big cardboard boxes and taken off to be gone through - at the Chairman's request they did promise to return it as soon as possible and in fact only four days later it was back and plugged in again, though I understand it took the secretary a while to sort out which files were now where. It had been clean. In the Rabbi's study there had been a monitor and the means to log in to the computer or send files to be printed in the office but no separate hard drive. Still, they went through his desk and so forth to look for external drives and sticks.

It was at home that he had given in to the temptations and the inner demons. Anyone who has ever fought an inner drive, an addiction, a laziness, an inability to relax, the desperate need for some nicotine, or sugar, or anything - we all have Something - knows the mental games one plays to put off submission to the *Yetzer HaRa,* the inner drive to do something that could be self-damaging or self-destructive. Painkillers, antidepressants, procrastination, pornography..... Some of these bad habits are more socially acceptable than others, some are less socially acceptable, some are absolutely taboo.

Needless to say, he resigned immediately he was released, from the congregational post and - sadly – from the rabbinic conference too. I say 'sadly' because colleagues of all people should be the ones to whom one can turn to for support even in difficult times when one has committed the dual sins of doing something, and being caught for doing it. What can one do after such a public humiliation? In the *Talmud* it suggests one should put on a dark cloak and go somewhere else, relocate. In former times the Colonies provided adequate shelter and employment for soldiers, policemen, engine drivers and others who had lapsed in their professional standards, gave them another chance to build up a career and a life. I have known rabbis who, having been caught in a moral lapse, made a new start in another hemisphere. It could be done. But that was then. And now? Is there anywhere left to where one can go?

Now nobody thinks any more about the perpetrator who has, by many standards, become also a victim. Nobody thinks about his marriage or his kids or his bank account or his pension. To be drummed out of the Army is one thing, to slip away and look for another post somewhere is entirely different. To discourage others. But something about the hysteria worries me. The extremism. A taboo has been broken, but there are other taboos which do not get the same reaction. Lives have been damaged but they have not been ended. Suddenly nobody, not even my other colleagues, want to mention his name. Suddenly his congregation cannot work fast enough to delete him from the letterhead and all publications, from the website, from the entry in Jewish calendars and similar. In the monthly newsletter no mention is made of anything, not of his being, not of his going, not of any reasons. No traditional smoothing-over of rough passages with terms such as "We regret to say that due to health reasons our Rabbi has had to..." As though nobody knew. It is as though he had never been. "*Yimach Shemo*" is traditionally the worst curse one can inflict on anyone - "May his name be wiped out" - may it be as though he had not been. To be utterly forgotten. To have not been worth being conceived and born. Everything he has done is as though it had not been done.

Priestley has a play in which two couples discover that the minister who officiated at their weddings had not been properly qualified and so the question arises as to whether their marriages are valid. Well, what of the weddings this colleague has officiated, his signature on the *Ketubot*, what of the *Bar-Mitzvah* services he has led and the funerals he has done - do the dead become unburied suddenly when he is removed like this? Rising again in disgust, demanding a second funeral from 'someone better"?

It's been a couple of years now, a new rabbi took the position, they were glad to get someone at short notice and learned later why he, too, was available and looking for a position, but so far it seems to be working out. I have no idea where the other chap is. He has literally dropped out of society. Nobody has an address or a mail address or a number for him. Nobody even seems to care. Well, I care. Whatever the sin may have been, the sinner is someone separate. A human being. Just like you and me, in fact.

****

JASENOVAC

What stays in my mind is the knife. It is a short, curved blade attached to a band that goes around the wrist like a watch strap. According to the explanatory label it was used for gouging people's eyes out. While they were still alive.

I shudder every time I think of it but the image stays with me. When people think of the Holocaust they usually think of Poland where we have the big contrasts..... Auschwitz I for example is still there and there are those big glass windows allowing shocked visitors to view the piles of hair, toothbrushes, suitcases and more, the sound in the rooms is the sound of a lot of people staying very quiet apart from the clumping of shoes on the wooden floorboards or the concrete. Auschwitz II, Birkenau, is the vast expanse of foundations of the barracks which have gone, the symbolic iconic gatehouse with its entrance for the railway track, the three parallel tracks themselves... and at the end the ruins and rubble of demolished buildings, crematoria, gas chambers.... Auschwitz III, the former Monowitz industrial area, is now a housing estate, pleasant bungalows and a plaque. Treblinka and Sobibor - basically vanished, at Stutthof there are some of the buildings and some wagons, Belzec has gone.... The ghetto in Krakow has been dolled up to make it into the film set and tourist attraction it has been, whereas that in Warsaw is replaced by post-war blocks of flats and here and there a memorial. But look elsewhere and what is left at Westerbork, or at Drancy? Or at Gurs? Sachsenhausen and Ravensbrück and Dachau have some of the buildings and a few recreated barracks and plenty of gravel to walk around, Buchenwald too. Flossenbürg is now mostly a pleasant housing estate.

These are the sorts of places Jewish tourists go to. Babi Yar was deliberately covered with housing.... other ghettos and places of horror survive here and there as memorials but without the smell, the stink, the smoke, the blood, the excrement, the fear.

But people often overlook the Balkans. There was Trawniki. The Jasenovac camp was one of several and one of the most horrible. The Yugoslavs have a habit of treating each other as horribly as possible and some of the things they thought of doing to each other made even the Nazis gasp and feel queasy, according to some accounts. I mean, it is one thing to be a heartless mass murderer, following the Führer's orders, it is another to be a mass murderer who actually enjoys the close-up slaughter. Not shooting people into a pit, standing safely at a distance, not gassing them in an enclosed room or vehicle, where you couldn't actually see unless you wanted to peek through a spyhole, but actually gouging them with a knife attached to your wrist........ who would think of that? It was a place where the Croat Ustase killed Serbs and Jews and Sinti and anyone they didn't like. It wasn't actually a German, Nazi camp at all. This was home-grown brutality.

There wasn't much left of it, the only time I went there, but even that was enough for me. A big concrete Communist-style memorial in the middle of an empty space, one of those black holes in the surface of the Earth that suck in all energy, all humanity, all light. Along one side a railway track and on it stood as part of the memorial a typical Serbian 2-6-0 freight engine and several goods vans - from our side looking quite intact, but the other side was covered in shell holes and bullet holes because, ironically, this camp now lay on what had become the border in the NEXT war, a war also marked by torture and mass rapes and the murder of innocents and the massacres of entire villages, sometimes while the UN soldiers stood helplessly by, mute witnesses to the inhumanity of mankind and its inability to learn any empathy. From the opposite side of the River Save people had shot at other people (I don't know why, what did they hope to achieve?) and had shot at the memorial to people killing other people, the ultimate proof that Homo Sapiens NEVER learns.

The prettier the countryside, the nastier the people - this isn't a fixed rule, but it often seems to apply. It is an interesting question to what extent entire societies are defined by their geography. Those who live in flat plains experience the endless horizons, the wide-open skies and are aware of man's puny insignificance and the vastness of the heavens and the God there; those who live in deep narrow valleys where the sun penetrates only for a few hours around midday see the towering mountains and again are aware of man's puny insignificance but also dream of climbing to those mountain tops to get closer to the heavens and to God. But the people who live in the next valley are strangers with whom one has little contact since they are so hard to visit. Those who live on island archipelagos have the sea around them but also other islands, those who live on isolated islands somewhere in the Atlantic see only the sea all around them. All have their myths, how their world was created, what forces enabled it to happen or tried to obstruct it.

But life is hard enough, so why do we constantly make it harder and shorter for our neighbours? To get here one passes through countless villages of pretty white houses with red tiled roofs scattered in the dark green valleys. It is only as one gets closer and passes through that one sees they are deserted, the windows empty, traces of smoke from the interior staining the white plaster, holes in the red tiled roofs. Each has been systematically destroyed, not by a natural catastrophe but by other people who saw what people had carefully designed and built and probably saved for and paid for and then set about destroying it. By now, with the conflict declared over for now, the bodies have been collected and buried, the raped women have found some shelter somewhere else, the orphans have been gathered in urban institutions, the animals that had been left to starve have been slaughtered and eaten or stolen and put to pasture elsewhere. If this is normality, then normality has been restored. If this is normality. Unfortunately, it so often is. But nobody has come back to live here yet, to reclaim the properties, to rebuild the houses, to fill them with family life once again. If they ever can, if they ever will.

That knife. I cannot put it out of my head. Thank God no-one put it into mine.

****

A SIGNATURE

This is it. The right name on the sign. I press the buzzer and go in. Take the lift to the fourth floor. Find the name on the door, knock, am let in. The man, to be fair, looks a little embarrassed. But he has been commissioned to perform a task, a legal procedure, and to get my signature on a piece of paper. We sit at a big wide desk, the type that only lawyers ever seem to have. He slides across the smooth varnished surface some sheets of A4. I look through. All is quiet. We set this appointment for the evening, after normal office hours, the offices are empty, the streets are empty, there was no problem finding a place to park. My heart is empty too.

It seems a bit strange to be signing one's own death sentence, so to speak. Of course, I exaggerate a bit but this document draws to an abrupt end eleven hard years of dedicated work, brought to a sudden and early end because one person did not like one sermon. And because no-one else had the balls to stand up to her. Not the other board members, not the congregation's members, not the colleagues, not the Movement busybodies. Oh, again I exaggerate, some tried, tried to call her, tried to stand up and speak at a meeting, but nobody was prepared to fight. Really fight. And I was forbidden to. Forbidden to talk, to communicate, to go public. Even my colleagues, who should have known better, who should have realised that now was the time to draw a line in the sand, that if they let this pass then we could all be at risk for any tiny, insignificant argument, that our contracts are worthless, that all the nice words and the applause at conferences mean nothing when it comes to getting, no demanding, a dignified departure, a reasonable payment, a decent reference...... Well, they will also find that out in due course. All those people who say "Don't fight, it will only make it worse" - would they have said the same to the Maccabees, or to the fighters in the Warsaw Ghetto, I wonder?

What really, really worries me is that I suspect the answer for some of them at least would be "Yes". There is the old joke of the three Jews standing before a firing squad, the commander of which offers each of them a last cigarette. Two accept it, the third refuses and spits on the ground. "For heaven's sake, don't make it worse" says one of his fellows.

That's the way it goes. The pen is mightier than the sword, spear, halberd and revolver put together. The bastards don't care about my family or my mortgage or my hire-purchase payments on the car, they don't care that my pension fund is now frozen and that to open a new one will mean paying more to get less, since I have spent over ten years with this organisation. They don't care that our social life is dead and the marriage under stress. They don't care that the only way to get another job will mean to leave the city and go elsewhere, because there is not exactly a vast choice of similar firms or schools around to which one could apply, to which one could transfer. Not only that, but many know what I have not been allowed to tell them, that this overreaction is because the person in question thought that in my sermon I was referring to her, for she had done the same thing I was criticising! Which, ironically, I had not known at the time, until someone told me later....

There were two copies. One for him, or them, one for me. My pen scratches a bit. It is not ink but my soul's blood that it writes with. Outgunned, outmanoeuvred, delivered on a tray to my enemies, I have no choice. I sign. He thanks me. We shake hands. All very calm, business-like, professional. Nobody else dared be here, of course, they were paying him to do the dirty work for them. As is so often the case. The law must be observed in a minimalist way, morality and humanity can go to hell. Me too. Then there is the quiet drive back home.

There will be no Farewell Service, no Presentation and Good Wishes for the Future; no Farewell article in the newsletter thanking everyone for their help and support over so many years. There will be no continuity, no handover to a successor to whom I can explain outstanding issues, conversion candidates in the middle of their learning, long-term patients who will miss rabbinic visits so abruptly ended, files of correspondence. But nobody cares about that, of course. Nobody knows one tenth of what one does. For me - It is time to start looking for another job. There is a family to feed, a mortgage to pay. The world will not stand still, despite the stillness in this office now. But the wound is deep and the scars will remain. They way scars do.

This is the way my world ended. Not with a bang, but a whimper.

....

There are two Postscripts.

A few weeks later I had to return to the synagogue's office to get some official forms signed and stamped in turn. From the Employment Exchange. When had I started working here? - that sort of thing. The Honorary Secretary complained. Why had I registered as "Unemployed'? Surely Rabbis didn't do this? This could be SO embarrassing for the congregation!

I won't give my answer here. The publisher would only want me to cut it out......

And then, ten years later, when things had calmed down, the dust had settled and they had struggled for a while to find a successor (for rabbis talk to each other as well, you know) and there had been some major changes in the Board - I was invited back to a big anniversary celebration. After some thought, I accepted. But - It is hard to say 'Hello' to people again, when you never had a chance to say 'Goodbye'.

****

DOWNFALL

One of the things I have learned is that when Catastrophes come they almost always come from a clear blue sky; they come when you are not expecting them, when you are feeling good, when you feel your work is going well, that you have successfully completed several projects, that you are respected for your hard work and admired for your ideas and initiatives, that you are at last getting some reward for the blood, sweat and tears that accompany (but out of sight) so much of what one has to do. Things are going well one day and - next day - it is all over; there are just dust and ashes, torn trust, destroyed relationships, a darkness and a hopelessness and a bewilderment at how quickly this has all happened. It happens to many of us - not to all, and those colleagues who have not experienced this, or at least claim not to have experienced it, seem unable to comprehend what it is like when one day the people you have worked with and for over many years turn suddenly against you. One rabbi's wife once told us, as a warning and as well-meant advice, that "it takes years to realise you cannot trust even the people you can trust" and I learned the hard way what she meant. Those colleagues who have never experienced this, for some reason, often look askance at those of us who are licking our wounds and anointing our sores and tend to feel, as so often happens, that the victim is somehow partially at least to blame for what has occurred. All one can do in such cases is to say "Just wait and, when it happens, Remember Me..."

"Surprises normally come unexpectedly" wrote the old German comic writer Wilhelm Busch, and he put it in a nutshell.

So it pays to keep your powder dry, to have as few debts and mortgages and hire purchase arrangements as possible and as much flexibility as possible; and an independent pension fund. One issue is that, outside the major conurbations, seeking a new position means seeking a new city to live in, for there simply are not that many congregations in each town. As a secretary or a teacher or a sales executive you might be able to find another job that allows you to stay in the same home, the same district, but when you hold such a minority position as a rabbi any move means not just a longer commute but a full move. If one's spouse also has a job, then one needs to think what to do. Whose potential salary is the greater? Should one of you commute to work in a different place?

When it hit, after several successful years, it was because a couple of Board members did not like a sermon I had delivered to a near-empty synagogue one morning, after a very full and successful evening service attended by civic guests at which I had apparently preached the best sermon of the century. But it really, really is true that you are only as good as your last sermon and this turned out to be in fact my last sermon at that congregation! For the next day, a Sunday, I was formally asked to return my keys..... Really, as quickly as that.

There are always some people you may upset at a meeting, in a committee, or with a sermon. This is a given. It is not your job, nor is it possible, to please all of the people all of the time. It is your job to teach and to challenge, to deny people the chance to misuse their power or their religion, to stand up for the weak and the powerless, to argue unpopular corners when somebody has to do it. So, to have a few opponents and enemies is fully normal. But you don't expect the people with whom you have shared a great deal of your life, shared dinner parties at your home and at theirs, had their children playing with your children.... that these are the ones who will suddenly turn against you and play the morally superior form of creation and will watch calmly while your family faces disintegration and despair. The ones you thought you could trust.

Then there was the time I wasn't there. No, the times, in the plural. One had been earlier, when there was some large formal reception and I felt I ought to attend, despite not feeling very much in common any more with the then-Chairman and his coterie. These worthies stood in line at the entrance shaking hands and murmuring the sweet complimentary nothings that one does on such occasions - until my wife and I reached them, at which point they all turned their backs and made as if to walk into the hall for a short stroll. There was little we could do but smile and continue into the hall ourselves though, I must say, even a couple of my enemies were shocked at this treatment and came up to me later in the evening to say they had felt it a painful matter. THEY had found it painful? What in hell's teeth did they think WE had felt? But we bore up. There is after all a certain game that is played here; The rules are unwritten but known by all. The Game consists simply of walking into a room with ten people and seeing only five of them. To these five one advances, extends the hand, kisses the cheek, greets, whatever, whereas the other five are as though invisible or absent.

A few weeks later a friend from another city wanted to attend the synagogue service and I said that out of politeness I would accompany him. I was after all still a member. We walked in - I timed our arrival carefully - just before the service was due to start and I walked us along the long, long aisle to the front row and took up seats in the middle of the row. And the amazing thing is that none of the three Wardens walking about or any of the committee saw us at all. One does not need a Cloak of Invisibility in these circumstances, one simply has to be whom one is. And put up with it.

A couple of years later one of the fellows wrote a history of the Jewish community which mentioned my predecessor and my successor but somehow did not mention me. At all. Not even in passing. Not even in the Index (I checked straight away.) These of course are the people who scream most loudly at any falsification of history as they see it, who demand that every detail of past sufferings be remembered and memorialised. But they are not above it themselves. Until this point I confess I had disliked the fellow intensely, but had still had some respect for him, at least as an historian. Now that, too, was gone.

And let us not forget that the one who writes the History has the power to define it. There is the old line about the difference between God and an Historian being that God can no longer change something that has already happened.....

So, it happens. One reels with the blow, one has to take time to catch breath. Lawyers don't have a clue. Most labour law does not apply. One has no Union. You learn that no colleague wants to take risks on your behalf. You learn that the people who run Movements run Movements because they like to run Movements and the one thing they cannot cope with is the presence of someone who might, even indirectly, lead to internal conflict or, heaven forbid, a split in their Movement. It isn't just religious movements that are like this, of course, but the point is, you learn, the hard way, that they are no better than any other.

There are bills to pay, children in school; a mortgage; insurance; all the rest of modern complexity. Life moves on, and you move with it, as best you can. At best, the time may come when you can write about it all, calmly and from a distance, emotion recollected in tranquillity as Wordsworth put it. All you need is some Tranquillity. Last I heard, there was a whole Sea of it, on the Moon......

****

THE RELUCTANT GRANDMOTHER

There is only one reason I can think of, for what she has done. Only one. Nothing else makes real sense at all. I think she simply does not want to become a Grandmother. And she is being terribly consistent about it.

It is a long story and I have no idea where or how it really began. What made her fear this state? My part in it began when I got a call one evening. Her daughter was in a manic-depressive state and was being taken to hospital. It sounded like a visit was quite urgent, one of those priority ones where you put aside the plans for the evening and get out the car keys. The story as it unfolded was quite a tragic one. The daughter had become pregnant, the way girls do from time to time even before their mother has had time to argue about the colour of the flowers for the wedding or the table settings. In the nature of things, if all goes well and follows its ordained path an embryo becomes a foetus and a foetus becomes a baby and once the baby is born it becomes, well, in this case, it would have become a grandson. Whatever the circumstances of his conception, however the insemination took place and from whom, the baby himself is a new innocent being, a new blank sheet of paper upon which deeds can be drawn, if given the chance. At least half his genes belong to the maternal family which can now accept him into their own. According to ancient Jewish law it is the mother who makes the child Jewish, because one usually knows at least who the mother is, whereas one could so very rarely be 100% certain who the father is.

I recall reading as a student of the medical research project performed on new-borns and their parents at a major hospital in the Midlands, whereby blood was taken and the Rhesus Factor amongst other factors was noted; according to the report, it transpired that in at least 50 per cent of even those births where the new-born child actually had two identifiable married parents, about a half of the total sample, the child could not be the biological child of both parents..... simply through the way the Rhesus factor in their blood was distributed. A lot of cuckoos fly around the Midlands, it seems, and lay their eggs wherever they will.

So of course, such an extramarital motherhood is socially embarrassing, but a healthy grandchild is a healthy grandchild and most parents would learn to cope with the initial shock and adapt as quickly as they can to their new roles as grandparents. I have known of cases where this happened with enormous suddenness, once even when a young girl went into hospital with stomach pains and suddenly a baby was born and NOBODY had realised it beforehand, nobody had had time even to buy a packet of nappies and look for a cot.

In this case, however, the baby had been given up immediately for adoption. Given - or taken? That is the question. In fact "taken", for the new grandmother had decided upon this move, not the new mother who was now, in reaction - and still under all the hormonal stress of giving birth, still with milk in her breasts, still with the feeling of unaccustomed emptiness in her belly but also an emptiness in her arms where a sweet-smelling suckling baby should be - cracking up. Understandably. Denied any pride in accomplishment, denied the sight of her new child, denied the feel of lips sucking at her nipples, denied the feel of the new soft skin, denied the presence of what she had carried and produced. Denied the proud love of her own mother. But it was her mother who was in denial, not she....

It was not an easy time for anyone, because the family did not want anyone to know what had happened.... something which is hard to keep secret in a relatively small community. Not only that, but the availability of Jewish babies for adoption is very small and the demand from Jewish couples with fertility problems is high, which is why so many make the trek to South America.... to acquire by whatever legal means may exist a child, not necessarily new-born any more, and maybe born with a variety of medical conditions due to the diet or the addictions of the biological mothers... So it was a shame that this healthy Jewish baby, if it really WAS going to be given away (or taken away) was not being made available to the Jewish Social Services - but that, of course, would have meant making the story too public. So nobody knows where this child is - by now he will be a teenager, at least. There was of course no *brit milah* to organise or celebrate.....

It was a sad case and one was pretty well helpless but it seems - for reasons that were obvious to me - that the girl did not really want many visits from her mother flapping about and trying to sound caring, considerate and compassionate. But I did go twice more, to talk, to listen and the second time was the real humdinger - because the girl's older sister had come to visit at the same time. It was simply a coincidence, I had never met her before, she lived elsewhere and had come to see her sister in the mental ward. And it was here I learned of the enormity of the situation. It seemed that this young lady had also become pregnant, also without the benefit of a wedding ring, and her mother had forced her to have an abortion - she herself had wanted to keep the baby, but the mother had said 'No!' and put all in train to make the termination happen. The daughter had left town soon afterwards and was now in a settled job and a new partnership, it seemed, but had decided not to have a family. Not with her mother - dominating, interfering - as a grandmother.

I left the congregation a couple of years later and keep only vaguely in touch and it was some time ago but, so far as I know, neither daughter has had a child since or shown any interest in having one and so the reluctant grandmother - her husband of course was totally side-lined in all these matters, his voice was silenced - has managed to achieve her ambition. Her line will in fact end with her own daughters. I sometimes wonder whether this is what she really wanted. But it is what she achieved. What the neighbours may think counts for her more than what God thinks, or for what the other family members think. The prophets of old fought against the practice of sacrificing babies to *Moloch,* but nowadays babies get sacrificed on the altar of respectability.

And Respectability is the most powerful god of all.

****

THE MINUTE TAKER

It was a bastard thing for the Bastard to do but, sadly, not untypical. It has been said before that a Committee is an organisation that keeps Minutes but wastes Hours. As Rabbi it was expected I should be present at Board meetings, without a vote of course and only allowed to speak at the Chairman's discretion. And these meetings were dreadful. Really dreadful. Acrimonious, repetitive, disrespectful of one another, the stages on which sad egos played out some of their more obscure power fantasies, where individuals pleaded ineffectively for recognition of their meagre achievements, where bitter squabbles blew up over trivialities, where insults were sensed at the end of every sentence... Threats of legal action were not unknown though rarely carried out - unless the congregation would be meeting the bills, of course, to defend its "good name" against some unrighteous but correct accusation.

These were evenings to be endured rather than enjoyed, though it was clear that some of the others did indeed enjoy these monthly bouts of verbal violence. Only once, in my many years of experience, did it get beyond verbal, but even so it was often brutal enough. Sneers and accusations and implied insults and all the rest. Some people become truly expert in all this. Some seem to have nothing else of interest in their lives, they look forward to these regular occasions.

Of course, let us not forget that all these conflicts were being carried out not to raise our market share or profit margin or to destroy our competitors, but in the name of Peace, Love and Harmony, to run a "Holy Congregation", a "*Kehilla Kedosha*", devoted to the teaching of God's word and maintaining Jewish values.

In theory, at least.

I would even be asked formally to read aloud a prayer or invocation before each meeting, urging all to listen to each other with respect and to see the image of God in each other as we carried out together our holy tasks. Something like that. Most of those who had already arrived - there were always a few late-comers - would be chatting to each other and looking through their folders as I read aloud.

Well, certain tensions had been building up for a while now and it doesn't really matter at this distance whether it was about the Building Fund or the Religion School or some new liturgy being introduced or some issue in the private life of the Executive member involved - I know and he knows but nobody else need know all the murky, grimy details. Suffice it to say that I sat there at the table as usual from 7.30pm onwards and, because I had promised to be home by 10pm, I apologised and got up to leave at 10.30pm and left the room and -

- and by 9.15am next morning when I got to my office the entire congregation seemed to know about it. Immediately after I had left the room the Chairman had formally called a 'Closed Meeting' and had announced that the Rabbi had to go, that his contract - my contract - would have to be terminated as soon as possible, even forthwith if this could be arranged. That no reasons should be given for this decision, "to protect his reputation". Hah! The bastard. It's a very clever technique, calling out "I see smoke!" where there is no smoke, and then letting everyone else assume that there must be a fire.

What interested me right now was that nobody had called me late the previous night to warn me or inform me. I had to wait until the morning and then hear when a congregant who was NOT on the Board called me to ask if this were true? That meant that even those I classed privately as 'Allies' or at least

'Neutral' had either chickened out or voted against me and had not dared to tell me. Each assumed that someone else would let me know, I suppose.

Religious organisations are in practice beyond any laws, even (or especially) divine laws. There are theoretically civil laws as to how to treat employees, laws concerning 'constructive dismissal' and aggravation and abuse of power and the breaking of labour contracts and all that sort of thing, laws that have been hard fought for by unions and parliamentarians over the centuries, laws that even say how long one should work in one stretch as a railway signalman or airline pilot or lorry driver and of course there is a law way back in Exodus chapter 20 that states that everyone, even the slaves, even the cattle, is entitled to one day off per week. Try explaining that to a Board member who has just HAD to schedule a VERY important meeting or life-cycle event on what is technically your free day, try to explain that to someone who sees no reason why a committee meeting, ABSOLUTELY important to the future of the human race or at least for the future of the Ritual Committee, need not go on till midnight after you have already had a hard day of work..... Show weakness and the battle is half lost before you begin. Don't go to a meeting, and you will have no control over what happens or what is Minuted. But this time, this bastard knew that I HAD gone to the meeting, Had taken part where matters affected me, Had contributed to discussions, and then he had waited till I left the room to put the dagger between my shoulder blades. Bastard.

It is interesting to consider what sort of person fights so hard to become and to stay a synagogue chairman or chairwoman - each are as bad as each other, in this respect we have complete equality. Why risk so many friendships, spend so much time, to become leader not of a mighty nation but of a tiny group of people? To be mightily significant among the pitifully insignificant? There is a difference in Germany, where many of the communities are effectively small companies with large budgets and control can have benefits, direct or indirect. One of the most useful and important lessons I learned as a rabbinic student - from a wise old colleague - was to look carefully at the people who spent too long at the synagogue, rather than just grumbling about those who did not come enough or stay long enough. What were the problems at home that led them to take on roles in committees? Some, it is true, were idealists, persuaded against their better natures because somebody had to take on a specific responsibility and it might even be that their professional skills as an architect, an accountant, a teacher might be useful. But there are others, there are always others, who have basically never achieved much with their lives, or at least not as much as they considered they were entitled to; those who had problems with their spouse or issues with their children, who had never been promoted above a certain junior level, and who yearned for a forum where they could have and exercise Power, any power, however small the circle, however minor the budget, so long as they were in control. I have to add here that in England all this work is honorary, but in Germany there were often financial inducements as well, paid positions as Chairman in some larger communities, substantial allowances for 'compensation for time and expenses' at smaller ones, the ability to divert funds with nobody challenging. I knew of one chairwoman who paid herself to lead the services - as a chairwoman she could not draw pay, but since she organised the services and sang at them, she reckoned she could pay herself for that task instead. Or apply to external sponsors for extra funding so that she could arrange a festival concert in which the performers would be well paid. The Treasurer supported her, other Board members were not even informed for some time, the financial reports were a muddle for years...... and when they did start to suspect something and tried to find out more, they were edged out quite brutally. But - in England, this would not have been relevant. In English communities it is a matter of power and pride, not of pennies and pounds. People fight elections, try to influence votes, slander other candidates, manipulate meetings, all to get elected to an honorary position where they are technically responsible for the smooth running of a religious organisation largely dependent on enthusiastic volunteers. I have known cases where someone denies he will stand again for office and then submits their application half an hour before the deadline, just to put all possible rivals onto their back feet. Where someone gets the constitution changed five months before his term of office ends to ensure that his main rival is disqualified ("has a non-Jewish spouse... lives too far away... has not been a member for long enough..." etc.) Or to get themselves appointed "for Life". Of course, if you have a 'Life Warden' or 'Life President' or some such title it is an open invitation to someone to find an alternative way to shorten the period involved....

The worst ones, the absolute worst, are those who wanted to become Rabbis themselves but, for whatever reason, were unable to manage this. These 'Rabbis manqué' as they are (sometimes politely) referred to have a grudge against every Rabbi for daring to have gone and got qualified. Especially when you are new in post it can be that you are now some years or decades younger than they are and so they assume that their accumulated life-experience, as plumbers or administrators or whatever, qualify them to tell you what a Rabbi should be, do, think and say.

The Bastard was one of these. The story is complex and sad but at one point he had, it seems, even managed to get accepted to a rabbinic college but had then been dragged back by his mother who was concerned for her darling's creature comforts and worried he was so far away from her. The classic Jewish Mother syndrome - but this was no joke, the experience had trapped him and embittered him and made him jealous of anyone who had the title for which he had craved. We had begun on a reasonably friendly basis, but I learned later that he was just testing me all the time. To see how I would react. The fact that he was an alcoholic - not really a secret - did not help but he pushed it a bit when drinking half a bottle of vodka during a meeting with me and then losing his temper. At that point, I realised later, I should have gone out all guns blazing and registered a complaint somewhere higher up. But the greatest wisdom in Life always comes when looking backwards, not forwards.

But now, now, there was a problem. It was obvious the whole town would know by lunchtime that something had been decided about me the previous night and that, whatever it was, I must have done something truly awful if such swift and draconian action had 'HAD' to be taken. How to salvage, if not my job, at least my reputation?

By the time I had left at 10.30pm several others had also made their apologies and got up and gone so I reckoned the meeting was still just quorate but not complete. That was important. Not all had been involved. Nobody from the Board had contacted me by 11am. Not the Chairman, nor the Vice-Chairman, nor the Hon. Secretary nor the Hon. Treasurer nor the Chief Warden. Theoretically all could be just a false rumour, there might be no point in calling a lawyer - yet. So I decided to try to find out some other way. I checked the list and called Stanley at his work. I had only had to do this once before - to inform of a death in the community - and so I knew he had an office somewhere and a secretary and could be called. You cannot call a dentist at work, or a hairdresser, or a bus driver. But a chap in an office - well, he has a desk, a chair and a phone and so he is available. And when he came to the phone I told him, "Look, Stanley, I know something happened late last night at the meeting. But I would like to know what, exactly. You were taking the Minutes - can you tell me?"

He was, of course, taken aback. It was a very direct approach. I interrupted some "Hmms" and said, "Look, it is not breaking any confidences, I am entitled to the Minutes in any case, I am *ex officio* a member of the Board, I am entitled to know what happens at meetings where I cannot attend. Can you tell me more?"

More Hmms. Then, "Well look, Rabbi, I don't have time right now and my notes are at home, I haven't even typed them up yet. Can you call me this evening, after I get back?"

On the one hand, this was sensible, and who knew who else might be listening in at his office? On the other hand, by evening more hours would have gone by and maybe the Bastard himself would have found the guts to call me. And Stanley surely had little need to refer to his notes about such a conversation, such a vote? But there wasn't much I could do about this. "Thank you, I will," I said, and put the phone down and wondered what to do next. Go to my office? Go out for a walk? Visit the two sick old ladies I had planned to visit and who had nothing to do with this fuss? One at her home, one at a Home? Continue working, pretending that nothing had happened, fulfilling at least those pastoral responsibilities I could?

That evening, as promised, I called. The news was not good and I was tense and it was taking its toll upon me and, of course, on the family too. What Stanley said made me furious. The chairman, the Bastard, had told him not to let me have any information. Not to have a copy of the Minutes. That he, the Bastard, would prepare the Minutes! This was not only irregular, it was downright illegal - except, of course, for this problem that the term 'legality' has such little meaning in the communities. In vain I pointed this out to Stanley, in vain I demanded, in vain I pleaded; the 'closed meeting' had been 'closed' and therefore proceedings had to remain confidential. Even from me. Ridiculous. A nasty trick. Manipulative. One is totally undermined. "Constructive dismissal" it may be called in some organisations, but in so-called religious institutions the normal laws do not apply.

Without seeing them I know already what the Minutes of the next meeting will be. At most there will be two lines announcing the departure - not the dismissal, not the resignation, not the expulsion - of the rabbi. And then the meeting will continue to discuss the leaking window frames in the religion school classrooms and the matters of reports from the Security Committee. And the meeting after that will formally accept the Minutes and the Chairman, the Bastard, will sign them as "a true and lasting record" of the previous meeting. They will become the historical record.

The Germans have, as so often, a word for this. The "*Schreibtischtäter*". The person who, sitting at their writing desk, performs the evil deeds or enables others to perform the evil deeds. In his hand is nothing more violent or dangerous than a pen or a typewriter or a keyboard, but in his mind is the same dark cloud that enables Evil to flourish and Lies to be spread. I am sure Stanley wouldn't have a clue what I was talking about, were I to take him to task on this. He is, after all, just taking the Minutes and writing down what the Chairman tells him to put in the notes.

The next day I called the rabbinic association but got, as expected, some moral support but only minimal help and - to cut it short - a little while later I was indeed looking for another flock to shepherd - although one sometimes wonders why one bothers with the metaphor, when half of them are in fact wolves in sheep's clothing, the enemy is already inside the fold. Still, the bills had to get paid. On dark nights I fantasised this bastard becoming a rabbi himself and experiencing the same thing.

It was a bastard thing to do. But the Bastard knew he could get away with it. And he did. One learns something new in every phase of life. "Keep Away from Bastards" would be good advice, but they rarely teach a class on this at the Seminaries. Maybe it is time to start.

****

HOWLS

FRIEDHOF HEERSTRASSE

A grey morning.
Humid.
Threatening.
Car park full, knots of people, all in black. Most smoking.

The mother sits on a bench and howls. The chapel is filling.
Chairs filling. She sits and howls.

Someone gets her a chair. A folding chair. She sits and howls.
The cantor sings. I read. I speak. She howls.

Now we have moved to the grave. She places some sand in the grave. She sits on the folding chair. Massive bosoms heave. Once her son clung to those breasts. Now they are as empty as her heart. And she howls.
And sits.
And watches as the others take turns, slowly, gravely, hesitantly,
At filling her son's grave.
Her only son's grave.

A group hovers round her. A woman comforts her. A sister?
Maybe. I have not been introduced.
A man clutches a bag with several packets of pills.
Tranquilisers? He looks embarrassed.
A girl is holding a plastic bottle of water. She gives some to the mother. The mother tries to drink. The mother howls.

The diggers heave sand into the hole. The mourners truly mourn. Not an eye is dry. Several young women. Not family. Attractive. Close friends? Very close friends? Very very close friends? They too howl and sob.

"*Maspik*". Enough. The sand has covered the coffin. Time for *Kaddish*. A man wishes to say it with me. But cannot. Needs guidance. Repeat after me..... *Yitgadal..... Yitgadal; Yitkadash..... Yitkadash.*
Slow and painful.

We shake hands. We mutter something. A brief hug? It is hard to know what to do.
We shake hands. And more hands. And walk away. Slowly. Slowly. Following the mother, borne between two women in black. They sob. She howls.

Back at the gate. Wash hands. Get bag. Escape. The mother howls.

Inside, I howl too.

****

HONOUR YOUR FATHER

After a few decades in this field of endeavour there are few things that shock you anymore. Mild surprise is still quite normal, for one never stops learning and human nature is an infinity of new possibilities, many of which would be incomprehensible if one were simply an academic behavioural scientist gathering data in a research project rather than a counsellor and pastoral worker working as best one can with those involved. Depression and frustration is still frequent, and occasionally rage at the stupidity of it all and even at the repetitiveness of some of the foolishness and the mistakes. It is not that Jews are better or worse than anyone else - somebody once described Jews as "like everybody else, only more so!" If one speaks to community leaders of other faiths, if one really speaks with them - it takes time to build up such trust, but this is where what is naively called "Interfaith Work" really works - one hears similar if different examples of human behaviour and misbehaviour. From time to time however something comes along, a wide ball, a curve ball, whatever metaphor one wishes to use, that still takes the breath away.

Once more one stands before the dilemma what to tell, what to hide, what to change, what to fudge and to leave vague. "Only the facts have been changed to protect those responsible". Let me try to explain it in this way:

Mr. and Mrs. Schwarz had married young and had only one child, a son, born (as one could work out later when one had access to all the forms) only five and a half months after the wedding. Nothing strange about that, as such, nothing out of the normal throughout human history. The son - we shall call him Ronald - grew and flourished and at the time I came to the congregation he had himself become married to, let us call her Antonia. Ronald had become a dentist with a practice in a small town about half an hour's drive to the East and by all accounts he was doing all right. Antonia, a familiar story, had been one of his Dental Assistants and had converted to Judaism through one of my predecessors before the wedding. It often happens that people are thrown together by their work, spending many hours together in an office or a practice or a staff room or whatever and if both are young and single the chances are pretty good that a relationship might flourish and deepen and, if all goes well, to mutual advantage rather than one taking advantage of (usually his) position over the other. I can think of at least three or four similar cases in the community. If you think about it, this is so much better than meeting someone by chance at a disco or a sports fixture or party because you get to learn a lot about their character, their background, their knowledge, their discipline, their ability to earn a living, their general hygiene and punctuality and a whole host of other characteristics before one even makes a tentative mild flirtatious remark, before one first asks them for a more private and possibly intimate conversation. She had curly brown hair and a charming smile with full lips and - of course - perfect teeth, a trademark of all those working in the field.

At the time Mrs. Schwarz died, fairly suddenly of a brain tumour or something like that, it was all diagnosed and over within weeks, a major shock, she had been a dynamic member of the Ladies Guild and one of those people with a cheery disposition that you need so badly in any community, Ronald and Antonia's little girl was about four and at Kindergarten and Antonia was working again but part-time and at a different practice, closer to home, which made sense in terms of the daily routine, who brings, who collects, who is available if a child gets ill and so forth. Mr. Schwarz took things very badly and turned rather depressive, which is also not a surprise, and to make it short after about three months it was decided by Ronald, with Antonia's agreement, that he should move in with them, at least for a while. They had a spare room in their semi-detached and although it was the sort of typical house of any young family with toys and clothes and things lying around the atmosphere was also one of Life, with his son, his daughter-in-law a young mother, and in the late afternoons a small child. Maybe if he pulled himself round he could do the afternoon run and pick little Carlotta up from Kindergarten, that would give him something to do, something to focus on during the day...... keep him from brooding on following his wife, and also mean less stress for Antonia because as we all know sometimes a brief dental appointment can take much longer and become more complex and the Assistant cannot always leave halfway through with the excuse "I must collect my child". One can easily see the sort of totally logical and sensible reasons behind such a move. Without going into too much timetable detail a routine developed whereby Ronald took Carlotta to the Kindergarten in the mornings, then drove on to open his practice and spend his day poring over opened mouths going "Ngaaah", while Antonia and - I shall still call him Mr. Schwarz - had time free for a slower breakfast once all the fuss of getting a kid ready and packed off was over, once the bathroom was free, once all was quieter, and so forth. Mr. Schwarz had a Bereavement Clinic to go to twice a week and medication to take, anti-depressants, a bit daft in some respect for one who is still going through mourning, but he needed brightening up a bit when the black moods hit so that he could look forward again. Occasionally, I know, he took a bus and went by himself to the cemetery - I actually bumped into him there once while officiating at another funeral a couple of months later. Ronald and his father were only about eighteen years apart in age and Antonia was about the same as Ronald, I think she was maybe a year younger.

How can I describe the next bit? Sometimes you can kick yourself for being so stupid, so blind, so naive, so gullible, so trusting, whatever. Hindsight may be good, but it comes at the expense of not having looked forward beforehand. One can make thousands of excuses and make hundreds of attempts to understand, but sometimes one just stands there, perhaps the telephone at the ear, perhaps the partner in conversation sitting opposite, and one's mouth drops open and one wonders "Bloody hell, now what?"

Antonia 'fell pregnant' as they say here and all seemed to be going well for some months. It was Ronald who called me and asked for a meeting, urgently, and I made a slot the next afternoon. He had a lot to say. Much of it very, very angry. Angry at Antonia, angry at his father, pretty angry at God and most of all angry at himself. Waves of hurt and anger and bewilderment and pained incomprehension waved over me as we sat and - well, mainly I listened. There was indeed a lot to be angry about. His father, and his wife...... alone at home, he away earning the money for the mortgage, the little girl away till the afternoon.... had started an affair. How it had started he could not quite say. As I have mentioned, the age gap was not that enormous, she was an attractive young woman and he was what one might call early middle age, he had been quite an active sportsman until his wife's sudden illness and all that followed it. At some point he must have reached out to her and she must have allowed it, he must have touched her and she must have accepted it, he must have moved his hands further and she had encouraged it.... Until it had gone further, indeed all the way. Since it was all "in house" as it were, nobody outside needed to see the two of them together or have any cause for gossip. At least, not until now.

I confess, I was stunned. You don't learn this sort of stuff at a Seminary, you pick up a lot of experience and hopefully some practical skills along the way but sometimes the gap between what you know and what is happening is simply bigger and deeper and darker than anything you have encountered before. The situation now was that Ronald was simply not sure whether the new baby on the way was his child or his half-sibling. Mr. Schwarz had moved back quickly to his own home - but Antonia went to visit him there, as a good dutiful daughter-in-law might do, bringing succour to her widowed father-in-law, even while she was carrying - again, such a plausible cover story that the neighbours would have little cause to suspect anything more sinister, unless they noticed when the upstairs curtains were closed. Ronald did not know what to do. he wanted to avoid a scandal. He wanted to keep Carlotta. But his marriage was over and his relationship to his father was over and his mother was dead and he felt very, very, very alone with his hurt and his grief and his loss. Could he demand a DNA test? What would this prove, if so much of his own and his father's DNA were so close? How could he say the prayers that start "Our Father, our King"? How could he continue to honour his father?

The irony is that, with the exception of the 'Levirate marriage' issue for brothers who were also brothers-in-law, such relationships were prohibited in the *Torah* precisely because they were feasible and, who knows, maybe even common in patriarchal polygamous societies - maybe your son died or was killed in battle, leaving an attractive widow as your daughter-in-law.... What this means is that in those lists of prohibitions in Leviticus 18 (this one is verse 15) that people like to skim over squeamishly there is actually some good advice and some valid warnings that we neglect at our peril.

Things happened. Mostly in an incredibly sensible and discreet manner. "For the sake of the child". Things were certainly said. Much of what followed had - thank goodness - nothing to do directly with me. Mr. and Mrs. Ronald Schwarz were divorced by mutual consent - unusual, of course, when the wife was by now quite heavily pregnant. I helped them, separately, fill in some forms for the '*Get*', the religious divorce which was performed by the *Beit Din* at a distance without anyone having to be present. A little later, but very privately, Mr. Schwarz and Mrs. Antonia Schwarz were married. Only a civil ceremony, no religious one. Mr. Ronald Schwarz did not attend his father's nuptials. There is now a little boy, whose birth certificate (I presume) shows that his father's surname was Schwarz but I have never asked what they did with the forename, though I think they made an agreement that Ronald would allow his name to be used but would not take any further concern or responsibility for the child. The boy is called Carl because the late Mrs. Schwarz had been Carol. Ronald left town a short while afterwards, he comes back now and then to see Carlotta and I believe he has got engaged - to another Dental Assistant. Carl and Carlotta – yes, there is room for a rare smile there – are brought up as siblings with an absent father and Antonia did not even have to change her name. Mr. Schwarz has retained membership of the congregation since he wishes to be buried next to his former wife in due course, but we don't see much of the family, they keep discreetly away for now. The story that is told is that Ronald left Antonia and then these two found each other. That sounds much better and I am one of the few (there are some solicitors too, of course) who knows more of the background. Not the whole story, but a bit more than was put out for public consumption. For Carl's sake, if not for God's. In due course - only a few years away now - there will be a *Bat-Mitzvah* for Carlotta and then things might start to get, shall we say, 'interesting'.

I have only ever, until now, told one person a part of the story – a Catholic priest at a short residential conference on pastoral training, where we were paired off for an afternoon session to discuss between us some of the 'challenging challenges' we had faced. I found it wonderful to let something out, it must be what Confession is like. You can sit on just so many secrets for so long and then it all gets too much, it clogs up the brain. Anyway, he had, to my amazement, smiled. Why? I asked. He smiled again, cleared his throat and said "Father, Son and Holy Spirit. You know, we Catholics have to believe that Joseph was also a child of God and yet God made Mary give birth." I hadn't thought of it that way and we found ourselves laughing loudly and disturbing the two other pairs of clergy talking in different corners of the dark hall.

"Eeeh, you've got to laugh, eh?" as the comedian said.

****

THE GERMANS ARE NOW ALL JEWS !

1. A SECRET MEETING

It was a secret place. Not a synagogue, of course; that would have been too..... too obvious, maybe. Perhaps also too dangerous. Who knows? Whatever the reason, 'WE' had found a place, a German place, indeed a very significant and symbolic place – yes, very symbolic. This was important so that everything would work properly.

Who are 'We'? A couple of colleagues and I – all Rabbis. The names of course are strictly secret, because it is like this with all Jewish conspiracies – everything has to stay secret. A few months ago we met at a secret place and together we solemnly formed ourselves into a *Beit Din*, a rabbinic court of justice, and we declared all Germans to be henceforth Jews.

May one do this? Simply to declare people Jewish, without their knowledge, or consent, maybe even against their wishes? Yes, of course one can! In Germany there is a long tradition of such measures. For example, in the 1930's and 1940's the then-Government declared people to be Jewish who had no idea at all that they were so or who did not even wish to be so. Many of them had been baptised, some had even become vicars or nuns! Many simply had somewhere, hidden in their family trees, a Jewish grandfather or some other relative. The end results of this forcible labelling of these people as Jews are unfortunately well known.

Or another example: In the 1990's many immigrants came to Germany from the former Soviet Union as so-called 'Contingent Refugees', on the understanding that they were Jewish – whether they were really believing that or not. Here in Germany they were all registered as Jews, even though a half of them or more were not really welcomed into the Jewish communities, because they only had a Jewish father. Interestingly, when it came to Money then All these people were welcome in the communities – not as worshippers but simply as members in the statistics. They did not have to appear in the synagogues. It was simply enough that they had been registered in the Population Registries as 'Jewish', because then many Jewish communities could get additional funding from official sources – and indeed they still do so – because this funding is calculated simply on a *per capita* basis and so it was only important that those concerned had a head; What was in or on this head was not so important. Probably many communities would in these circumstances have been very happy to have more members with Two heads, although the congregational leadership is not a good example of this principle – most communities only have ONE Head and he alone decides everything.

...

2. A LONG TRADITION

To this theme one can add that many of the Germans who have an interest in Judaism and who express a desire to convert also have Jewish roots somewhere (or at least maintain that they do so). Many of them speak proudly of their 'Jewish ancestry' or even describe themselves also as "we victims". And of course, many Germans – especially those on the right-hand side of the political spectrum – also yearn for a national role as Victims. It would only be logical to combine these two Victimhood roles somehow.

And then, in schools and in school playgrounds, all over Germany, schoolkids curse and insult each other as 'Jews' only because they are for some reason not fully part of the 'cool' group.

Of course, this sort of thing did not only happen in Germany. The Inquisition, that began in Spain, sought out people in many lands to label them as Jews in order to condemn them, torture them, murder them – they became literally fire offerings for their God – perhaps only because they had put on a clean shirt on a Saturday, or had not laid a fire at home that day. That was considered evidence enough for the Guardians of the True Faith – these were clearly 'Unbelievers', they were 'secret Jews'. Europe is still full of '*Marranos*' – this word is actually an insult but is usually used to mean people with Jewish ancestry who are not 'Christian enough' to be 'proper' Christians. Whatever that is meant to mean.

To which one might add: From the 12th Century onwards, if not already earlier, many Jews were forcibly baptized – in London there were at this time already two '*Domus Conversos*' – hostels for those who had converted to Christianity – which must mean that there can hardly be a single person in Europe who, if one could only go far enough back to check, does not somehow have some Jewish ancestor......

And in addition, for many Islamic fundamentalists all Americans are '*Yahud*'. For the old Soviet regime all the children of a Jewish father were also classed as '*Evrei*'. So we see that it is nothing new in declaring whole swathes of the population as 'Jews'.

...

3. EVERYONE IN GERMANY IS NOW DECLARED TO BE JEWISH

If so – then why should Jews not also do this? If all people were Jewish, then we Jews could at long last finally control the world - and no-one would have any problem with this....

One could perhaps raise the question: What about Circumcision?' But here too we have precedents to fall back upon. It is naturally important that, according to the *Halachah* - the Jewish legal system – all men (but ONLY the men) should be circumcised. But as we know, many of the Jewish immigrants from Eastern Europe and the FSU were not circumcised – and yet, nevertheless they counted for the statistics as Jews. In Germany we already have hundreds of thousands of men who are indeed circumcised but who do not (yet) count as Jews. These men would have no problems and would not have to do anything else.

Therefore we rabbis debated with each other and eventually decided unanimously, using a secret formula from the deepest section of the Kabbalah, the mystical tradition, which goes all the way back to the Creation of the World and maybe even further back beyond that, to the Book that God Himself used in order to create the Universe, we decided to declare every man, woman and child in Germany to be Jewish.

As regards the Deceased, we decided not to worry ourselves any further with them – as far as we are concerned, they are already in the hand of God and, although the Mormons are keen to sign up all those who have died to be their members, we didn't want any more posthumous Jews. We already have far more dead Jews than we would want. So: From Sundown on the 15th. Day of the Jewish month of Adar in the Jewish year 5776 (corresponding to the holy Jewish festival of 'Purim') this decision was made final, legally binding and irreversible.

...

4. ONE PROBLEM FEWER

Why did we do this? Because there are so many advantages to this course of action, so many advantages for all those affected, if they can only accept and start to learn what it means for them now to be Jewish. For instance: With one stroke we have resolved the entire problem of Antisemitism! If all Germans are now Jews, then - whether they want to be or not is immaterial, for after all, how many of us really want to be taxpayers? - then all arguments and conflicts are now only *internal Jewish Conflicts*. We are "amongst ourselves". And that means, all fights should from now on be carried out according to Jewish rules. Former bitter Anti-Semites can now be classed simply as 'Self-Hating Jews'. And everyone who wishes to immigrate here will have to understand: At the moment when they cross the German border, with or without valid papers, they will also automatically become Jewish! This could help to reduce appreciably many of the tensions and fears here. Those who really do not want to become so, should simply stay away, whilst those who do come here will be automatically integrated!

We Rabbis understand that behind many of the fears within German society is the fear of so-called 'Islamicization' – excessive Moslem influence. (Hardly anyone worries any more about undue 'Jewish influence', as they did in the past century – only the few really mad fanatics.) If all the refugees in recent years had been Christians, even if from different forms of Christianity – such as Maronites, Copts, Orthodox, from Iraq and North Africa and the Near East – then for the people running 'Pegida' and the 'Alternative for Germany' populist political movements this would have been one problem fewer to worry about or to capitalise upon. Then the larger Churches would at last have found cause to speak up and speak openly. And privately, when many Politicians speak about 'Integration', what they really mean is that all the new arrivals should become Christians. (Just think about the reservations concerning the entry of Turkey as a Moslem country into 'Christian Europe'.) There are even some fundamentalist Christian groups who are attempting missionary work in refugee hostels. This can lead to potential conflicts. There are even conflicts – which spill over in overcrowded hostels and refugee camps – between refugees from one country and another, or between Moslems and Christians, or between different denominations of Moslems – Sunni and Shiites, or between both these groups combined and Alawites or Achmediyyas. If, however, <u>all</u> of them were Jewish, then they would not need to fight like this any more!

…

5. ARGUING IS NORMAL

Grumbling – why yes, of course! Screaming and shouting? Absolutely! "*Bediyuk*!" Arguments about congregational elections and parties, about autocratic Presidents and incompetent Executive Boards? Why, ALL Jewish communities occupy themselves almost non-stop and exclusively with such themes. So much energy and time is used for such conflicts, that there is none left for the other problems in the world. But nevertheless: We would remain "amongst ourselves", "*unter uns*'. We are no longer Jihadisten but Jehudisten.

We Rabbis have now declared Judaism to be the new State Religion. Judaism is indeed not pacifist, but there are certain specific and fundamental rules. One of these is that one can have several different opinions and one can even present several different opinions, and your discussion partner can do precisely the same - and that is totally in order. Naturally, those who have a different opinion to yours are absolute fools and idiots - but they are nevertheless still your fellow Jews. Only very, very rarely do such conflicts spill over into violence. The very rare exceptions – think for example of the murder of Yitzhak Rabin – are shocking and essentially confirm that rule. One could at this point state that even though many people consider Judaism to be a religion of Rules and Laws, which is indeed the case, that there are at the same time more Exceptions than Rules.

Arguments are normal. One finds this in our religious texts. Abraham and Moses argue with God; The Prophets argue with the corrupt Priests; The Rabbis argue also with the priests but mainly with each other. In a Rabbinic Bible edition – a '*Mikra'ot Gedolot*' - one finds numerous commentaries from various different rabbis, who all have different opinions and interpretations, but all these are printed on the same page, they all have the right to be read and the Reader has the opportunity to read all the different argumentations and to compare the responses and they may then make up their own opinion based on these.

In the sole Jewish State of Israel the Ultra-Orthodox ('*Haredim*') and the secular Jews ('*Chilonim*') fight with each other in order to win more seats in the Knesset. *Sephardim* and *Ashkenazim* fight with each other about almost everything – but none of them actually wants their own state or their own Enclave, like the Basques or the Kurds or the Flemings or other Nationalist groups do. No, they all share the desire to remain in the same State of Israel, so that they may continue arguing with their fellow citizens. In Israel there are countless churches and mosques, there is a Baha'i Temple and a Mormon University; there is Gay Pride in Tel Aviv, there is almost everything – ironically it is really only the Liberal Jews and the Feminists who have to keep fighting for their rights – just like here!

...

6. ONLY BOOKS AND NEWSPAPER ARTICLES AS WEAPONS

We have never had and we have no Burnings at the Stake or *Autos da Fé*; We have not committed any massacres against each other. We do not plant bombs at wedding parties; As Weapons we employ only books and newspaper articles and sermons. We do have almost endless conflicts about minor matters - but then, is not every issue that so concerns mankind only a minor one, when compared to the entire universe, to the expanse of Eternity? It may be that one person thinks 'so' and another person thinks 'so' and a third stands somewhere between the other two – but so what? Is this really a good enough or important enough reason to take a human life, to destroy a family? With all the consequent damage to the families involved and the whole of society? "No," says Judaism; "No, we don't want that, we do not allow that. We want no human beings to become victims in the name of God."

And this is precisely the point: In spite of all the stupid, ridiculous, racist, obscene, false, lying, hate-filled prejudices against Jews, the vile accusations that we drink blood or murder children or do even worse things – actually we are BETTER than the others. Much better. We do not commit murders. And even though many Jews are relatively ignorant of their religion – and we are about to acquire a further 82 Million new ignorant Jews in Germany, who will all have to start learning the rules of their new faith – it is only a question of time before all these new Jews learn how they should behave. For a start, we should no longer speak or write of "The Germans and the Jews"! Instead, we should simply refer to "We Jews." Then people will start to learn, for example, what it feels like to be Jewish; even when, or even though one is no longer in the minority but indeed a part of the majority within our German society.

...

7. A SPECIAL MIXTURE OF HOPE, CYNICISM AND PRAGMATISM

Of course all this will cost something, but Jews willingly spend money for Education. In the Talmud already it is stated that one should show respect to teachers and pay them appropriately. Also, payment of teachers is seen as a duty in Jewish tradition and in Jewish communities. This means that it should be possible in due course to find enough teachers and appoint them in order to bring some elements of civilisation to all these New Jews. One can, if necessary, save money in other departments. We will not, after all, require so many expensive Airport projects – we can get into the heavens even without them! If one only learns, how......

Perhaps it is only in this way that we can yet save the World. Judaism is a special and unique mixture of endless Hope, Cynicism and Pragmatism. Only in this way has it managed to survive so much – so many historic catastrophes, so many expulsions, so many Empires, and other intolerant Religions.... Judaism says, There is a God, but this God is ONE; Judaism says that this God has created EVERYONE, therefore we are all a part of Creation and in this respect we are all the same.

This does not mean that all are equally intelligent, and also not that all should be equally rich, but nevertheless all do have an equal right to live and to earn something and to rest and to be respected and acknowledged as human beings.

If God has made many people as Non-Jews, then this is no problem for we Jews – we are tolerant; we have had until now no theological problem with this – only now and again a political problem or even a problem of Survival. We have no problem when Christians are Christians or Moslems are Moslems or Hindus Hindus or Buddhists Buddhists – or even when Atheists are Atheists. That is their God-given right, they can be so if they wish and then they can later, before the Heavenly Throne of the Highest of Judges, explain themselves. This is no problem for US.

...

8. WE DO NOT INDULGE IN MASS MISSIONISING

For thousands of years we have not carried out widespread Mission amongst the Non-Jews. In the Book of Esther or in one of the Books of the Maccabees one can find brief references to conversions, and in the Book of Ruth a widow from Moab decides for herself to join the people of her deceased husband – but any mass missionising is totally alien to us. In the Biblical times it could be that the head of a tribe decided who could become a member and who not. Normally, say we rabbis, one knows who the Mother of a child is and so if the mother is Jewish then her children are also classed as part of the Jewish community. Whoever cannot prove this, may choose to convert, but then they must also demonstrate (to a *Beit Din*) that they take this step seriously and that they will know what it means to be able to live as a Jew and to pray as one. But there should not be any pressure upon them. And those who decide not to do this are nevertheless still Human Beings and they may have their own individual connection and relationship to the same God. And the right to continue living. There is Freedom of Thought.

Only when missionising has been used against us, when we were compelled to convert or when we were publicly humiliated in so-called 'Disputations', only when people attempt to influence us or other Jews by 'love-bombing' to encourage us to leave Judaism – only then does our Tolerance reach its limits.

...

9. THE PARTNERSHIP BETWEEN MANKIND AND GOD

In our Theology (actually we have never really developed a proper systematic one) Mankind learns very early to distinguish between Good and Evil. This means that Mankind has no excuses any more. Mankind can no longer give God the blame for everything or say, "Well, we were born already laden with Guilt, we came into the world from our mother's womb already heavily laden with Sinfulness." A person may not say that they are helpless, powerless, that Fate will decide everything, that one just has to wait fatalistically for whatever has already been decided for you to happen. No, in Judaism the human being has Rights but also Responsibilities, Duties, and even if some of these duties – the so-called '*Taryag Mitzvot*', that is to say the 613 Commands and Prohibitions which one can interpret out of the first five Books of the Bible, plus the calls of the Prophets and in addition those commands added in the rabbinical literature – even if some of these are no longer relevant, applying as they do only to certain ritual practices or only for the Priests or the Kings or the agriculture in a single specific land – nevertheless the basic fundamental principles are pretty clear.

A Human Being, as a Creature of God, stands also in a Partnership with God. They are a Junior Partner, admittedly, but nevertheless a Partner with all the rights and duties which this implies. It is only together with God that we can improve our world – not through God alone, who needs us, and not, in that we leave everything to God or hand over everything to God – no, we must also take an active part in this task. Social Justice does not just happen by itself, as a natural law. "*Letaken Olam beMalchut Shaddai*" – means to make the World better and to repair it – as a part of God's Kingdom.

....

10. TABLE MANNERS

In Judaism there are rules as to how we are to relate to God and to our other fellow human beings. To God? Well, yes, it is true that the old methods are now out of date and no longer relevant – there has been and there continues to be progress in living religions. Although some peoples believed that they should bring human sacrifices, the Torah has told us: "No – instead, only animal sacrifices and foodstuffs." We brought to the altar bullocks, rams, lambs, goats, doves, fruit, grain, flour, olive oil and wine – ingredients for a joint meal, which could be divided between the humans down below and God up above. If we ourselves couldn't eat it, then obviously we wouldn't sacrifice it, for then we could not take part in the meal! We are not cannibals: Therefore it was all quite clear and understandable for those times.

Later this method was lost for us – there was no Temple anymore, no Priests, no Altar, no Sacrifices – and the Rabbis created a wonderful new alternative system whereby we eat down here, just like normal people, but invite God down to join us. Now we are the hosts and we can thank God for the gifts that God brings. This system too is relatively simple and comprehensible – a few *Berachot* – Blessings – to be said before or after the meal – and everyone is satisfied!

But there is no real conflict over the question of Who may be allowed to serve the meal or whether what is served is somehow transformed and transubstantiated, it is a meal but not a Last Supper. Yes, of course we argue with each other over the question of who has the authority to declare something *kasher*, which Rabbi with which authority. There are Jews who avoid eating in this or that synagogue or in an allegedly '*kosher*' restaurant. As has already been mentioned, we have many, many internal Jewish conflicts, indeed a culture of argumentation – but we do not commit murder as a consequence. THAT is the difference.

....

11. WHAT COULD BE SIMPLER?

And the duties we have towards other people are also clear. In Leviticus 19:18 (Jesus of Nazareth quoted this concept in Mark 12:31) the basic principle can be found: "I am who I am; I know what I like, and I know what I do not like, what hurts me or upsets me or causes me worry. I can therefore assume that You are in this respect just like Me. You also do not like Fear, Pain, Hunger, Cold, Desperation, Homelessness, Loneliness, Sickness, Worries, Poverty – therefore I should do my best in order that You can avoid these in Your life, or at least not make them any worse.... Just so. I can indeed not manage to do EVERYTHING in order to make things better, but I can at least do Something, and at the very least I should do my best not to make things any worse." What could be simpler?

And that applies to ALL people, even for those who serve us and work for us, or for those who come from other countries, even for those who are poor or widowed or handicapped, and who look different. Even for those taken as prisoners of war – men or women – there are Rules They have lost, they are indeed prisoners, but nevertheless they have specific rights.

The details for these Rules – there are thousands of them – fill many books and there are constantly new problems which need new interpretations from our learned experts: For example, How can one define 'healing' when the invalid is lying in a coma or is clearly past all methods to cure a condition? How can one help somebody who rejects all help and is actually prepared to commit suicide? How can one use modern technologies and methods to help and to build instead of destroying? There is no place for Dogmas, for the World is constantly changing, and in consequence one needs this pragmatism, this flexibility – one must always be in a position to make a new beginning, and that is not always easy. But the basic ideas are really simple. "My life is My life, not Yours, and it is certainly not your plaything; My property is My property; I am allowed to possess it – You may have Yours, but then I should not steal what is Yours and not lust after it, fantasise about owning it or envy You for it. My marriage is My marriage and Your marriage is Your marriage, and if we have each decided to get married, to become someone's spouse, then we have made a vow and we also have the right to assume that others respect this. You and I – we are similar in so many ways! I should treat you in the way that I myself would wish to be treated, and I expect from You, that You will treat me in the same way and following the same principles.... for the same God stands over both of us."

And this principle extends further – even into the animal kingdom. The beasts of burdens also have rights – the right for rest and to be treated fairly, to be fed punctually (even on rest days and festivals). Yes, it is true that they are our servants, but they are also entitled to enjoy a day of rest; Yes, it is true we are allowed to kill them and eat them - But they should not be slaughtered in a brutal and painful manner, they should not be forced to watch when their own young are being slaughtered. The mother bird and the egg should not be taken at the same time.... the ox and the ass should not be forced to pull together..... It is not as though we are forbidden to kill mosquitoes or dangerous snakes, it is not as though we are compelled to do without consuming meat altogether – that would go too far for us; But a certain respect for other parts of God's Creation – that belongs to Judaism, and that is important for us. We should not be wasteful with things. We have only this one World, at least in this dimension – "*Olam HaZeh*."

...

12. OH YES, THE SOUL.....

The Beyond, whatever comes next, that is a different world, an "*Olam Habah*". But we have very little information about this and principally just hopes, It should however be open to ALL. WE are not those who decide who may purchase an entry ticket – or exactly when other people should be despatched there, often before they feel ready to go.

Oh yes, the Soul. All people have one, who have been born. (Incidentally, those who have not yet been born do not yet have one – this is a difference between a Foetus and a Person.) But the Soul – this power, this energy, this individuality, personality, feelings, the 'Software' within the 'Hardware' of the Body – this soul has an existence of its own, its own purpose, independent from the Body – and it can, it should at some point later make a report, or make a confession....

...

So, my new Brothers and Sisters in the Jewish Faith: "*B'ruchim HaBa'im*" – Welcome into the Jewish People! There is a lot to learn. From now on we can have arguments with each other, insult each other, criticise each other, just like real Brothers and Sisters. Yet nevertheless we must continue to live together and share the same destiny and accept this fact. And perhaps in this way we will make the World – Our World – God's World – a little better. Should other countries then start to ask, "What is it, this Specialness? Why is it that things are suddenly going so much better in Germany?" Then .....

But no! No! *Ssssshh*! This should remain OUR secret. Just between Us, yes?

****

Glossary

A brief Glossary cannot be and should not aim to be a full explanation of complex religious terms and concepts; There are other books for this. But a brief clarification may at least help the normal reader. However people use a mixture of Hebrew, Yiddish and Aramaic terms and also different dialects and accents, which makes transcription complex. Some Hebrew letters have no direct English equivalents and approximations are employed.

Aleynu : One of the closing prayers of a standard synagogue service. "It is our duty to praise God..."

Amidah : The core prayers of the service, said standing. Also called 'The Eighteen Benedictions'.

Ark, or *Aron Kodesh* : The cupboard or niche for holding the *Torah* Scroll(s).

Aufruf : From German/Yiddish: Used for a call to the *Torah* reading (also known as *Aliya*) but especially to the ceremony of calling a bridegroom to the *Torah* on the *Shabbat* before his wedding.

Bar-Mitzvah : coming-of-age ceremony. (For girls, later: *Bat-Mitzvah*). Lit. 'Son of the Commandment', marked usually by being called up to read from the *Torah* during a public service. For boys, usually, at 13, for girls at 12 and a half.

Beracha, pl. *Berachot* : A blessing, also a blessing formula to be recited at specific occasions.

Brit : lit. Also *Bris*. Covenant. Used also to mean a *Brit Milah*, a circumcision whereby by removal of a small piece of skin a young male is brought into the covenant.
Chag (or *Hag*) : A festival or holy day. The greeting is '*Chag same'ach*!' - 'Have a happy Festival'.

Chasan : Cantor, sings the service in some synagogues.

Chevra Kadisha: 'Holy Brotherhood' (Aramaic); the voluntary associations of those who will wash the dead and prepare them for burial and comfort the mourners.

Chumash : A volume containing the five Books of Moses and the *Haftarah* readings, for use in the weekly synagogue ritual of readings.

Chuppah : Wedding canopy, refers also to the wedding ceremony.

Get : A Jewish religious divorce document, freeing both parties to remarry.

Haftarah : A reading from the books of the prophets, following the Torah reading, in the synagogue on certain occasions (Sabbaths and Festivals)

Havdalah : A brief ceremony on Saturday evening that formally ends the Sabbath.

Kabbalah : A general term for a range of mystic teachings.

Kaddish : An Aramaic passage read at the end of the service and also at funerals and memorials, praising God and asking for peace.

Ketubah : A wedding contract document.

Kiddush : The act of sanctifying wine and bread, also used for a buffet following a service.

Kippah : Ritual Headcovering, usually round and fairly flat. Also called *Yarmulke.*

Kol Nidrei : The opening Evening Service of the *Yom Kippur.*

Levayah : A funeral.

Machzor : The prayer book containing specific passages and prayers used for Festival as opposed to Daily or Sabbath services.

Mazal Tov! : An expression either wishing good luck or congratulations.

Meyt : A dead person, corpse.

Mi Shebeyrach : A blessing, "May the One who blessed so-and-so, also bless this person..."

Mitzvah : An action, usually refers to a good deed which one is commanded to do.

Pesach : The springtime Passover festival, commemorating the Exodus from Egypt and marked by several rituals and prohibitions on what may be eaten.

Purim : A festival in springtime, based on the Book or Scroll of Esther, celebrating deliverance from a planned genocide in ancient times; marked with festivities, alcohol, food, costumes, a carnival atmosphere.

Rabbi : A teacher, preacher and religious judge. (Yiddish: *Rebbe*).

Rosh Hashanah : The Jewish New Year festival, in the autumn.

Rov: A Yiddish term (from Hebrew Rav) - for a Rabbi.

Sefer Torah : The parchment scroll on which the five Books of Moses are written by hand, and placed on two wooden rollers. At certain services one reads one or more sections from this, rather than from a printed book.

Shabbat / Shabbos : The seventh day in the week, a day (theoretically!) of rest, meditation, religious services. Corresponds to Friday evening till Saturday evening.

Shema : A section from Deuteronomy, declaring the Unity of God and the duty to speak of this at all times. An important declaration and a part of most synagogue services.

Shivah : lit. 'Seven', the seven days of intense mourning following a death; also used for the services held in the home of the deceased or of the mourners.

Shul : Yiddish, reflecting that a synagogue was also a school – but now used to mean a synagogue.

Siddur : Prayer book used for Daily and Sabbath services. (see '*Machzor*').

Sidra : The section of the *Torah* selected for the weekly reading.

Tachrichim : Grave clothes.

Tallit / Tallis / pl. *Tallitot* or *Talleisim*: Prayer shawl, with tassels on the edges and corners.

Talmud : A lengthy collection of rabbinic comments and commentaries regarding biblical texts and their interpretations - as first gathered in the *Mishnah* around the year 200 - and further commented and edited around the year 500.

Torah : The five Books of Moses; also used more generally for 'Learning'.

Yad : lit. 'Hand', a pointer used for reading from the *Sefer Torah,* often shaped like a small hand and finger.

Yahrzeit : The anniversary of a death, usually calculated by the Hebrew calendar, not the secular one.

Yom Kippur : The Day of Atonement; in the autumn, the High Holy Days. A 25-hour fast day.

Zachor (*Yiddish: Sochor*) : Remembrance, a commandment to Remember events of the past.

About the Author

Rabbi Dr. Walter Rothschild

"How people think a Rabbi's Life is"

Photo credit: Joyce Rothschild

"How it often is..."

Photo credit: Margrit Schmidt

Walter Rothschild was born in Bradford, Yorkshire, England in 1954 - son of two teachers; His father Edgar had been sent as a boy from Germany in 1939; his mother Esther had been born in Bradford but her family's roots were in Riga and Vitebsk - so, one could say, it was a typically mixed background. (Some of the maternal family history has been fictionalised and is now published as 'The Kreutzer Chronicles' by his aunt Irene Chavert). The congregation was small and for many years lay readers, even teenagers had to assist in leading services on a rota basis, since there was no full-time rabbi. (He has written a biography of Rabbi Dr. Erich Bienheim, the rabbi of his early childhood.)

After school, half a year working on the railways in Hamburg, three years studying punting, romance and Theology at Cambridge, a year's Teacher Training and a brief, inglorious but educational career teaching Religious Studies in Hemel Hempstead, the 'Call' came (quite literally) and he applied to the Leo Baeck College, London. Following six years of rabbinic studies, including one year in the Netherlands and one in Israel, with student pulpits in Woodford, Bristol and Newcastle, he was ordained as a Rabbi in summer 1984 and took a post in Leeds, where the congregation had originally been founded by European refugees in 1944. The duties however involved working all over the North-East of England, serving also the smaller communities in Bradford (his home synagogue), Hull and - after helping to found it - Sheffield. As the only Reform Rabbi in the whole of Yorkshire one was also called upon to visit universities and prisons in the region. He also wrote 'Jewish By Choice', a Basic Judaism course for conversion classes.

In November 1994 the then-Chairwoman's dramatic over-reaction to a sermon on local communal political issues led to a sudden and unexpected but interesting career change - initially working for the World Union for Progressive Judaism, commuting regularly to Vienna, with additional trips to Brno, Bratislava, Graz, Zagreb, Sarajevo.... Then taking a position in Oranjestad, Aruba - a small community of European, North American and South American exiles with a large number of visiting tourists to serve in addition.

In 1998 an invitation to take a post in the large and formal Jewish Community of Berlin seemed attractive - until it was too late. Experiences here were horrific but when the community's Chairman (who himself wanted to become and then became a rabbi) broke his contract twice, he was freed of further responsibilities. From 2000 he has, whilst staying in Berlin, worked instead part-time as Rabbi in a multitude of small Central-European communities including München, Freiburg, Halle/Saale, Köln, Wien, as 'Landesrabbiner' in five congregations in Schleswig-Holstein, in Hamburg, Warsaw and Gdansk, and has been active in Beit Din activities in Berlin, Beograd, Skopje, Krakow, Bratislava etc.

He has written "The Honey and the Sting" (in German, "Der Honig und der Stachel") - a Basic Course in Judaism for all who are interested, including but not restricted to those who wish to convert; A Polish translation has also been prepared. "99 Questions about Judaism" has appeared in German as "99 Fragen zum Judentum" (GTB) and also in Italian as "99 domande sull 'Ebraismo" (Giraudi) and is also available in English. The parodic "Tales of the Chutzper Rebbe" (first published by Alef Design in California) is an 'Acidic Anthology' for Mitnagdim, the opponents of Chasidism.

In addition, several volumes of "Tales from the Rabbi's Desk" have been published, reflecting some of the stranger experiences in a career in Britain and Europe - This is the volume in this series. "Auf das Leben" (a German version of some of these stories, translated by Miriam Pressler z'l, published by Goldmann) has appeared also in Korean.

In addition, there have been numerous articles, radio talks and of course sermons. An edited autobiography of Bert Dyke, Royal Engineers is in process of publication by Mainline & Maritime, who also published 'British Military Railways of World War 1' (B.O.R.H.T.) for which he wrote the chapters on Egypt, Syria and Palestine. Other projects are in progress, including a biography of his grandfather Landgerichtrat Walter Rothschild, a history of Palestine Railways, one on Lebanese Railways, and also further collections of short stories.

His interest in railway history has led to a PhD from King's College, London on 'Palestine Railways 1945-1948'; the founding, editing and publishing of a quarterly magazine 'Harakevet' on Railways in the Middle East (see: **www.harakevet.com** for details) and many contributions to the 'Bulletin' of the World War 2 Railway Study Group- (Now the Military Railways Study Group).

He has written the texts – song lyrics and 'Aesop's Foibles' - for 'The Minyan Boys', a jazz band of international disrepute in which he performs; A CD 'Minyan Boys Greatest Hits Vol. 2' is available, though 'Songs My Dybbuk Taught Me' has remained under limited distribution. He also performs together with Max Doehlemann cabaret on Jewish and personal themes all over Germany – the 'Leiderabende'. A CD of Schubert Lieder updated to reflect modern travel experiences - 'Die Winterbahnreise' - is in preparation.

He is a father of three children but is not (yet) a grandfather...... and he has written hundreds of 'Naughty Stories for Naughty Children' as well as other series of short stories; Two collections of 'The Bookcase of Sherlock Holmes' have appeared on Amazon and Kindle. He is currently working on 'The Greatest Novel Ever Written'.

Working as a Rabbi in Europe in these decades from the 1980's to the 2020's has often been exhausting, frustrating and depressing - and sometimes even a little bit frightening - but it is also very rewarding and it has never, ever been boring.

Further information about him can be found on:
www.walterrothschild.de
www.rabbiwalterrothschild.de
www.rothschild-comedy.de
www.harakevet.com

Other books by the Author

The Honey and the Sting

A Study Guide for Conversion to Judaism, written with a love for Judaism and with British Humour. (JVFG, London 2016)

Many introductions into Judaism are available, but only few teach about how to become Jewish and how to practice Judaism every day; almost none describes this from a European Progressive Jewish perspective. This book fills this gap. It is based on materials circulated under the title “Jewish by Choice” used in European Jewish congregations for several years, written by a Progressive Jewish rabbi for his students. In the appendix it contains a list of possible questions that the Beit Din may ask and some test-yourself quizzes.

Rabbi Dr. Erich Bienheim

"Rabbi Dr. Erich Bienheim came from a small village in northern Germany, studied in Berlin, served as Rabbi in Darmstadt, then suffered the horrors of Nazi concentration camps and exile and British internment, before coming to serve as rabbi in Bradford for the last thirteen years of his life. Sadly, he left few records and no close family but Rabbi Dr. Walter Rothschild learned his first Hebrew letters from Bienheim - he was only seven when his first rabbi died - and in a way the seeds were sown for a mirror career that has led to him leaving England and serving as Rabbi in Germany. Some rabbis become famous, others do not and Bienheim was one of the latter but he served faithfully and well and deserves to be remembered, at least, as one of those who toiled in the vineyards of the Lord - even if the harvest was often but bitter grapes. This is a personal biography, written from a rabbi's perspective - and who would know better what that means?"

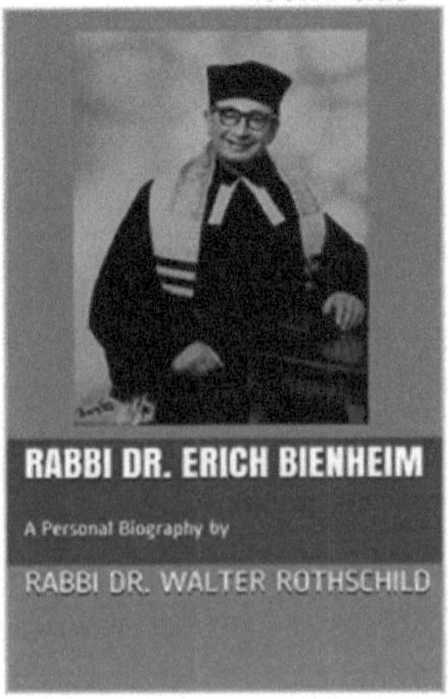

99 Questions About Judaism

Not-Quite-All You ever Wanted to Know about Judaism but were Afraid to Ask..... In just 99 Questions and personal Responses (not Answers) one cannot cover everything but one can make a good start. 99 is an arbitrary limit but one has to start - and end - somewhere. This is an updated and expanded English version of a book which has already been successful in German and Italian, written from decades of rabbinic experience concerning the questions that are most frequently asked at interfaith meetings, schools etc. concerning this mysterious and - for many - intimidating yet fascinating religion. Filled with surprises......

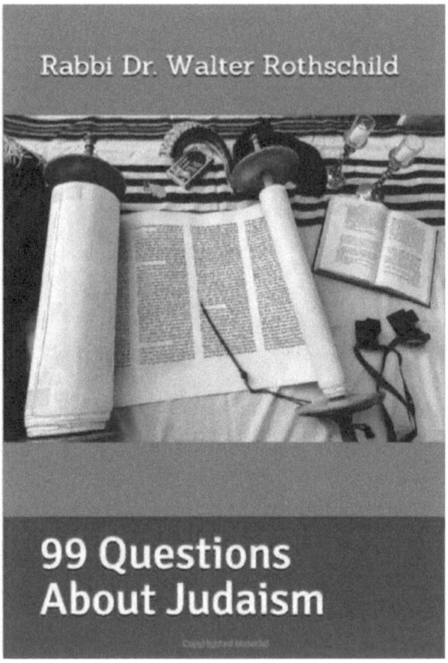

Tales of the Chutzper Rebbe

Lost in the mists, swamps and forests of Eastern Europe, plagued by mosquitoes and Cossacks (though not necessarily in that order) lies the almost-forgotten Shtetl of Chutzp. Here is the seat of one of the lesser-known Hasidic dynasties - The Chutzper Hasidim, that mystic, anti-intellectual, ecstatic sect that placed so much emphasis on a close encounter with Hashem, facilitated when necessary through a haze of schnapps. With a tinge of nostalgia we look back at some of the founders of this Hasidic school, their disciples and others whose lives were touched by their unique view of this world and the next.

Tales from the Rabbi's Desk

Volumes 1, 2 & 3

As a Rabbi I had been taught always to look behind a story, to see what is hiding in the spaces between the letters and between the lines...... to be aware of other dimensions; To be sensitive, like Elijah the prophet, to still, small voices." Rabbi Dr. Walter Rothschild brings us a collection of stories, some fictional and many based on factual experiences, based on several decades of work as a congregational Rabbi in England and in Europe.

These stories give an insight into the rich tapestry of human lives that he and his colleagues have touched.

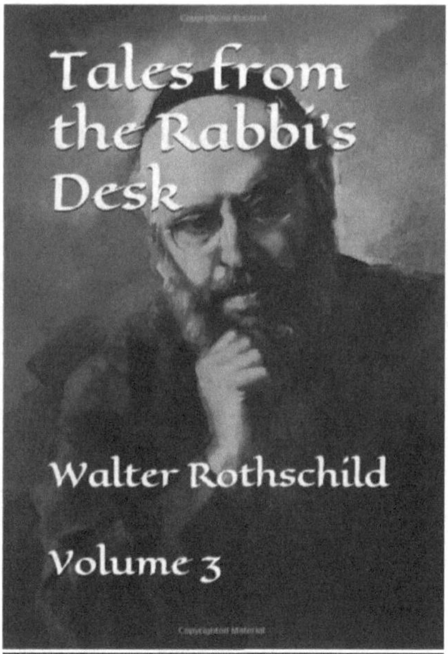

Sherlock Holmes' Bookcase

Volumes 1 and 2

The term 'Sherlock Holmes' has come to indicate an ascetic, meticulous observer, one whose deductive powers were useful for the detection of many a criminal and the resolution of many a literary mystery. But surely there was another side to the man, and also to his faithful companion and 'Boswell', Dr. John Watson? What sort of men were they, what were their backgrounds, what were their concerns? Over the years many have tried - with varying degrees of failure - to emulate Arthur Conan-Doyle's original writings; there are even humourless obsessives who will criticise every comma they deem misplaced. Nevertheless, we now present a new collection of stories, discovered by accident, possibly even written by accident, and designed to be read by accident. Rather than the detective's Casebook, this is more a Bookcase, mixed volumes standing side by side and on those vague borders between fiction and fantasy. The reader may explore further at their own risk.

Cryptic Tales From The Crypt

Memoirs of an Undertaker's Undertakings
Or: My Apprenticeship with Death.

By Henry A. H. Longbottom - As told to Dr. Walter Rothschild.

Mr. Henry Longbottom spent some years in his youth as an Apprentice at Thistlethwaites' Funeral Directors and we are fortunate to have some recorded interviews in which he recalls some of the events of that period. Apart from keeping the premises tidy - it is the Apprentice who usually has to Brush with Death - he had to accompany the senior staff on many jobs and picked up many a fascinating tale from those who had worked there longer. These 'Cryptic Tales' are now presented by the Shadley Local History Society, edited by its Chairman Dr. Walter Rothschild.

THERE'S TROUBLE DOWN AT T'PITCH!

Football as it really was. Memories of Huddersfax City and Cleckheckmondsedge Rovers in the glory days.

As told by a Father to his Son.

Football in Yorkshire, back in the 1920's to the 1950's – How was it really? These affectionate tales of the glory days of Cleckheckmondsedge Rovers and Huddersfax City won't exactly give the answer to this question, but hopefully they will enlighten and entertain – and may even explain a little of what went on inside the heads under those cloth caps huddled under the rainclouds in the old pictures in the papers.

The Kreutzer Chronicles

"The Kreutzer Chronicles" written by our late aunt Irene Chavert and edited after her death by Walter, Joyce and Sylvia Rothschild is also available on Amazon. It is a novel which reflects the family history in Northern England from the 1890's to the 1930's.

Printed in Poland
by Amazon Fulfillment
Poland Sp. z o.o., Wrocław

35722197R00158